The Power of Events

The Power of Events

An Introduction to Complex Event Processing in Distributed Enterprise Systems

David Luckham

✦✦Addison-Wesley

Boston • San Francisco • New York • Toronto • Montreal
London • Munich • Paris • Madrid
Capetown • Sydney • Tokyo • Singapore • Mexico City

The publisher offers discounts on this book when ordered in quantity for special sales. For more information, please contact:

Pearson Education Corporate Sales Division
201 W. 103rd Street
Indianapolis, IN 46290
(800) 428-5331
corpsales@pearsoned.com

Visit AW on the Web: www.aw.com/cseng/

Library of Congress Cataloging-in-Publication Data

Luckham, David C.
    The power of events : an introduction to complex event processing in distributed enterprise systems / David Luckham.
        p. cm.
    Includes bibliographical references and index.
    ISBN 0-201-72789-7
    1. Electronic data processing—Distributed processing. 2. Management information systems. 3. Electronic commerce. I. Title.

QA76.9.D5 L83   2002
004′.36—dc21   2002018357

ISBN 0-201-72789-7
Text printed on recycled paper
1 2 3 4 5 6 7 8 9 10—MA—0605040302
First printing, April 2002

To John Salasin,
a patient mentor and a friend

Contents

Preface

Complex event processing (CEP) is a set of techniques and tools to help us understand and control event-driven information systems. And today, any kind of information system, from the Internet to a cell phone, is driven by events. What is a *complex event?* It is an event that could only happen if lots of other events happened.

For example, suppose you see a car you like at your favorite car dealership. That car is on the showroom floor only because a number of other events took place—events in the inventory control systems of the dealership and the manufacturer, shipping events, customs events at the port of entry, and so on. Of course, when you see exactly what you want in the showroom, you don't ask how or why. But if you don't see the model, make, or color you want and ask why not, you'll get an explanation about allocation quotas, backlogs at the factory, or some other factors that affect events in the causal history leading up to the event you wanted.

This illustrates one of the ideas behind CEP. Events are *related* in various ways, by cause, by timing, and by membership. CEP applies to electronic information systems. It makes use of relationships between events to answer questions like, "Is our system providing the correct level of service to our customers," "Will our shipment arrive on time," and "Is someone trying to steal our information?" CEP adds a new dimension of event processing to what our event-driven information systems already do.

Why is there a need for CEP? Let's look at the situation briefly.

Today's information society is founded upon gathering and sharing information. All our organizations—commercial, government, and military—are dependent upon electronic information processing. Their foundational backbone is the kind of distributed computing system based on computer networks that is nowadays called the "information technology layer" (or IT layer) of the organization. The use of these systems has expanded rapidly over the past ten years to meet the increasing demands of automation, electronic commerce, and the Internet explosion. Investment in technology has focused on making IT systems faster, capable of handling larger and larger amounts of information, and able to collaborate with one another. We now live in the world of the *open enterprise,* where commerce and information move across the boundaries of organizations and nations. Our society has become dependent upon IT systems.

Less investment has been devoted to develop technology to solve the increasing problem of understanding what is happening in our IT systems. Whenever there is a crisis—a denial-of-service attack or a system failure— at first we don't understand what is going on or how to fix it, and then in the aftermath, we scramble for weeks to find out what caused it. We need to understand and control our critical information infrastructures better than that!

A lot of the information in IT systems is never recognized. Messages— or *events*—pass silently back and forth across our information systems as unrelated pieces of communication. They are a source of great power, for when they are aggregated together, and correlated, and their relationships understood, they yield a wealth of information. A new technology is needed to harness the power of events in global information systems. This book is about such a technology.

A few words about CEP—what it is, and where it applies.

CEP consists of very simple techniques, a mix of old and new. Some of them are well known in other kinds of computer applications, such as rule-based systems in intelligent programs. Some of them are new techniques, such as tracking causal histories of events in large distributed computer systems. Or using patterns of events and event relationships, to recognize the presence of complex events that are signified by hundreds or thousands of simpler events in our IT systems. In CEP, new techniques are combined with well-known techniques in a unified framework.

An example of the kind of electronic complex event we are talking about is the *completion of a financial transaction* involving a bundle of financial contracts. Several merchant banks and brokerage houses may participate in the transaction. They use a global trading network. The event itself, the completion of the transaction, might be the result of hundreds of electronic messages and entries into several different databases around the world over a span of two or three days. These events don't necessarily happen in a nice linear order, one after the other. Some of them might happen simultaneously and independently of others, mixed in with events from other transactions. We can apply CEP to the trading network to recognize not only when that complex event happens, but, more importantly, whether it is going to happen, or if it is getting off track and may not happen, and why.

CEP applies to a very broad spectrum of challenges in information systems. A short list includes

- Business process automation utilizing the Internet and electronic marketplaces
- Computer systems to automate the scheduling and control of anything from fabrication lines to air traffic

- Network monitoring and performance prediction
- Detecting attempts to intrude into computer systems or attack them

There is a fundamental reason for this broad applicability. It is simply because information systems are all driven by events. To be sure, each system, or application running on top of a system, depends upon different kinds of events. Network events are different from database events, which are different from financial trading events. But one of the major themes of CEP is that different kinds of events are related. CEP provides techniques for defining and utilizing relationships between events. CEP applies to any type of event that happens in a computer application or a network or an information system. In fact, one of its techniques lets you define your own events as patterns of the events in your computer system. CEP lets you *see* when your events happen. This is one way to understand what is going on in your system.

That brings us to another point—flexibility. CEP allows users to specify the events that are of interest to them at any moment. Events of interest can be low-level network monitoring alerts or high-level enterprise management intelligence, depending upon the role and viewpoint of individual users. Different kinds of events can be specified and monitored simultaneously. And the specification of the events of interest, how they should be viewed and acted upon, can be changed on the fly, while the system is running.

The users of CEP can be human, or they can be autonomous processes. The processes that manage our enterprises are becoming more complex. Linear workflow processes that epitomize document processing in commercial transactions are not capable of managing the open electronic enterprise. In the future, enterprise management processes will be designed to incorporate complex event processing in order to get the kind of events they need to operate.

Now, a few words about the book itself and what the reader should expect. First, there are two parts to this book.

Part I is for a broad audience of people with an interest in various aspects of the information society, such as electronic commerce, the Internet, B2B collaboration, or, generally, electronic information processing. Part I deals with two questions about CEP: what it is for—that is, the kinds of problems in the information society that CEP can be applied to; and what it is—a simplified view of CEP, the basic concepts and easy examples of applications.

Part I includes Chapters 1 through 7. The first four chapters describe the problems and issues in IT systems that CEP applies to. The next three chapters describe basic concepts of CEP, such as what an "event" is, causal and timing relationships between events, patterns of events and event hierachies, and how to apply them to solve the problems described earlier.

Part II consists of Chapter 8 onward. It is intended for information systems specialists with some background in software. Part II presents how-to-build-it details and case studies of CEP applications. The goal of Part II is to describe what is needed to build applications of CEP that are capable of solving real-world problems. It includes first a detailed description of a complex event pattern language, reactive event pattern rules, and event pattern constraints. Second, Part II shows how to build solutions by using the event pattern rules and constraints to build event processing agents and architectures of communicating agents. Part II also includes case studies, as large and as detailed as we can fit in a chapter of a book.

The final chapter of this book deals with the question of how to develop an infrastructure for CEP. We can look around the event-driven applications being developed in the commercial world today, utilizing the power of distributed computing, the Internet, and private networks. An almighty commercial struggle is brewing for market share in the world of eMarketplaces and electronic commerce. It is quite predictable, considering the trends in middleware, the Java world, the .NET world, the security world, and so on, that CEP will be developed as a competitive advantage. This chapter deals with leveraging these developments to build an infrastructure for CEP—now and quickly!

A word about references. This area of Internet technology is changing so quickly that any attempt to give comprehensive references would be outdated in six months. Not only that, but any less than complete set of references would be unfair to some. I assume that any reader has access to the Internet and can search for current references to, for example, "middleware" or "application server." So I have tended to include only a few references, either general references to Web sites or citations to seminal research papers that are not easily found.

At this time in our society, any technology that attempts to view and control IT systems may be seen by some as conflicting with issues concerning privacy. In fact, CEP may provide a foundation for resolving some possible conflicts. However, I cannot deal with this topic here, and I do not.

Just a little history. CEP has grown out of a research project at Stanford on event-based simulation called the RAPIDE project. This research took place between 1990 and 2000. Out of RAPIDE came some early experiments in CEP applied to viewing small communicating systems built on commercial middleware, or applied to recognizing security threats in progress on the IT layer of a large university, where hackers love to play. These projects are documented on two Web sites:

- http://pavg.stanford.edu/rapide/
- http://pavg.stanford.edu/cep/

Acknowledgments

I must acknowledge the efforts of all those who have contributed to developing RAPIDE and CEP. First are the students and staff who participated in the research of the Stanford Program Analysis and Verification Group (PAVG) over the past ten years, particularly in developing the RAPIDE event-based simulation system and early prototype CEP systems. Their names, too numerous to mention, appear as contributors on the Web site http://pavg.stanford.edu/rapide/.

Special thanks are due to the long-term PAVG members who debated endlessly the ideas described herein, implemented them, and proved experimentally that they work: Doug Bryan, Walt Mann, John Kenney, Louis Perrochon, Sigurd Meldal, James Vera, Wolfgang Polak, Alex Santoro, Benoit Gennart, Woo-Sang Park, and Frank Belz (TRW). As I look back on it all, they are a great group of researchers, and it has been my good luck and privilege to work with them.

I also owe thanks to the Defense Advanced Research Projects Agency (DARPA) for supporting the research of the PAVG on these projects.

Finally, a grateful thank-you to the reviewers of drafts of this book who have helped in many ways to improve it: Armond Inselberg, Doug Bryan, Geoff Mendal, and Louis Perrochon.

David Luckham
Professor of Research Emeritus, Electrical Engineering
Stanford University

A Simple Introduction to Complex Event Processing

Highlights in Part I:

- *The challenges involved in keeping the human in control of today's electronic information systems*
- *The basic concepts of CEP*
- *How CEP can be employed to meet the challenges*

Chapter $\boxed{1}$

The Global Information Society and the Need for New Technology

- *Events everywhere in our information systems*
- *The Internet and the growth of global communication spaghetti*
- *Layers upon layers in enterprise system architectures*
- *Global electronic trade—understanding what is happening*
- *Agile systems—future reality or just a dream*
- *Can an open electronic society defend itself?*
- *The gathering storm—global coordination or global chaos*

Information processing using computer systems on a global scale has become the foundation of twenty-first-century life. It runs our governments and industries, our transportation systems, hospitals, and emergency services. It is the foundation for global economics and global electronic trading in the new millennium.

Information processing systems have grown up around the globe at *"Web speed,"* only slightly slower than "warp speed" in science fiction. The Internet or "Web" has been a driving force. The technology to build these systems, to make them faster, capable of handling and routing larger and larger amounts of information, has developed to help drive this growth. New applications are appearing all the time to entice us into new ways of using IT systems.

But there is no similar development of foundational technology for monitoring and managing the information that flows through global information systems. And the fact is, if we do not know what is going on in these systems—and I mean "know" in the sense of human understanding—we cannot protect them, and we cannot use them to maximum advantage. This chapter describes our event-based world and some of its challenging problems.

1.1   Distributed Information Systems Everywhere

Typical examples of distributed computing and information systems are systems that automate the operations of commercial enterprises such as banking and financial transaction processing systems, warehousing systems, and automated factories. The Internet has promoted and speeded the growth of distributed information processing beyond the single enterprise, across the boundaries between enterprises. Information is shared between different enterprises and provides the foundation for trading partnerships and the automation of business collaborations.

Figure 1.1 shows a multi-enterprise financial trading system. These systems are distributed over various networks worldwide and often use the Internet as one of the networks. When viewed at a macro level, the various enterprises and organizations are simply components of the system. Each of them has its own internal information processing system. The figure shows these components, including the stock market information system, brokerage houses and online customers (or more accurately, their workstations), the Federal Reserve, investment banks, and the networks through which all these components communicate. Messages (or "events") flow across networks between these enterprises. They react to the events they receive and issue new events that are sent to other components. The system is *"event driven"*—it lives or dies based upon the messages flowing across its IT networks. This is a rather large system with high volumes of messages flowing through its networks. For example, in 2001, 5,000 or 10,000 messages per second flowed through a single large brokerage house's information technology layer. Soon, that number will be higher.

Financial trading systems are but one example of distributed IT systems. Generally speaking, the business operations of any global coporation are supported by a widely distributed, message-based computer system. Figure 1.1, by the way, shows tools for complex event processing added to the distributed system—we will explain this later. In fact, that's what this book is about.

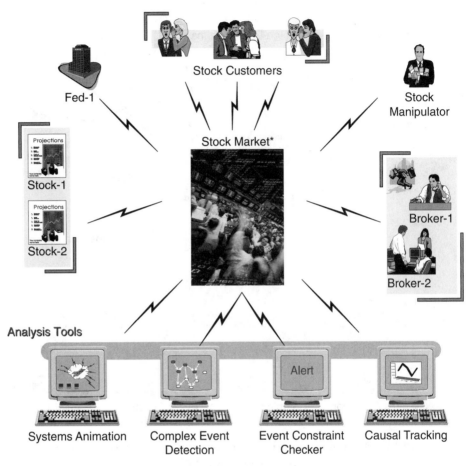

Figure 1.1: A system of distributed communicating enterprises
(*photo by Wonderlife USA Corporation)

Government and military information systems are also distributed systems. Figure 1.2 depicts a typical military command-and-control system that links command centers, intelligence-gathering operations, and battlefield units of all services—a so-called C^4I (command, control, communications, computers, and intelligence) system. At first look, a military system may seem to be entirely different from a commercial one. Certainly, the military goals and operational conditions are very different, and many of the types of component objects in military systems are different from commercial systems. But military systems also contain a lot of commercial components, such as operating systems and databases, and often parts of their IT layer use the same publicly available networks, such as the Internet.

In fact, all three kinds of systems have a lot in common. In all cases—commercial, government, and military—the underlying architectural

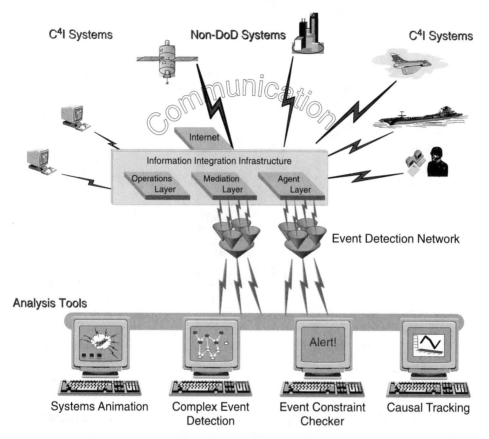

Figure 1.2: A command-and-control system monitored by an event processing network

structure is the same: a distributed information system consisting of a widely dispersed set of several thousands or hundreds of thousands of application programs (or *component objects,* as they are often called) communicating with one another by means of messages transmitted over an IT layer containing various kinds of media.

All these systems have come to be collectively called *"enterprise systems."* They all have a common basic problem. Their activities are driven by the events flowing through their IT layers. And they produce zillions of events per hour or day. But there is no technology that enables us to view those events and activities that are going on inside these systems in ways that we humans can understand. To be sure, given the primitive tools we have at the moment, we can *see* the events. But making *sense* of them is the problem!

Enterprises invest as best they can in tools to monitor events in the basic networks that carry information. So we are told, for example, that "the router in Hong Kong is overloaded." We have to figure out that the router problem may be holding up completion of an important trading agreement between our New York office and our partner's Tokyo office. We need to be able to answer questions about events that are not simply low-level network activities, but are high-level activities related to what we are using the systems to do—so-called business-level, or strategic-level, events. We need answers to questions like these:

- "What caused our trading system to sell automobiles (a business-level event) to a customer in Texas?" The answer could involve several other trading transactions.
- "Is the system, at this moment, under a denial-of-service attack?" The answer requires real-time recognition of complex patterns of events, the patterns that indicate such attacks.
- "What is causing the system to fail to execute this trading agreement?" The answer could be a missing set of earlier business-level events, like failures of several suppliers' systems to respond within time limits.

These questions are about *complex events,* which are built out of lots of simpler events. Answering them means that we need to be able to view our enterprise systems in terms of how we *use* them—not in terms of how we *build* them, which is the state of the art in enterprise monitoring technology today.

1.2 The Global Communication Spaghetti Pot

The World Wide Web and all large-scale networks are constructed on well-understood network engineering principles, protocols, and conventions. They allow the ultimate flexibility in communication whereby any two computers have the potential to communicate with one another. This flexibility, or "openness," allows communication to take place, and information to flow, in patterns we do not understand.

Consider for a moment what happens when you visit a Web site today. Suppose you are the client in Figure 1.3 visiting a Web site, say, www.anymumble.com. You click on something on the Web site screen. You get a screen full of banner advertisements, blinking applets, links to other sites, and, maybe if you're lucky, the information you were looking for. Is all this stuff coming back at you from www.anymumble.com? Very unlikely. What you see on your computer screen may actually be coming from several

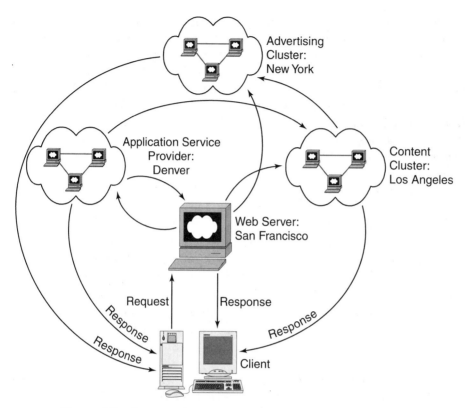

Figure 1.3: Communication spaghetti across the Internet

different places on the Internet, as Figure 1.3 shows. And the next time you visit www.anymumble.com, what you get may be coming from a totally different set of Web sites. In fact, what you get and where it comes from may depend upon who the anymumble site thinks you are and what you did the last time you visited it. That's communication flexibility for you!

Another simple example of communication flexibility is the now very common e-mail virus attachment. The "I Love You" virus in 2000 was a fine example. Released in the Phillippines as an attachment to e-mail, within a few days it wrought havoc in computer systems across the world, estimated in the billions of dollars. The virus even took down chunks of computers within the U.S. Department of Defense, supposedly protected from cyber attack behind communication firewalls. How did it travel so far so fast? Through the simple communication flexibility of forwarding e-mail across the Internet, together with the address book features in our mailer programs that let us do that easily.

Communication flexibility is one of the great powers of the Internet. We certainly don't want to restrict this flexibility in any way. On the positive side, it is enabling rapid growth in new kinds of business activities. One example is *outsourcing,* which enables a Web site that supplies services to subcontract with other Web sites to supply some of those services. When you go to a Web site that offers home mortgages, for example, it communicates with lenders over the Internet to get you the latest bids that fit your requirements. If you apply for a mortgage, it may outsource a credit check to a credit agency. All this happens in a second or two. Another example is *automated trading Web sites,* or "eMarketplaces" as they are called. These let many enterprises, buyers and suppliers of goods, communicate to complete multistep transactions in a matter of minutes. An automobile manufacturer can reduce inventory costs by tracking parts suppliers' inventories and prices, and placing orders "just in time" that are spread across several suppliers to reduce costs. eMarketplaces are connecting together and may eventually morph into the "global eCommerce Web."

The flip side is that the communication flexibility of the Internet makes it difficult to track the causes of events. Because events can come flying at us from anywhere on the Web, we often cannot figure out why they happened or what other events caused them. For example, when a trading transaction fails to complete, there is nothing to tell us why. Whenever we need to know the causes of a message, we have to resort to searching through very large, low-level, network log files and, often, lots of them. It is tedious, expensive, and very primitive. And often fails. We have no *causal* tracking that can tell us what events caused another event to happen. There is no technology that lets us detect when events at different places—say, Web sites in New York and London—at different times, have a common cause, or if complex patterns of events happening globally are repeating.

For example, at a staff meeting of a large commercial Web site, the CEO might ask the IT manager, "There was an unusually high number of complaints from customers in the New York area about delays in getting pages on their screens—why?" A reply might be, "We think it was the XYZ advertisement server we outsourced to for those banner ads directed at the Northeast, but XYZ says their demand loads were light. And the ISPs aren't taking any blame either."

Communication flexibility on the Internet has led to a very dynamic communication architecture in which the links between various computers are constantly changing. At any given moment in the life of any large IT network, we don't have a global view of who's communicating with whom, nor what is causing what, and we have to work very hard to find out. This is communication traffic we do not understand.

What we have today is *global communication spaghetti.* We can't tell where it starts and where it ends, we can't unravel it, and most of the time we don't know how it happened.

The challenge is *not* to restrict communication flexibility, but to develop new technologies to *understand* it.

The technology of monitoring and managing events in IT systems has been completely overrun by the technology of communicating events. This is a global problem in search of new ideas on how to solve it.

1.2.1   Event Causality

A key to understanding events is knowing what *caused* them—and having that causal knowledge at the time the events happen. The ability to track event causality is an essential step toward managing communication spaghetti.

Events are flowing all the time through our Internet-based systems from one part of the world and causing events in another part of the world. For example, suppose I send you an e-mail message, say, M, and you reply with another message, say, N. Then my message, M, *caused* your message, N. This is so obviously important to my being able to understand your reply, which may come back days later when I have forgotten my M, that the "reply" feature of mailers usually attaches M inside of N.

Another example is pointing a browser at the www.anymumble.com location, which is an event. This event then causes all those applets and banner advertisements to appear on our screen—that is, lots of other events. This example is not so simple because there are a lot of intermediate events flowing between the anymumble Web site and other Web sites before we get the events on our screen. So tracking how we got the stuff on our screen is not so easy.

In examples like these, the causal relation between the events is sometimes called *horizontal causality* to emphasize that the causing and caused events happen on the same conceptual level in the overall system. In the e-mail example, N is an event caused by M, and both events happen at the level of using e-mail applications. So the causal connection is "horizontal"— that is, at the same level. Events can also be components of other events, in which case the component events are thought of as happening at a lower level. The component events of an event also cause that event. This kind of causal relation between events is called *vertical causality,* as described in the next section.

1.3   Electronic Archeology: Layers upon Layers

Enterprise systems are *distributed, event-driven systems.* But they all have another property in common. They are *layered systems.* Layering is a design technique for controlling complexity. But it is also a side effect of unplanned or uncontrolled growth. In some systems the situation bears analogy with the multiple layers of civilizations of different historical periods, one on top of another, that the archeologist Heinrich Schliemann discovered at Troy, back in the 1870s.

Layered IT systems present another dimension in the search for new ways to understand the events that happen in them.

1.3.1 A Layered Enterprise System

Figure 1.4 shows a common layered structure of an enterprise system.

Applications and Users at the Top

The top layer is called the *business level* or *strategic planning level* because it is the layer at which an enterprise plans and transacts its business. It contains the applications that people use to transact business and do their

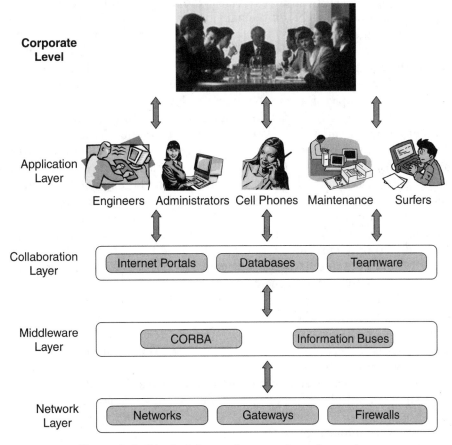

Figure 1.4: Typical layers in an enterprise system

work. This layer contains user interfaces to the enterprise's services, planning and forecasting applications, inventory and accounting applications, spreadsheets, calendars, Web browsers, document preparation tools, e-mail, communication devices such as cell phones, system administration tools, and so on. The contents of this layer are expanding rapidly. Different kinds of applications are appearing all the time, each requiring different types of information.

The application layer is the level at which human users work and conceptualize their goals—for example, "I want to send e-mail to so-and-so," or "I want to initiate a process to purchase item X from the cheapest supplier." Events that signify activities at this level are the ones humans can understand most easily. These events result from using applications.

The high-level events that are of greatest significance are not explicitly generated by users using applications, but they are *consequences* of sets of other high-level events. For example, a single *business-level* event could consist of a sequence of events indicating uses of various applications. It could signify a completed supply chain transaction with business partners, negotiated by messages across the Internet. It is a *virtual* event signifying a very real activity with contractual and economic implications. These inferred events are aggregated from sets of other high-level events and are the events of interest to the business level or strategic planning level of the enterprise.

Another example of a complex business level event is a stockbroker, or a group of brokers, in a financial trading enterprise trading stocks on many different accounts, including those owned by the trading house itself. Some patterns of trading activities on various accounts might violate Securities and Exchange Commission (SEC) regulations. But high-level events signifying trading violations have to be inferred from the explicit trade events generated by the brokers when they make trades. It depends on an ability to recognize *complex patterns* of events involving timing and relationships between the events. We understand a "violation event" when it is pointed out to us—no problem! But it isn't actually generated. That's the problem! It is a *virtual event* signifying a very real activity. It has to be recognized from the morass of actual events.

There are myriads of similar situations going on in enterprise systems all the time that have the potential for similar kinds of violations of the enterprise's policies—for example, in online Internet-based auction houses and in "dot-com" retailing, where violations of the regulations of various states may happen.

Conceptually, the events of interest to the highest layer of an enterprise, or a system of multiple cooperating enterprises, are virtual events comprising sets of application layer events. The *strategic planning layer* must be fed aggregations of application-level events.

But application-level events are not subjected to a battery of monitoring and analysis tools as the network-level events below it are. This is unfortunate but understandable, because such tools would need a new kind of technology that deals with complex patterns of events to be effective.

So, in a layered system, understanding at the highest level what is going on in the enterprise, at every layer, is one problem. But there are more problems to come because causality between events crosses layers.

Collaboration and Enabling Layer

Next in this figure comes the collaboration layer, which contains components that help make applications available to users. Here we find components that we have come to expect, such as databases and servers for e-mail groups, news, and chat rooms. We might even go so far as to include the operating systems, such as Windows and Linux, in this layer, although it could be argued that they belong in layers below. The collaboration layer now contains a growing number of products that enable more sophisticated uses of distributed information processing. For example, Web sites that service applications (so-called application service providers, or ASPs). And business rules engines that enable trading agreements and correlation of information. The collaboration layer contains more and more tools that enable users and applications to interact intelligently on complex projects, like building software systems or putting together multistep trading deals. This layer is the target of a growing industry in business-to-business products and services (often called B2B).

The dividing line between the collaboration layer and the application layer is not a definite, rigorous line. Sometimes, for example, a database would be more appropriately viewed as an application rather than as an enabler of applications, in which case we would put it in the layer above.

Middleware

The next layer down is the *middleware layer,* which lets all the stuff above communicate. Included are Object Request Brokers (ORBs) and messaging systems such as information buses. This level of communications sits on top of the basic networks and lets all the applications and application servers talk to one another. It contains the system components that are often categorized as Enterprise Application Integration (EAI) products. It is called "integration" because it helps link business-level applications by letting them communicate. And it is called the middleware layer because its components are viewed as lying "in the middle" between applications and networks.

Before 1990 this layer and the products in it didn't exist. It came about by design, to make it easier to get applications to communicate over networks. Middleware is a go-between, translating the message communication between applications into low-level messages called packets that networks are designed to carry.

Communications middleware has become an industry in itself. Middleware for distributed applications includes ORBs and various kinds of message-oriented middleware based upon message queues, publish/subscribe (pub/sub) services, and so on. These products provide a layer of communication protocols, together with Application Program Interfaces (APIs), that the enterprise business applications use to communicate. At present there are several widely used commercial middleware products that form the basis for the EAI industry.

The Under-the-Hood Layer

At the bottom is the network layer—the essential plumbing for transporting information from one point to another, both within an enterprise and across enterprises. The kind of networks we are talking about here first appeared in the 1970s. Before that, applications had no way to communicate with one another.

The network layer is the core of the information technology layer (IT layer) in an enterprise system. Newspaper articles refer to it as the "under-the-hood" part of an enterprise's IT system, or the Internet for that matter. It is generally looked upon as something the common man should not know about and certainly not tinker with—it is a source of many system problems. And when it collapses in one of many well-known or not so well-known ways, the whole system grinds to a halt. We often hear "The network is down." Network crashes can become a critical concern to the higher-level echelons in a distributed enterprise. And they certainly affect business. Spectacular network crashes make newspaper headlines—for example, when online stock-trading systems clog up and stop the customers from trading, or when hackers orchestrate a denial-of-service attack on Yahoo and other popular Web sites.

So the network layer has become the domain of a powerful new kind of expert, the specialist in network and IT systems management. Often this person has a title, like IT director. The job is to keep the network layer running at all costs—otherwise, the enterprise is out of business. It's the first point of pain for a distributed enterprise.

Consequently, network management products have proliferated. There are all sorts of tools for the IT director to use. They track resource consumption (CPU use and memory or disk space use) on every machine in the network and provide statistics and summaries in every color in the rainbow. They log alerts or warnings from network components such as routers and servers, slice and dice them by the minute or hour, raise the alarm, and page the IT director out of bed at any hour of the day or night.

But keeping the network running is not the IT director's only problem. Additionally, there are issues of security and privacy. And *cyber warfare* is an increasing headache for all enterprises. Everyone knows it is going to increase. Plenty of tools and products try to help the IT director solve cyber warfare problems, but again, they don't do too well.

The IT director's problem is making sense of all this network-level information. The importance of this task is well understood by enterprises today. They invest heavily in whatever technology is available to help. For example, the network operations room in a large global banking enterprise represents a billion-dollar investment these days.

1.3.2 Vertical Causality: Tracking Events up and down the Layers

Although there are no general layering standards for categorizing enterprise systems, the picture in Figure 1.4 is typical and captures the general idea.

- The applications that humans use and understand (sometimes) are at the top.
- Network plumbing that carries the messages and information is at the bottom.
- Several layers are in between, depending upon the complexity of the system.

Activity at each layer is translated into activities at the layers below and conversely. Those lower-level activities must complete successfully in order for the higher-level activities to also complete successfully.

So, we have a general principle of layered enterprise systems: An activity at the top *causes* activities at successively lower levels, which in turn *cause* other activities to happen at the top.

Layering adds another dimension to understanding events. Discovering the causal relationships across layers, between high- and low-level activities, especially in real time, is another outstanding issue in enterprise systems. We call this *vertical causality*.

An ability to track vertical causality in a layered system has at least two important uses in managing our enterprises. First, knowing how a business-level event is broken down by your system into sets of lower-level events is very helpful in understanding properties of that high-level event, such as its timing—for example, why it took so long or failed to complete—and how to improve performance at the business level. Sometimes we may only need to understand the breakdown of the business-level event into calls to applications, while at other times, we may need a breakdown all the way to the network level. This is the kind of information that might have helped the IT manager answer the CEO's question about what caused customers in the New York area to complain about slow service.

Second, if we were able to track vertical causality, we could use it to group events at lower levels according to the high-level events they signify. That would help us make sense out of the mountains of low-level events that network monitoring tools give us.

Tracking vertical causality is not a simple problem because there is almost as much dynamism in the layers of our enterprise systems as there is in the communication between them across the Internet. For example, the ability of a service provider to load-balance incoming requests may depend on the loads of lower-level servers that are continually changing. A high-level complex event, such as defaulting on a service-level agreement, can happen in many different ways. It may result from lots of different sets of lower-level events. Moreover, our enterprise systems are dynamic in their composition and structure. The sets of components at each level are changing all the time, as are the kinds of activities the system is being employed to do. So the kinds of events that can happen at every level are changing too. Keeping up with what our systems do is not an easy task.

1.3.3   Event Aggregation: Making High-Level Sense out of Low-Level Events

What about those strategic-level complex virtual events that we talked about earlier? Virtual events are not actually generated in the system—nobody sends a message saying, "I violated law XYZ." The activities signified by high-level virtual events have to be recognized from among sets of events at the application layer or below. These policy and contractual events are top-level events of immediate interest to the corporate level of the enterprise.

We have just discussed the potential usefulness of an ability to track vertical causality. But there needs to be a high-level event in order to track its causes. Often, all there is at the highest levels is a perception, a suspicion, a list of complaints. But the business and strategic implications are very real.

The complementary operation to downward tracking of vertical causality is the aggregation of sets or groups of lower-level events into a single higher-level event that expresses the meaning of the lower-level events, taken together. These are some examples:

- A group of stock-trading events, related by accounts, timing and other data, taken together constitute a violation of a policy or regulation.
- A large set of network-level operations, originating from the same machine and repeating similar accesses on different target machines, may signify an attempt to intrude into a network.

- In an application service provider, groups of events signifying accesses to distributed applications, such as those illustrated in Figure 1.3, together may imply a violation of a service-level agreement with a customer.

Recognizing or detecting a significant group of lower-level events from among all the enterprise event traffic, and creating a single event that summarizes in its data their significance, is called *event aggregation*. The aggregate event will appear at a higher level in the enterprise's operations.

Event aggregation is a capability that needs to be developed. It is a very powerful technology for monitoring and managing our enterprises. It will in turn depend upon technology for recognizing patterns of events in large amounts of lower-level event traffic, in real time. And it depends first on an ability to express patterns consisting of multiple events together with their common data and timing. If event aggregation is implemented properly, it can give us the ability to track the lower-level events that were aggregated to create a high-level event—so-called *drill-down* diagnostics for tracking vertical causality.

1.4   The Gathering Storm of New Activities on the Web

There is already an urgent need for new technologies to help us understand the information in our IT systems, at every level from low to high. This need is going to become even more urgent. In the next three sections, we look at some of the newer activities hosted on the Internet.

We pick out three main themes among the activites now developing in the Internet world:

- Global electronic trade and the emergence of the *open enterprise*
- Agile systems—new kinds of highly flexible information-gathering systems
- Cyber warfare and cyber defense—the battle for the information society

Each of these themes, we shall argue, is making increasing demands for new technology for information gathering and delivery. Widely distributed fragments of information must be gathered and pieced together into forms appropriate for electronic processes to tackle the problems at hand, and for humans to understand high-speed business situations and stay in control.

Demands for new design technology also abound in each of the themes. We must be able to deal with increasingly complex systems, demands for high reliability, and frequent, rapid modifications. Demand for a design technology that applies across the complete system lifecycle will appear in each of these themes, systems of electronic business processes that span multiple collaborating enterprises, agile information-gathering systems, and cyber defense systems.

1.5   Global Electronic Trade

The Internet is fast becoming the ether by which enterprises transact all forms of business. This is the next stage of Internet development. It goes beyond the electronic retailing and trading that we have all come to know, and love or hate, as the dot-com industry.

Global electronic trade involves collaboration between enterprises to transact business electronically on a scale unforeseen a few years ago. This is the *electronic collaboration* model of doing business. The stakes are high—reduced costs, lower inventory levels, faster time to market—all adding up to increased profitability and increased competitiveness.

The various visions and predictions for how this will happen can all be captured in the idea of the *global eCommerce Web,* shown in Figure 1.5. It is a grand scheme.

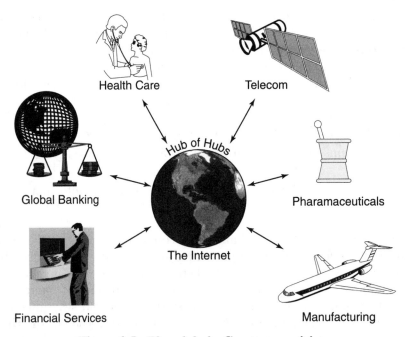

Figure 1.5: The global eCommerce vision

At present special Web sites called trading hubs, or eMarketplaces, are being developed for particular industries, such as retailing, automotive manufacturing, aerospace, financial products and services, telecom provisioning, and the like. Each of these trading hubs provide services that let enterprises in that industry collaborate by integrating various business processes—for example, supply chain processes between buyers of automobile parts and the suppliers.

A trading hub is set up to enable electronic commerce between enterprises in a particular industry. It provides standard formats for electronic trading documents used in an industry, and a range of services to support eCommerce between enterprises in that one industry. Services include, for example, demand forecasting for the industry, inventory management, partner directories, transaction settlement services, and so on. The role of the trading hub is to serve as an integration medium for the electronic management processes of enterprises that wish to collaborate in business.

In electronic commerce, trading documents are contained in messages that drive the steps in a trading process. There are standards for representing the trading documents within the industry. So the processes in each enterprise can easily understand documents from another process and respond intelligently by taking the next steps in a mutual trading process. The current trend is to base these standards on Extensible Markup Language (XML). Various services available on the hub may be supplied by different individual members. Then there are *content managers,* which are applications such as a distributed master catalog. Each participant manages its own content, and the master catalog keeps a constantly updated view of all the inventories of all participants in the hub. Anyone can get a globally consistent view of the "content" of the hub. Global content management is a critical facilitator to encouraging electronic trading agreements on the hub. The highest-level services are *transaction managers* of electronic business processes that automate the trading agreements between enterprises. These applications are process workflow engines that automatically initiate the next step in a trading process each time a message completing the previous step is received. Electronic trading across a hub can take many forms, from collaborative integration of individual business processes to auctions and exchanges of goods (electronic barter). The hub provides aggregation and settlement services.

The advantage of trading hubs is reduction in the costs of doing business. For example, procurement costs of a Fortune 100 manufacturer can run annually into billions of dollars. Just-in-time purchasing on the hub saves a significant percentage of these costs.

Now, the grand vision is that the trading hubs for all the various industries will be linked together across the Internet into the global eCommerce Web—that is, a global trading *hub of all hubs.* It will be event driven, of course. As one visionary puts it:

> The traditional linear, one step at a time, supply chain is dead. It
> will be replaced by parallel, asynchronous, realtime marketplace de-
> cision making. Take manufacturing capacity as an example. Enter-
> prises can bid their excess production capacity on the world eCom-
> merce hub. Offers to buy capacity trigger requests from the seller
> for parts bids to suppliers who in turn put out requests to other
> suppliers, and this whole process will all converge in a matter of
> minutes.[1]

To what extent will this vision ever happen? It implies an awful lot of
very complex high-level business events flying around, causally dependent
upon sets of other high-level events. Will these global trading processes "all
converge"? Or will there be a lot of timeouts and thrashing about with
no convergence? This kind of real-time marketplace decision making will
be driven by events. It is clearly going to need a new technology, beyond
master catalogs and workflow engines, that enables us to detect event patterns that signify market situations of interest. These patterns will need to
specify sets of business- or trading-level events and their data, timing, and
causal relationships. What kinds of "situations of interest"? Here are some
examples.

- *Risk mitigation.*   Certainly, in the real-time marketplace, automatically recognizing and avoiding risky situations is going to be
  necessary. For example, an enterprise may want to abort a multistep
  purchase process in midstream if events happening in the hub's
  current context signify purchases by other parties that are likely to
  drive up the overall cost by the time the process has completed.

- *Policy enforcement.*   Enterprises will need to maintain strict
  limitations on real-time trading processes because of the speed with
  which they could get out of hand. Each enterprise will have its own
  private policies. Policies could range from constraints on the data in
  events that are driving the trading process, such as "no parts manu-
  factured in country XYZ," to avoidance of processes that can be indi-
  rectly influenced by competitors. The former kind of policy is a
  constraint on the data in events, while the latter may require detecting patterns of events happening in other trading alliances.

- *Opportunistic trading.*   The flip side of risk mitigation is recognizing
  when trading processes should be speeded up or changed in midstream
  to take advantage of favorable situations. Again, such situations may

---

[1] Jay Marty Tennenbaum, EE 380 Seminar Lecture Series, Stanford University, May 2000.

often be signified by patterns of events, not directly related to the executing process, but happening in the global trading context.

- *Regulatory monitoring.* This is the same kind of issue as policy enforcement, but on a global scale as agreed to by all participants. Electronic trading will be subject to regulations placing limitations on trading processes, perhaps local to one industry's hub, or perhaps the result of international trade agreements across all hubs. It is well beyond the scope of this book to try predicting what the regulations of the global eCommerce hub might be. But what can be predicted is that the technology to monitor compliance will be event based, will involve recognition of complex patterns of events happening in the total global context, and will need to be flexible enough to be changed frequently without disrupting the monitoring functions.

Real-time marketplace decision making may well become a cybergame of cat-and-mouse, where the advantage goes to those with the best event monitoring and event pattern recognition capabilities. Players in such a game will need to analyze and adjust trading processes frequently. Tools to help analyze multilevel trading processes will need to track causal relationships between events, both horizontally and vertically. So we can expect that analysis tools incorporating causal tracking and complex event pattern detection will be used to monitor the business event layer and the layers below. This kind of monitoring and viewing activity (we will discuss "viewing" later) will need to have the same real-time scalability at higher levels that network-level tools have today.

1.6   Agile Systems

An *agile system* is defined as a system that is able to adapt rapidly to changes in its environment. What people have in mind, particularly the military, is large systems of small autonomous agents that share information across the Web and other networks. An agent is a small program or software object that peforms one task with the information it is fed, usually a stream of events, and passes on the results. The agents perform their individual tasks and are in constant communication with one another to achieve some overall objective—such as guiding a missile to its intended target or making a profit on arbitrage between several stock markets. As the environment changes, which may involve part of the system being destroyed, the community of agents adapts, spawns new members, and continues as best it can to achieve its objectives.

This kind of system model is appropriate not only for military command-and-control systems, but it could also be a model for business intelligence gathering, collaborative stock-trading strategies, and all manner of cyber warfare activities as well.

The major activity of agents in agile systems will be to process events fed to them from various sources, including but not limited to the Internet. In military systems like the one shown in Figure 1.2, other sources of event inputs will be special networks and sensors (radar, unmanned aerial vehicle [UAV], and so on). There will be a layered organization of communicating agents. Sets of agents will be organized into layers, with lower layers performing information gathering, filtering, and aggregating streams of events, and higher layers performing analysis and decision making. A second dimension of organization, orthogonal to layering, is also envisioned. Communicating agents will also be organized into enclaves or cells, to achieve specific goals and to improve the security and resilience to destruction of the system as a whole.

Agile systems are expected to deal with quite challenging situations, well beyond the scope of workflow engines and business process integration. Intelligence gathering requires the ability to correlate events from different domains of activity, such as manufacturing and transportation statistics on one hand and satellite image processing on another. Events may arrive from sources that are not normally associated as being related or relevent, and the events may arrive at the processing agents in a different time order from the order in which they actually happened. Furthermore, agile systems must make decisions based upon incomplete information. In the battlefield, information gets fragmented or destroyed en route. Nevertheless, global views of a situation must be constructed in real time and actions taken.

If the agents are to be sophisiticated enough to be the building blocks of agile systems, they will need to be based upon a new technology of event processing. Each agent will perform one or more functions, such as recognizing a complex pattern of events, or aggregating lots of lower-level events that match a pattern into higher-level intelligence events, or detecting relationships between events that differ widely in their source and time of arrival at the agent. Agents will be needed that can perform these functions on any level of events, from low-level network events to high strategic-level events. So the underlying technology must apply generally across all layers of events, actual or virtual—a technology that can only process network-level events, for example, will not be adequate.

An agile military system is expected to carry out military doctrine, strategies, and processes, which may be dynamic and change on the fly during operations. The underlying technology must allow for continuous construction of new classes of agents that can recognize different patterns of events and perform new functions. It must enable us to easily add them into a running agile system without disrupting its operations. And it must let us build agile systems that have the ability to respond to certain situations by adding agents and reconfiguring themselves automatically.

The agile system vision has more of an artificial intelligence (AI) flavor to it than the global eCommerce vision. But it is a safe bet that AI will play a role in a successful solution to either vision.

1.7 Cyber Warfare and the Open Electronic Society

What would happen to us if our computer systems suddenly stopped working for a few days? Nobody knows! Of course, given the redundancy and tolerence to failures in our computer systems, that is very unlikely to happen. Or is it? It is quite surprising what havoc a rather unimaginative virus attack can cause. And hackers seem to be able to invade corporate Web sites and government computers almost at will. The reality is that we do not know what is happening in our information systems minute by minute or day by day.

Cyber warfare involves the development of new ways to defend our IT layers against an increasing set of criminal and destructive activities. The battleground is the Internet and every corporate IT layer. These are some of the current problems:

- Intrusions into computers. An intruder is someone who is not an authorized user and who anonymously gains privileged (or "root") access to a computer. The purposes for an intrusion vary widely and include the following examples:
  - Using a computer anonymously to set up a chat room for drug trafficking
  - Accessing databases (supposedly secure) to steal information such as credit-card numbers
  - Using a network server to launch another kind of attack at some other site in the network
- Denial-of-service attacks on Web sites and networks
- Computer viruses, propagated from machine to machine by file transfers and e-mail messages
- Spam, unsolicited e-mail, and other nuisance activities

Present security technologies such as encryption, firewalls, network-level intrusion detectors, and virus scanners defend against well-known, "textbook," criminal activities on the Web. When a new kind of attack is discovered, the IT security managers scramble to include it in their log file search scripts, and the security tools manufacturers try to add a defense against it to their products. But new tricks and techniques to exploit vulnerabilities in the defenses are being devised all the time. This kind of crude rearguard response we have at the moment—fix the defenses *after* we know what happened—is totally inadequate for dealing with the coming wave of electronic crime.

It is a total myth that it takes an expert or genius to break into a computer. Breaking and entering an operating system is something that's taught nowadays—it is a very good way to learn how operating systems and network protocols work. There are chat rooms on how to break in and scripted attacks that can be downloaded. The majority of those breaking into systems do not understand how their exploits work any better than a clerk understands how the operating system running his inventory program works.

When a new kind of intrusion is devised, it does take an understanding of the detailed workings of an operating system, or a network protocol, or an application program. From then on, that method of intrusion can be applied using scripts that carry out the steps of the method automatically.

Experts often publish new attacks on the Web to encourage manufacturers to plug the holes in their operating systems and application programs. But of course, the "crackers" and "kiddies" can read the expert's techniques too! And even when holes are plugged by the manufacturers, the patches are often not downloaded to many of the computers on the network. A vulnerable computer is usually the weak link into a subnet or a whole IT layer.

At present it is generally admitted by anyone in the know, including those who build or manage IT networks or advise on Internet policy, that our present abilities to defend our IT infrastructure against attacks, both old and new, are dismal. Let's list a few of the problems.

1. We don't have powerful enough technology, even at the low level of network events, to detect nefarious activities in real time and cut them off. And new ones are springing up all the time.

2. At the network level, the current crop of detectors have absurdly high false alarm rates. We can't correlate the outputs from various network-level detection products to get a more accurate picture of whether or not an intrusion attempt is taking place. Correlation of the various detectors produced by the security industry would need a lot of planning and agreements. First, we need standards and conventions for the formats of detector outputs, so-called alerts. This first-step problem has been recognized by the Internet Engineering Task Force (IETF) and other organizations. We may have some standards for alerts and alarms soon. Then we need event processing technology beyond what is presently available from the security industry to do real-time correlation of alerts.

3. Some kinds of attacks are difficult, if not impossible, to detect at the network level. They would be easier to detect if we had application-level

monitoring—but we don't. We don't have adequate monitoring to provide defensive tools with the kind of information they need. To do this, we need detectors that work at all levels of an IT system.

4. New Internet applications and activities, such as global eCommerce, for example, present new opportunties for electronic theft and destruction. We need technologies that enable us defend at the highest levels in enterprise operations. Just imagine being able to mess with your competitor's electronic trading processes—insert a few false events supposedly coming from a partner at the "right" time, or intercept and divert process events between trading partners, or relay process events to competitors.

5. We, as a society, have become far too dependent upon the Internet. Most of our essential services, from telecommunications and financial transactions to food distribution, now operate over the Internet and IT layers that are accessible from the Internet. In many cases there is no backup mode of operation, should the Internet be taken down. A denial-of-service attack on the Federal Reserve's Fedwire funds-transfer system could, if successful, bring the banking system to a standstill.

6. Traditional security technology—firewalls, for example—and open eCommerce are in direct conflict.

The first four problems all indicate the need for event processing technology that applies across all levels of enterprise operations and applies uniformly to a wide range of the security industry's products. The fifth problem is a political and national policy problem, beyond the scope of this book.

But the sixth problem is one of the most perplexing problems with the Internet explosion—that is, the tension between traditional security based upon locking things up and denying access (firewalls, virtual private networks, and so on) and the need for open commerce. Industry analysts have written report after report on this problem, but the technology to allow openess, whereby anyone can communicate with anyone else and still have secure operations, just doesn't exist.

The sixth problem could become the great stalemate in developing visions like the global eCommerce vision. Unfortunately the "real" problem is not the sixth problem itself, but the lack of attention to it by the developers of grand visions. They are focused on making the vision happen. I have no doubt that the sixth problem can be solved. The question is whether a solution must be part of the infrastructure of the grand vision from the earliest designs, or whether it can be added piecemeal afterward when the cyber warfare really begins—rearguard actions all over again, but the stakes will be higher than ever.

There may be a lesson to be learned from the DARPAnet, the precursor of the Internet, which was built on open principles and little thought about misuse. The focus was on getting distributed communication networks to work. Could the DARPAnet have been designed differently, in hindsight, to make our present security problems easier to track, compartmentalize, and handle? Some experts feel that authentication should have been included in name servers from the very beginning, and that the messaging protocols should have been designed to always indicate the actual source of any message, no matter how many "hops" it makes in getting to its destination.

Following up on this early DARPAnet lesson, should the IT systems of the future be built with monitoring facilities and event feeds at every level from the network to the strategic level? And should they have backup duplication of essential monitoring and tracking facilities? This will be expensive, just like having security checkpoints at airports today. But it may become part of the cost of running the information society.

1.8 Summary: Staying Ahead of Chaos

The recurring theme of this chapter is that our event-driven global information society is heading into a lot of trouble if we don't pay attention to tackling and solving a number of related problems.

- Monitor events at every level in IT systems—worldwide and in real time.
- Detect complex patterns of events, consisting of events that are widely distributed in time and location of occurrence.
- Trace causal relationships between events in real time, both horizontally within a level of system activity and vertically between high and low levels of system activity.
- Take appropriate action when patterns of events of interest or concern are detected.
- Modify our monitoring and action strategies in real time, on the fly.
- Design our systems to incorporate autonomous processes for applying levelwise event monitoring and viewing and for taking appropriate actions.

What we are talking about here is developing an *event processing technology* applicable to every level of system operations in all our IT layers. Such a technology is a key foundation to managing the electronic enterprise and is critical to developing capabilities to defend our IT systems.

Chapter 2

Managing the Electronic Enterprise in the Global Event Cloud

- *The global event cloud*
- *How enterprises operate in the global event cloud*
- *Management processes—going beyond workflow*
- *Autonomous parallel, asynchronous processes*
- *The electronic enterprise*
- *Treating the exceptional situation as normal*
- *Enabling the human to control the electronic enterprise*
- *Technology demands for managing the electronic enterprise*

As we saw in the previous chapter, today's enterprises—business, government, and military—are adapting to and utilizing global information processing. This is a matter of survival.

This chapter discusses what kinds of capabilities a new foundational technology would have to provide to meet the challenges of managing the electronic enterprise.

2.1   How the Global Event Cloud Forms

Fueled by the growth of Internet-based information processing, more and more enterprises are engaging in trading hubs, either public or private, and other forms of Internet trading to modernize and streamline their business processes. Despite the dot-com bubble burst in 2000, this trend toward electronic business processing is continuing to increase in an effort to cut costs and gain competitive advantage.

One example that illustrates this activity is the outsourcing of applications to application service providers (ASPs).[1] The industry projections in 2000 for the growth of eCommerce activities are staggering. At that time, market research projections estimated the revenue in outsourcing to ASPs to increase from $900 million in 1998 to $23 billion in 2003. Some estimates predicted business-to-business eCommerce revenues to increase worldwide from $185 billion in 2000 to $1.26 trillion in 2003, with 34% of those revenues carried by eMarketplaces.

2.1.1   The Open Enterprise

As enterprises adopt the electronic collaboration model, described in Section 1.5, their boundaries become blurred. Events are being created internally, within the enterprise, and externally, outside the enterprise. These events flow in both directions across the IT layer boundaries, its network gateways and firewalls. Events are flowing between the enterprise and its trading partners, the electronic market hubs in which it is participating, and its outsourcing activities with its ASPs, as well as between its own operations. The enterprise is becoming *open* to permit the event traffic it needs to pursue its collaborations. This kind of openness requires sophisticated security technology, including new kinds of authentication and real-time policy monitoring, that defend the enterprise without obstructing its business activities.

2.1.2   The Global Event Cloud

Today's reality is that the enterprise is operating in a complex environment of events happening on a global scale. These are high-level business, logistics, and application-to-application events. They form the *global event cloud* in which the open enterprise is operating. The scale of the global event cloud that each enterprise must interact with is continually increasing. Today thousands of business-level events per second are being communicated across the IT layers of some enterprises. These numbers will increase with activity in the global eMarketplace.

---

[1] A Web search on "ASP" will provide more than enough references.

We talk of a *cloud* of events rather than a stream because the event traffic is not, in most cases, nicely organized. Events arrive from all parts of the global Internet. They do not necessarily arrive at the enterprise in the order they were created or in their causal order (see Section 1.2.1). They form an unorganized cloud of events, and the open enterprise has to deal with it.

Some of these events drive the autonomous processes that manage the enterprise's operations in this environment. Each stage in a management process may depend upon recognizing patterns of several events—not just one event—from within the cloud. And those events may arrive in unexpected orders or timing. Many more events from the cloud could be leveraged for electronic intelligence to aid the enterprise's processes, if only the technology were available to utilize the information these events convey.

2.1.3 The Electronic Enterprise

Event driven means simply that whatever tools and applications are used to automate business and enterprise management processes, those tools and applications rely on receiving events to monitor the progress of a process and issuing events to initiate its next stages. This is becoming universal for all business processing.

For example, simple document processing, such as moving purchase orders through a chain of activities or process steps—for example, authentication, inventory checking, payment, and delivery—is managed by workflow engines that rely on events from the process steps to drive the execution of the process. Typically, those events may come in the form of messages across the Internet from separate departments of the enterprise in different geographic locations.

Another example is manufacturing processes, such as chip fabrication. These processes are controlled by complicated sequences of events flowing back and forth between the fabrication line (fabline) machines and process-controller engines that track the progress and test results of each casette of wafers as they move along the line through a six-week manufacturing process.

Nowadays the highest levels of supply chain processes supporting just-in-time manufacturing are automated and integrated with the processes of other participants in a supply chain consortium. Here we see the trading hubs devoted to specific industries, such as automotive manufacturing, global banking, pharmaceuticals, energy trading and distribution, and so on, emerging as the integration layer for these B2B activities between enterprises.

As globally integrated business process collaboration becomes the highway to cutting costs and streamlining business operations, so also the sets of events that must be processed to execute these processes become increasingly complex and highly nonlinear. The enterprise must learn to operate in the global event cloud. Management processes must be event driven and automated.

The technological implication is that the modern enterprise is becoming, or has already become, an event-driven, autonomous, information processing system. This is the *electronic enterprise.*

2.2   Operating in the Global Event Cloud

Figure 2.1 shows a simple workflow business process, ProcessOrder, for processing customers' orders to buy product.[2] Enterprise management processes today typically consist of a large number of linear workflows like this one, loosely strung together and nested one inside another.

ProcessOrder is a process for handling incoming orders from customers in our typical electronic enterprise. Let us call it enterprise E. E is the vendor to the incoming customer, but it uses its own "vendors" to help fullfil an order. So E is an electronic middleman, perhaps using eMarketplaces to

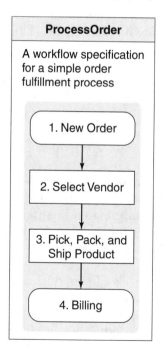

Figure 2.1: Today's business process: a linear workflow, ProcessOrder

---

[2]Web search on "workflow," "workflow standards," "workflow coalition."

select its vendors. ProcessOrder is initiated inside E by an event signifying that a customer places an order for product. A simple sequence of activities— a flow—then takes place to complete the process. First E must choose a vendor that can supply the product at the best price, and second, when the step 2 activity terminates successfully with a chosen vendor, E must request the vendor to pack the product and ship it directly to the customer. Finally, E initiates the activity of billing the customer.

In carrying out this simple linear workflow, the boundaries of enterprise E are crossed by outgoing and incoming events many times.

Figure 2.2 shows how this workflow operates when it is put in place in the enterprise's processes. The workflow specification is compiled (using one of a number of commercial workflow tools) into a set of rules that drive the process activities. Each rule triggers on an event from one step of the process and generates a new event that initiates the next step. The rules are executed by a workflow rules engine. In Figure 2.2 the ProcessOrder workflow is on the left, the global event cloud in the center, and the rules

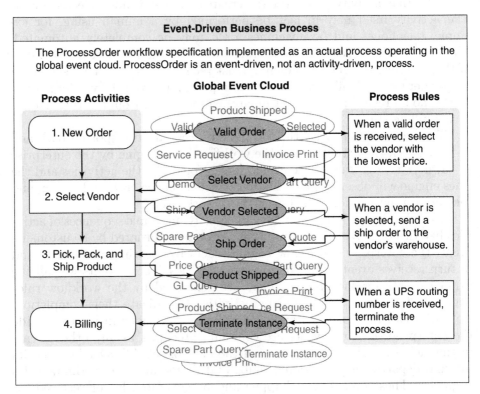

Figure 2.2: Enterprise operations in the global event cloud

that drive the workflow process are on the right. Events are depicted as oval shapes and their source and destination by arrows.

The rules that drive the process are *reactive rules*. The rules in the figure are written in English, but in actuality they are translated into a computer language that the rules engine can execute. Each rule contains an event pattern called a trigger. A trigger will match any appropriate event sent by one activity in the process, called a triggering event, and react by generating a new event. The new event contains the data needed to initiate the next activity. Rules that depend upon matching single events are sufficient to drive a simple process like this one. The rules to drive more complex processes may have trigger patterns consisting of multiple events.

Figure 2.2 shows that a lot of events are happening in the cloud. Most events are light colored—they are irrelevant to this process. Only a few of them, the dark events, trigger the workflow rules and drive the process. The process is initiated by a ValidOrder event. That event triggers a driving rule that issues a SelectVendor event, which initiates the next activity, "choose vendor with best price." If and when that activity completes successfully, that activity generates (or creates) a new VendorSelected event. The activity itself may in fact be performed by a human using, for example, telephones and fax machines, or it may be completely automated. The new VendorSelected event is transported by the IT layer and appears in the event cloud. The rules engine must receive it and react by sending a ShipOrder event. Similarly, a ProductShipped event from the vendor's warehouse should result in a final TerminateInstance event from the rules engine to the billing step.

These events that drive the workflow process are transported back and forth between the activities and the workflow rules engine by the enterprise IT layer. They are part of the event cloud. Hopefully, the activities and the rules engine will observe the events in correct sequence, as they happen, and take appropriate action. Then everything works well.

Workflow is a good methodology for specifying simple sequences of activities like this one. When an instance of a process is initiated by a customer's event, the enterprise's workflow engine reacts by creating new events and in turn receives events from the process activities. These events we call the driving events for the process. They are generated by the workflow rules engine to initiate activities and by activities to indicate their completion. Activities can take place in widely distributed locations inside or outside the enterprise. Driving events are communicated just as any other events in the global cloud of events crossing the enterprise's IT layer between its internal departments, its trading hubs and ASPs, and the workflow rules engine(s). These events must happen and be generated by, or received by, the engine, or the process will stall. That's when managers have to worry as much about the driving events and if they are happening, as much about the activities.

When a driving event fails to happen—a so-called *exceptional situation*—we have to find out why. The problems causing the situation could be in the process steps, or the event cloud, or the workflow rules. Then capabilities to view the process's progress intelligently and diagnostic tools to find out quickly what happened become very important. More about these issues later. Of course, we have simplified the picture. The rules are usually much more complex than simply "choose the vendor with the lowest price." The choice of vendor may be an auction process, as we shall see. Also, in practice many instances of the process are going on simultaneously for different orders. Events contain data that identifies which instance of the process they drive—for example, order Id, product, quantity, price, and timing. The data in the events is critical in enabling the rules engine to do its job of monitoring and prompting the right process instance. Also, we have omitted discussing details such as the need for event adapters. To access the enterprise's event cloud, the rules engine must be interfaced to the enterprise's IT layer by utilizing event adapters to transform events into formats used by the rules engine. However, the overall message that we want to get across in this section is simple: The process is *event driven*.

2.3   Going Beyond Workflow

We've said nothing about how the activities in our workflow example are actually carried out—for example, are they fully automated, or are humans still in the loop? In Figure 2.2 the events that indicate the completion of each step are shown by dark arrows as being sent from the workflow boxes through the event cloud to the rules engine. They travel in a left-to-right direction in the figure. In some enterprises some of the activities shown as boxes might be performed by humans. The completion events would be created by a human completing an activity, by making a database entry such as "I've finished this task" or sending that message on a pub/sub middleware. The rules engine receives completion events from the cloud, for example, by receiving callbacks from a database or subscribing to specific message subjects on a pub/sub middleware.

To enter the world of global Internet marketplace decision making, business and management processes must meet the reduced time scales and increased situational complexities that will be involved. Processes as simple as ProcessOrder will become the exception rather than the rule, perhaps occuring only at the highest levels of the enterprise. The management processes of the electronic enterprise will be built to optimize their execution times. They soon will be (or already are) parallel, asynchronous processes.

Three key technology demands toward achieving the goal of autonomous parallel processing.

- Enterprise management processes will
    - Be completely automated and event driven.
    - Execute in parallel.
    - Make decisions and communicate asynchronously.
- The human will be taken out of the loop to make all the activities in the process fully autonomous.
- The human will be kept in control over the processes by being provided with
    - Personalized, real-time viewing to make decisions.
    - On-the-fly modifiable process rules, including exceptional situation handling, to modify and control processes.

The first two demands are dictated by the speeds at which global eBusiness processing will take place and the complexity of the event processing involved.

The third demand is a matter of business life and death, for we cannot expect to build processes that perform correctly in every situation or to foresee every possible situation. Just as the airline captain can override the autopilot, so must the corporate executive be able to monitor and override the autonomous process.

But, wait a minute! Will all enterprise processes become fully automated? Probably not. Some kinds of manufacturing processes—for example, aircraft manufacturing or high-end products requiring human craftsmanship—will have humans in the loop in some activities.

Do these technology demands still make sense as a technology foundation for those processes in which the human is an active participant—that is, still "in the loop"? Yes. Parallel and asynchronous execution remains desirable to achieve greater flexibility in the process. The human, by the way, very seldom sticks rigidly to a linear activity flow and may wish to interact with the process flow control at several points concurrently. Stock traders epitomize parallel, asynchronous decision making. Also, the trend will be to integrate human in-the-loop processes with other processes that are fully automated. Integration is easier when all processes are based on similar driving technology. Finally, even in purely linear workflow with humans participating in the activities, having effective real-time monitoring with personalized viewing of the progress of the process is key to increasing the effectiveness of process management.

2.4 Parallel and Asynchronous Processes

As an example of an automated, parallel, asynchronous business process, suppose we interface our ProcessOrder process with our enterprise's operations with trading partners or with a trading hub. The SelectVendor step 2 (see Figure 2.2) becomes a complex subprocess that is not easily expressed in standard workflow.

SelectVendor must deal with real-time eMarketplace trading. The simple rule "select vendor with the lowest price" for step 2 of the workflow is expanded into a detailed set of rules for a complex process. This step is a parallel, asynchronous process for sending out requests for quotations (RFQs) for product and for making a choice from among the bids that respond.

Figure 2.3 shows an expansion of the SelectVendor activity in Figure 2.2. It is now a fully automated process. The SelectVendor process is expanded

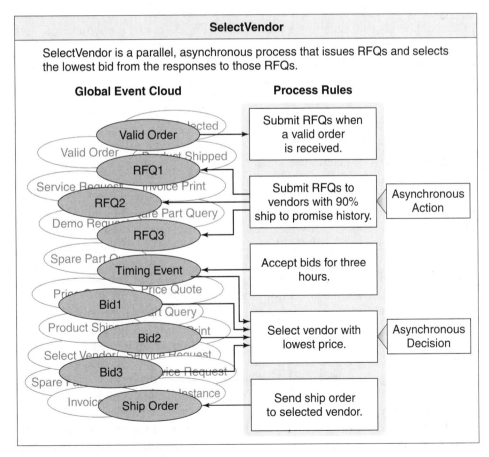

Figure 2.3: A parallel, asynchronous eTrading process

into a set of subprocesses that execute in parallel and asynchronously. The subprocesses issue RFQs and analyze the Bid events that respond. There is also a timer subprocess. All subprocesses can be executing at the same time.

All the subprocesses are interfaced with the enterprise's IT layer. The events driving the whole process are communicated to and from partners, suppliers, and trading hubs outside the enterprise. We assume all processing within the enterprise is fully automated. Consequently, the SelectVendor process compiles into reactive rules that are executed by a process rules engine or maybe several rules engines. All event interaction is between the rules engine(s) and entities outside the enterprise. All interaction to drive the process takes place through the event cloud. Rules engines with reactive rules interact with the global event cloud via the IT layer.

The event cloud is shown on the left in Figure 2.3, and the reactive rules are shown on the right. Arrows indicate which events are generated by the rules engine and which events it receives from other entities via the cloud.

As Figure 2.3 shows, a Valid Order event initiates the SelectVendor process. The process puts out a number of RFQ events by some method that can vary between instances of the process; it can be broadcast, or parallel point-to-point distribution, or whatever. The RFQ events go out into the event cloud, and Bid events come back from trading hubs and individual suppliers. The Bid events can arrive concurrently in no particular order, and we don't know how many there will be. The RFQ events may be interleaved with the Bid events. For example, the first wave of RFQs might lead to bids that result in modified RFQs and then more bids.

The patterns of events the rules engine creates and reacts to are much more complex than in the case of linear workflow. Rules trigger on sets of events (not single events), execute in parallel, and output sets of events. Rules will trigger on a set of events only *if* the events match a specified pattern *and* the context in which the events are received is the right one. Typically, context checking involves checking the state of the process—for example, checking to see if specified database queries return expected values. Context checking makes the execution of the rules more complicated.

For example, the SelectVendor rules might contain a strategy to accept sets of Bid events in case no single bid is satisfactory. A number of bids might be accepted together if they are all received within a small time window, and if they can be aggregated to satisfy product volume and cost, and if each of the bidders has a record that satisfies a reliability test. This kind of rule would trigger on a pattern that is matched by a set of several Bid events. A database query would be made to check the reliability of each of the bidders in a set of Bid events that matches the pattern.

This kind of process can only be executed if we have the technology to detect complex patterns of events and take into account the current computational state as part of the matching process.

Technology demands for achieving parallel, asynchronous processes include:

- Scalable complex event pattern matching, taking into account the context or state at the time of a match.
- The ability to reuse the data in sets of events that match a rule's pattern in the creating of new events.

We need a capability to match *complex event patterns* in the global event cloud. These patterns are needed to trigger reactive rules. Briefly, a complex event pattern is a template that specifies multiple events and their order and timing, the data they may contain, as well as other information (for example, values of database queries). A complex event pattern can match an unlimited number of different sets of events—unless it is specified to be very restrictive in what it can match. We expect to need complex event pattern matching that scales to thousands of events per second.

The rules for electronic enterprise processes will be constructed to trigger on matches of complex event patterns. They will react by creating new events and taking other action using data carried in the events that matched the patterns.

These technology demands are the foundation for implementing parallel, asynchronous real-time management processes. Our phrasing of these demands is somewhat technical, but we will explain them in detail later.

2.5 On-the-Fly Process Evolution

The business environment will change continually in the global information world. We cannot expect to design our processes to foresee or react to every situation. We will need to adjust them frequently by changing their responses to a situation or to recognize a new situation. Enterprise management processes will be in constant evolution. Adjustments to the processes and to their driving rules must be made on the fly during operations.

On-the-fly evolution means the ability to modify a process without halting the rules engines or disrupting the execution of other processes—and to effect the modifications rapidly, on the scale of minutes or hours rather than days or weeks.

Figure 2.4 shows changes to the process rules for accepting bids from suppliers. The modified rules for sending RFQs and analyzing bids are shown in dark gray. The timing rule has been deactivated—perhaps a bad decision that may be reversed on the basis of future performance. The criteria for sending RFQs and selecting Bid events are now quite different. Changes like this might be made for a variety of reasons that are not likely to be

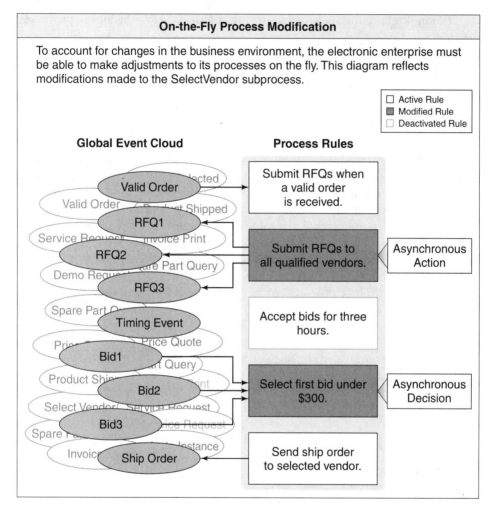

Figure 2.4: Process rule changes must be made on the fly

foreseen when the process is designed. The first wave of Bid events might not be satisfactory, so the requirements are lowered. Or business intelligence gathered from the event cloud and other sources might indicate that the product is about to become scarce.

This is an example of why the human needs to be in control of the enterprise's processes, at least for the foreseeable future. Humans must be able to see and understand the management situations in real time, as they develop in the global context, and how the enterprise processes are responding. "Being in control" requires humans to have understandable, personalized *views* of enterprise activity at every level of activity. Monitoring log files of rule engine activity, as provided by many of today's process automation tools, is not acceptable. A technology of viewing enterprise systems has to be developed.

Many technical issues are involved in on-the-fly process modification—for example, what to do about instances of an old version of a process that are still running when the modification is made. Another issue is how to analyze the effects of a modification to one process on other processes with which it may interact. In current technology, changes to a business process in a large enterprise often take weeks and lead to numerous meetings to form a consensus among affected parties.

Some technology demands for controlling and modifying electronic processes are

- Real-time, personalized viewing of activity at every level in the enterprise
- On-the-fly process modification
- Simulation of processes before going live

2.6   Exceptions Must Be First-Class Citizens in Process Design

If a process fails to behave in a given situation as specified or meets a situation for which it has no specification, it is said to have encoutered an *exception.*

For example, an exception situation would be when the SelectVendor process fails to select a vendor within the specified time. It fails to generate the Vendor Selected event.

There could be a myriad of reasons for such a failure. Some examples follow.

- The SelectVendor process did not receive any bids in response to its RFQs. A lack of response from the process could be caused by a missing case—for example, the process design did not specify what to do if no bids are received.
- The selection subprocess failed to reach a decision on the set of bids that were received. This could be a bug in the subprocess's selection algorithms, or none of the bids was satisfactory.
- The Submit RFQs and SelectVendor subprocesses did not coordinate properly, and the selection subprocess did not start. This could be another kind of bug in communication between processes.

The idea of exceptional situations being "first-class citizens" means that whatever design techniques are used to design and implement the normal and intended behavior of processes should also apply to designing them to deal with exceptional situations (see Figure 2.3). We should be able to add new rules to evolve our SelectVendor process to deal with the "no bids received" situation—for example, by generating an event reporting that situation. Figure 2.5 shows additional rules for dealing with a situation in which no vendor is selected within three hours, by relaxing the criteria for sending RFQs.

So, the process design technology should let us design normal processing and exceptional processing in the same way. We should be able to evolve processes to deal with exceptional situations by using the same on-the-fly rules change techniques that we use to evolve processes to meet changes in marketplaces or other operational environments.

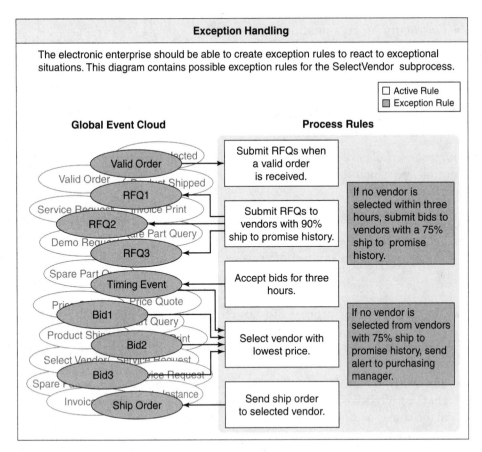

Figure 2.5: Rule changes on the fly to deal with an exception

However, there are some distinguishing problems in dealing with exceptions.

- We must be made aware of their presence in real time—that is, the process is not behaving as specified.
- We must be able to find out what causes them.

The first issue should be solved by the same real-time, levelwise, personalized viewing that is needed to support process evolution in the face of marketplace changes. But the second issue, finding the causes, requires new diagnostic capabilities. We need to know which subprocesses are involved in creating events that have led to an exception. The subprocesses are not necessarily known at design time because a process design can be dynamic, allowing different subprocesses to be invoked at runtime depending upon the actual situation that arises. Different subprocesses will be invoked in different situations. So we need a diagnostic capability to uncover the subprocesses and events that are causally related to an exceptional situation, and their subprocesses, and so on, and the state of each subprocess all the way down the causal chain. Indeed, we need to be able to track the causal, hierarchy of events leading to an exceptional situation, and to discover any missing events that should have happened. This kind of capability is called *runtime drill-down diagnostics*.

So, in dealing with exceptional situations, the technology demands will be, again, all the demands listed in Section 2.5 for real-time, levelwise, personalized viewing and on-the-fly modifications, plus one additional demand: runtime drill-down diagnostics for tracking causally related process activities.

2.7 Summary: Managing the Electronic Enterprise

In this chapter, we have described the event-driven operation of an enterprise's business processes and the challenge of managing them in the emerging global eMarketplace. Most business processes will become fully integrated with other processes outside the enterprise. The trend toward openness and collaboration will bring additional complexity to managing processes across multiple enterprises. At each step in the discussion, we have drawn conclusions about requirements for a technology foundation for managing this kind of processing.

It is unpredictable at the moment how far enterprises will actually develop toward finally achieving "autonomous electronic" status. The time such developments will take may turn out to be three years from now or ten years from now. But it is abundantly obvious that the trend is in the direction of Internet-enabled global electronic commerce. And anyone who wants to be a player is going to need some of this foundational technology. Of course, new technology is not a substitute for a good business model. It is an aid to making a good model work.

We summarize the technology demands as the following:

- An ability to design and deploy event-driven parallel and asynchronous processes that can recognize complex event situations in the global event cloud
- Process simulation as part of the design phase, before going live
- On-the-fly modifiable processes
- Design for handling exceptional situations as an integral part of process design
- Real-time, drill-down, event-based diagnostics, utilizing event causality relationships, applicable to process behavior

Chapter $\boxed{3}$

Viewing the Electronic Enterprise—
Keeping the Human in Control

- *Event monitoring—the standard technology today*
- *Enterprise viewing—a step beyond monitoring*
- *Recognizing sets of events from the global event cloud—a key to personalized viewing*
- *Information gaps*
- *Enterprise structure and abstraction hierarchies*
- *Hierarchical viewing—the key to human control of the enterprise*

Running the enterprise's processes, and recognizing the processes' driving events, is one aspect of enterprise management. The global event cloud contains a lot of other information that is relevant to understanding the performance of the processes, but not always in an obvious form. It has to be extracted.

The ability to get *problem-relevant information*—and get it in time for it to be useful—is a critical capability toward managing an enterprise. We need to be able to tap into the event cloud at every level of the IT layer (see Section 1.3) and observe the events. Whether we are engaged in next-generation inter-enterprise commerce or fighting cyber wars, we need relevant information to automate the complex decision making these kinds of real-time activities require—and to diagnose what goes wrong with them.

It would be convenient if we could observe and monitor events that are directly relevant to whatever problem we are trying to solve. As we will discuss in this chapter, the events we have access to are not always tailored to the problems we are trying to solve. Therefore, we need a technology that enables us to progress in stages. The first stage is recognizing relevant patterns of events in the sources of events we do have access to and can monitor. The second stage is aggregating information in those events to build up information that is needed to solve our problems.

Given relevant information, we can then design and automate our enterprise processes to make decisions and take actions based upon that information. Furthermore, our problems are constantly changing. So, we must have the flexibility to change both our event processing and our enterprise processes on the fly when our problems and goals change.

3.1　Today's Event Monitoring Is Too Primitive

Why is it difficult to get events that are relevant to the decisions we are trying to make? Part of the answer lies in the historical progression of problems that have arisen in running an IT-based enterprise, from the low-level network problems of yesterday, ascending to the high-level problems of today. At each step in the development of layered enterprises, technology has lagged behind the progression of problems.

3.1.1　System Monitoring Focuses on the Network Layer

The most common class of problems facing enterprise systems today is keeping them running. Major headaches happen when the performance of the communication layer deteriorates, or parts of it fail altogether. As we discussed earlier, this class of problems is generally lumped together under one category, *network management*. What makes these problems difficult is that *distributed behavior* is hard to track, understand, and control. And it is compounded by the fact that modern IT layers often have a dynamic architecture of their own.

Understandably, the bulk of the considerable commercial effort that has been put into enterprise system monitoring until now has been concentrated largely on the low-level IT layers. Even so, the IT layer monitoring tools leave much to be desired.

The network layer tools monitor and record both the network traffic and special kinds of instrumentation events. The kinds of events that are logged are typically TCP packets, warning events, alerts, and performance measurement events that indicate the performance of basic network components such as routers and servers. The event logs are fed to various commercial viewing tools that provide traffic statistics and warnings of various problems. All these tools give system managers a primitive way of keeping track of how the IT layer is behaving and a way of detecting overloading or failures on various pathways through it. Additionally, many intrusion detection tools monitor network traffic for sequences of events that are typical of known attempts to subvert the security of the IT system.

At present, the number of event viewing and analysis tools is growing rapidly to meet the demands of this market to improve network reliability and security. All this monitoring and analysis is focused on the events at the lowest networks layers of our enterprise systems, as shown in Figure 1.4.

3.1.2 Network-Level Monitoring Doesn't Even Solve Network Problems

Despite this growth in network monitoring, system managers still have a hard job. The tools contain very little "smarts" to tell a manager what the problem is and what to do. Network managers have to figure out from the event logs and statistical views of the event traffic exactly what is happening. They are faced daily with the following kinds of issues.

- *The network event logs can become very large and difficult to handle in real time.* In many cases, network management is reduced to "day-later" postmortem analysis. This is particularly true in monitoring for intrusions and information theft. Indeed, intruders routinely script intrusion probes to take several days, thus outlasting the analysis capabilities and "flying under the radar."

- *Tools to aid in picking out sets of related events are needed.* Events can be related because of the network topology or other factors not explicitly encoded in the event's data. An example is the so-called "event storm," in which many misleading alerts indicating potential equipment failures happen because of a single failure somewhere else in the network. Events that signify related system activities in the communication layer can happen at different times and therefore appear in the logs widely separated by a lot of irrelevent events. A history of related activities may last over several logs. Tools to identify related events are needed and should apply over large sets of log files.

- *Causal tracking is needed.* When we view a large event log in real time, and an event that indicates an error turns up, like a server going down, we need tools that can immediately point out the other events in the log that indicate which system activities caused the failure. At present we have to use a lot of knowledge about the network to try to figure it out.

- *Predictive monitoring is beyond the state of the art.* Recognition of patterns of events during network operations that indicate an approaching failure before it happens just isn't in the picture. At best, there are methods for extracting patterns from prior failures and trying to recognize when these happen again.

So, although network-level monitoring is already a multi-billion-dollar market, the analysis tools for network management need a lot of improvement. The diagnostic intelligence needed to keep the network running is not yet in the tools but still resides in the system manager's head.

To summarize, the present generation of IT layer monitoring tools do a poor job of aiding in network management, and they certainly do not deliver events that are relevant to higher-level operations and decision making.

3.2 An Example of Causal Tracking

Here we give a short example of how tracking both events *and* the causal relationships between events can yield more information than simply tracking the events by themselves. Our example applies causal tracking to monitoring a simple transaction protocol. Many transaction systems, particularly those dealing with database entries, use a *two-phase commit* protocol to terminate multistep transactions.[1]

As an example, suppose that we are monitoring the transactions in a financial trading system, as depicted in Figure 3.1. The middleware in Figure 3.1 is a financial trading network. Several banks and brokerage houses may be participating in a transaction. Finalizing the transaction depends upon finalizing several subtransactions between the participants. Either all the subtransactions complete successfully, or none of them are completed. This is often called *atomicity*, meaning that a set of subtransactions appear as one atomic transaction. To ensure atomicity over the set of subtransactions, we might suppose that the Electronic Trade Confirmation (ETC) system shown in Figure 3.1 plays the role of a transaction manager.

One of the banks plays the role of the transaction master. When it determines that the transaction may have reached completion, it asks the

---

[1]Web search on "two-phase commit."

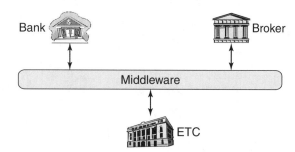

Figure 3.1: A financial trading network

ETC to manage the completion step. This step takes place in two phases:

1. *A polling phase.* The ETC sends a message to each of the participants, asking if they are willing to commit to their subtransactions.
2. *A commit phase.* All the replies are taken into consideration by the ETC in determining whether to request a commit to, or withdraw from, all the subtransactions. If one reply is negative, the ETC requests all participants to withdraw.

We can monitor the events between the participants by monitoring the trading network. We assume sufficient knowledge is supplied by the data in the events and by the participants about their business processes to track the causal relationships between the events.

The events resulting from the two phases are shown in Figure 3.2. Events are shown in boxes. If an event is a cause of another event, there is an arrow from the first event to the second one.

In Figure 3.2 there are three participants: P1, P2, and P3. Atomicity here means they all have to agree to commit their subtransactions. The Request from the master bank to the ETC, to commit transaction with identification number Tid, causes a polling phase to begin. A Request is sent from the ETC to each participant. For example, the event ETC_to_P1_Request is a request from the ETC to P1 to commit to transaction Tid.

In this example, each participant agrees to its subtransaction. There is a causal relationship between each Request from the ETC and the Agree reply from a participant. A Request *causes* a reply, either an Agree or a Deny. On the other hand, because the interactions between the ETC and the participants are carried out independently, usually at the same time, there are no causal links between the Request and the Agree events between different participants. So there are three independent causal chains in Figure 3.2 between the ETC and the participants in the polling phase.

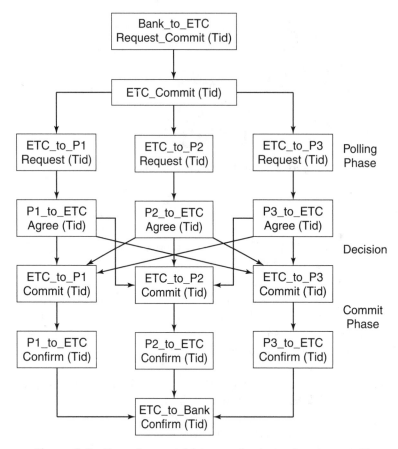

Figure 3.2: Causal event history of a two-phase commit

After the polling phase, the ETC makes a decision. As shown in Figure 3.2, every Agree reply is a cause of every Commit event that the ETC sends to the participants. These causal relationships exist because the ETC takes *all* the replies into account in the decision to issue commit events. For example, the arrow from P1_to_ETC Agree to ETC_to_P3 Commit means that P1's reply was a cause of the ETC's message to P3 to commit.

The causal arrows give us additional information about the ETC's decision making process that cannot be seen from the set of events alone. For example, at the decision point, if any of the causal arrows between the Agree events and the Commit events are missing, the ETC's decision making process is in error. A missing causal arrow would mean that the ETC didn't take one of the replies into consideration in deciding to send one of the Commit events to one of the participants. That reply might have been a Deny! If we look only at the events, we may not see that the process has an error, because the decision, say, Commit, could still be correct—that is, consistent with all the replies. Using only the events, we would not see that the decision process is erroneous, because the events show only a correct decision. However, an erroneous decision process will eventually lead to errors in other transactions, perhaps when the decision should be to withdraw. It would be less costly to catch the decision process error now, before it causes transaction errors later on.

Note that in the case when some of the replies in the polling phase are Deny, the commit phase instruction to all participants must be Withdraw. The causal structure between the replies and the Withdraw instructions can differ from the case when all the replies are Agree, because only one Deny is needed to make the decision.

In this example, the commit phase consists of three independent chains of events, a Commit and a Confirm, between the ETC and each of the participants. It results in the ETC's issuing a Confirm to the master bank.

3.3   Information Gaps

The problem of delivering relevant information does not stop with the IT layer monitoring tools. It's a problem with monitoring and management at every level in an enterprise.

Different people engaged in the operations of an enterprise, as shown in Figure 3.3, need different kinds of information. This is most obvious when people are operating at different levels of activity within the enterprise or at the same level but within different departments. This leads to *information*

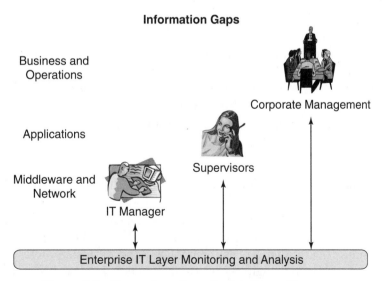

Figure 3.3: Examples of vertical information gaps

gaps between the kind of information people need to do their jobs effectively and easily, and the information they actually get.

An information gap generally has two dimensions:

- A vertical dimension, which is the difference between the level of the enterprise at which events and other data are monitored and the level at which the user is operating within the enterprise.
- A horizontal dimension, which is the amount of analysis needed to render the monitored information in a useful form for the user's tasks.

3.3.1   Examples of Information Gaps

Here are some examples of information gaps, having both horizontal and vertical components.

- A network manager for a manufacturing enterprise wants to view events carrying information about network functions such as node alerts, message traffic volumes, and overloads. The network manager has a large number of network monitoring tools to choose from. But the network manager must still infer from the data that those tools present what fundamental network problems are arising, or are likely to happen in the near future, before he or she can take appropriate actions. The monitored information is at the right level. But, as we discussed earlier, the analytical tools are weak. The information gap, representing the amount of reasoning needed to locate a problem, is largely horizontal.
- On the other hand, a production line supervisor in the same manufacturing enterprise as the network manager doesn't want the detailed network-level events. That kind of information is not relevant to the fabline supervisor's problems. The fabline supervisor is interested in a totally different view of the enterprise's operations that is relevant to such problems as
  - Utilization of machines on the fabline
  - Machine performance
  - Machine maintence time
  - Fabrication line status (machines in operation, machines idle, product flow, and so on)

To satisfy the fabline supervisor's needs, we can monitor the messages on the middleware communication layer between the fabrication machines, the fabline process controllers, and databases. Our source of events is somewhat higher-level than the network. But because they are controller messages, machine status, and test results messages, they are lower-level than the level of the supervisor's problems. They contain a lot of relevant information, fragmented and mixed up with irrelevant stuff. Large sets of these messages must be aggregated to give the supervisor a relevant view of the problems. So the information gap for the fabline supervisor is mainly vertical.

If things go wrong, the fabline supervisor will want to know if the network layer had anything to do with it. Here we see the need to drill down to the network level when fabline operations go wrong.

- Similarly, corporate management isn't interested in the network events or in fabline operations middleware messages. Management's problems center around a higher level of enterprise operations, involving the whole fabrication process:
  - Fabline product yield rates and product test results
  - Fabline operations costs
  - Excess production capacity
  - Orders for product
  - Delivery schedules

To deliver the information corporate management needs will require correlating events from different sources. Events from the fabline middleware must be aggregated with messages from industry trading hubs and the enterprise's business process and operations level. In this case, the information gap results from the range of levels of the event sources and the analysis needed to correlate them effectively.

3.4 Problem-Relevant Information

To bridge information gaps we need a technology for constructing problem-relevant information from whatever events we can monitor. What is "problem-relevant information?" The most important thing to consider in answering this question is that we monitor and process events toward solving a particular problem, the *problem of immediate interest*. It could be a specific situation that comes up during execution of a supply chain trading process. We need to know what's happening with the process—for example, why some suppliers are not responding within agreed time bounds, and whether to decide to complete the process with alternate suppliers. Or it could be an intrusion into our IT layers that's in progress, and we are watching it to see what the intruder will do next.

If the events we have to work with are relevant to the problem of immediate interest and contain information directly bearing on the problem, we will have an easier task to make decisions and take actions to deal with the problem. But, as usually happens, our event sources will not be relevant to our problem of interest but will present us fragmented information, diluted with lots of irrelevant events. So we have to process our event sources to produce problem-relevant events.

A second consideration in real-time decision making is that the problem of interest can change minute by minute. So we must be able to change our event processing operations on the fly as the problem of interest changes, to extract information relevant to the current problems.

Whether or not the events we get from our monitoring tools are relevant to our problem of immediate interest depends on how well they meet the following criteria:

- Relevance to the problem of immediate interest
- Ease of understandability
- Ease of analysis
- Ease with which multiple views can be coordinated

Relevance means that the events should be easily associated with factors in the situation and problem of interest. It is a subjective criterion. But we don't want to be looking at log files of TCP packets when we are interested in some corporate business-level problem, such as why our process for just-in-time auto parts acquisition is failing. As we will discuss later in this book, you don't always get events that are directly or obviously relevant. The underlying issue is what kind of technology can translate the events you are given into events that are relevant—whenever that is possible.

Understandability might be thought to be unnecessary if we could automate all our real-time decision making processes. Why would we humans need to watch what's happening? Let the rules engines do the work! It would take a very brave CEO to be that much "hands off." The situation would be analogous to an airplane pilot who didn't have an autopilot override. There will be bugs in our workflow engines, and situations we didn't plan or predict in our processes, and we have to watch out for cyber warfare too. So we will need technology that can translate our event feeds into situational views, graphs, and animations that are understandable and tell us how our problem of interest is progressing.

Ease of analysis is related to what kind of information the events contain. Among the data in the events should be data about their *relativities*. The events should contain information telling us which other events caused them, their timing as viewed from various system clocks, and how they are related to lower-level events. If an event contains data specifying its causality, timing, and aggregation, we have an easy task to build tools that let us drill back in time or causality, or drill down through layers, to find out how the event happened.

An ability to coordinate multiple views of a situation built from our event sources is needed whenever there is more than one problem of immediate interest. This puts us into multidimensional real-time decision making. We will discuss what a "view" is later. But it's important that whenever we have multiple real-time views of a moving or developing situation, we can synchronize them to give us a coordinated view of all dimensions of a real-time activity. As with ease of analysis, an ability to synchronize multiple views also depends upon the information contained in the events.

3.5 Viewing Enterprise Systems

A capability to construct problem-relevant views of a system's operations is the most important prerequisite for automating our processes for real-time decision making and managing our systems.

A *view of a system* is a selection of information about what the system is doing currently or did in the past that is processed to abstract or extract those aspects relevant to a problem of interest. A view can contain information from many sources, such as design and architecture documents, databases, and log files. But a great deal of it comes from the events generated by the system during its operation in its various IT layers and management tools.

These are some examples of views.

- *An application-level activity view:* A spreadsheet graph showing dynamically the percentage of the total communication traffic across the IT layer that is generated by the application-level activities on each workstation. Communication traffic is categorized into common application-level activities, such as e-mail, Web traffic, and FTP traffic, and plotted against time. So, for example, IP address X would show 5% of total Web traffic, 2% of total FTP traffic, and so on in time interval Y.
- *A who's-talking-to-whom view:* A moving animation of the messages flowing between applications shown on a picture of the system components and connections between them (actual network connections or virtual connections supported by middleware).
  - For example, in viewing a large ASP Web site, this view might show message flow between an application that does Web page rendering for customers and system components such as name servers and advertisement servers.

- A similar animation view of a command-and-control system might depict message traffic between the various components such as radar sensors, military strategy supervisor, track predictor, threat recognition, weapons controllers, and other components.

- *A network problems view:* A picture of the system's network architecture that shows by varying colors which network components are generating alerts or warning messages and how frequently they are doing it. This kind of view, typical in network management tools, would change the color of components such as servers and routers on a picture of the network architecture as those components issue more or fewer alerts and warnings from one time interval to the next.

- *A high-level system performance view:* A view showing the utilization time and downtime of the various components at various levels in the system together with what influence each component had on another's utilization time.

  - If the system is a factory automation system, a performance view might show the percentage of time spent in operation, maintenance, and downtime for each piece of equipment on the system.

  - For a large Web site, say, one being operated by an ASP, a performance view might show page rendering time and their breakdown into time spent by the page renderer on calls to other components such as servers and databases.

- *A corporate business process tracking view:* A view of the progress of each instance of a business process. The view initiates when sales notifies production of a completed contract, and that then tracks the high-level steps to start manufacture, report to corporate finance, deliver product, bill customer, and ship product. This view does not show any lower-level details of exceptions and failures within each department.

Each of these examples of a view has the following elements.

1. Each view has a problem of interest. In some examples it is a network-level problem, and in others it is a problem for some level of management.

2. Each view is event driven. Sources of events from any level of the enterprise system are monitored and processed to form the view. Examples of event processing operations include

   - Filtering out unneeded events

   - Categorizing events and counting events in a category

> — Aggregating events: recognizing sets of lower-level events and generating a higher-level event that summarizes the relevant information in the set of lower-level events

3. The views are provided in humanly understandable forms using graphics.

4. Each view provides relevant events that can be used to drive automated decision making processes. These processes may take actions such as generating events to drive the next steps in a process and issuing alerts, warnings, and requests to subprocesses for status and diagnostics.

5. Most important, a view must be easy to modify, on the fly, to incorporate new types of events, change the aggregation techniques, and so on. Commercial tools already provide some of these examples of views but are not easily reconfigured to change the view.

Viewing, as applied to an enterprise system, is a dynamic activity. It takes place while the system is running, although it is frequently also applied postmortem. Its purpose, in a nutshell, is to focus attention on, and thus understand, particular aspects of an enterprise's behavior, at any level of the system. It can be proactive so that action is taken to influence certain kinds of system behavior when it occurs.

3.6 Creating and Coordinating Multiple Views

Different people need different views. But to work together, they must all be "on the same page." Their views must be coordinated.

Simply, this is because different users are interested in different kinds of information about the system. And they need their personalized views of the system at the same time. The network manager and the stockbroker must have the views that are important to them—at the same time. In fact, it is usually true that two stockbrokers want different views of what is going on in a financial trading system. The capability to do this is called *multiple viewing*.

Not only do we need multiple views of a system, but each user needs to be able to customize their own view. It is quite likely that the demand for customized views of a large system will go well beyond what can be achieved by starting with some fixed set of views, say, as provided by some tool set, and combining those views according to a fixed set of combinators.

At present there are no principles for creating views or structuring them. The tools in the marketplace are quite ad hoc. But even more chaotic, there are no principles for *relating* views. One tool gives you one view. And another gives you a separate, unrelated view. As multiple viewing becomes possible, there will be an obvious need to relate different views so that users can coordinate their activities.

3.7   Hierarchical Viewing

A powerful technique to help in understanding a complex enterprise system is to separate the system's activities, and the operations that implement those activities, into layers—called *levels*. This is called an *abstraction hierarchy*. It allows us to view the system's activities one level at a time. And it lets us focus on what we want to think about. For example, we don't have to think about low-level concepts such as packets of bits, headers, and timeouts at the same time as we think about higher-level operations, such as sending and receiving e-mail. We might want to think about whether we spelled an addressee's name correctly or got their e-mail address right before we worry about whether the mailer is accessing the network properly—these are two different levels of concerns.

Viewing a system's behavior at different levels is called *hierarchical viewing*. It is one way to define techniques for creating and relating multiple views. The stockbroker and the network manager can be viewing the same system—the one they are both using—at the same time. But they can be looking at completely different views, one dealing with financial transactions and the other with network message activity.

To build hierarchical views we must first define an abstraction hierarchy. The sets of activities and operations of the system must be separated into different levels. Several problems need to be overcome to do this, some of them are technical and some, political.

- *Operational description:*   There must be general agreement on what the activities and operations of the enterprise are. This task has a political flavor because it involves forming consensus among the various users in the organization.
- *Hierarchical structuring:*   The levels must be ordered, top down, and the events signifying operations at any level must be defined as sets of sequences of events at the lower levels.

The operations of the communication layer will be at the lowest levels of an abstraction hierarchy for an enterprise. Above the communication levels are the application operations—the operations that are performed by using applications. The communication and application levels together form the *actual operations* of an abstraction hierarchy. The activities and events at levels above are *virtual* in the sense that they are composed of sets of actual events.

Hierarchical structuring is a foundation for building multiple views. The activities and events of any level are defined in terms of lower-level events. This lets us relate views. A view at one level can be refined (or blown up) into a view at lower levels using the hierarchy definition. As we shall illustrate later on, this is particularly useful when a view needs explanation, perhaps because something has gone wrong. For example, if a stockbroker's trade did not execute, maybe an explanation can be found by blowing up the trade view into a financial transaction view—maybe it would have violated SEC regulations because another trader was executing trades on the same account.

3.7.1 An Example of Hierarchical Viewing

To give an example of an event hierarchy, we return to our earlier example of causal tracking. The events and causal relationships in Figure 3.2 that result from the two-phase commit protocol activity together constitute a single complex event, say, Successful-Two-Phase-Commit. This event may have parameters that summarize the whole transaction, say, the names of the participants, the financial details, and the start and end times of the first and last events.

As Figure 3.4 shows, we view the Successful-Two-Phase-Commit event as being at a higher level, the *financial trades level.* All the two-phase commit protocol events and their relationships are viewed at a lower level, the *transaction protocol level.* Similarly, if the commit phase had failed, all the polling and withdraw events, together with their relationships, would constitute a Failed-Two-Phase-Commit event.

To define this hierarchy, we would need an *operational description* that defines the higher-level events, Successful-Two-Phase-Commit and

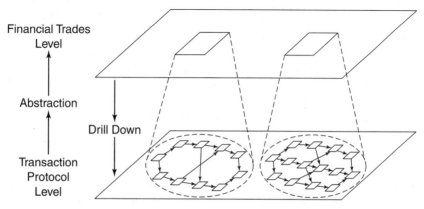

Figure 3.4: **A two-level hierarchy for viewing financial transaction activity**

Failed-Two-Phase-Commit, and a *hierarchical structure* that specifies the patterns of related protocol-level events that signify the high-level events.

Events at the financial trades level are called *abstractions* of patterns of events at the transaction protocol level. They abstract away, or hide, details that are considered unneccessary for a kind of user or view. Conversely, if we want to recover those details in any particular case, we can *drill down* from the higher-level event to the actual set of lower-level events and their relationships.

The events at the financial trades level give us different views of what is happening in the trading system from the view at the transaction protocol level. We can view, for example,

- The ratio of successful transactions to failures
- The timing of completed transactions, either successes or failures
- The numbers of concurrent transactions in progress at any time

At the transaction protocol level, the events give us detailed views of the actual transactions—how long a polling phase took versus a commit phase and so on.

If we are viewing at the financial trades level and want to know, say, why some financial trade took too long, we can drill down from that event to the protocol-level events that are its members. Maybe one of the participants took a lot longer to agree to commit its sub-transaction than the others.

A technology is needed that would allow us to implement hierarchical viewing and drill down—that is, to create the higher-level events whenever the patterns of related sets of lower-level events happen, and to recover the lower-level events from a high-level event. Such a technology has to be very flexible to easily allow for changes in the definitions of the event hierarchy.

Some abstraction hierarchies have become international standards, such as the International Standards Organization (ISO) Open System Interconnect (OSI) reference model for network-based systems [9]. This is because even before viewing became an important consideration, abstraction hierarchies were helpful in the design, standardization, and integration of systems—making them fit together. In the ISO standard, protocols are defined to specify the activity at each level in terms of the operations at that level. Relations between the operations at different levels are also defined precisely.

A complex system does not necessarily have one fixed abstraction hierarchy. This fact may be one measure of complexity. It may also result from variations in the user community. But this does not stop us from defining abstraction hierarchies as a first step in defining views and relating different views.

We may begin an effort to define an abstraction hierarchy using English as an easy-for-everyone starting point. But we can't stop there. When an abstraction hierarchy has reached community consensus, we must define it mathematically. We need precise techniques to define multiple abstraction hierarchies whose operations and levels may overlap. Mathematical precision is the key to being able to use an abstraction hierarchy to coordinate views dynamically, while the system is executing.

3.8 Summary: Viewing the Electronic Enterprise

Summarizing our discussion in this chapter, a brief list of the technical challenges for personalized viewing to keep the human in control of the electronic enterprise is as follows:

- *Personalized viewing:* An ability to create views, driven by the enterprise's event traffic, that can be defined or modified in real time to meet changes in enterprise operations or user requirements
- *View coordination:* Principles for coordinating multiple views
- *Hierarchical viewing:* Principles for defining event abstraction hierarchies corresponding to enterprise activity, and building views corresponding to levels of the hierarchy

Chapter 4

Designing the Electronic Enterprise

- *Rapid process modification to meet the demands of the eMarketplace*
- *The roles of process architecture in the process lifecycle*
- *Using process architectures to reduce errors in mission-critical process systems*
- *Constituents of process architecture—reactive behaviors, design constraints*
- *Dynamic process architectures*
- *Layered architectures and plug-and-play systems*
- *The abstraction principle for layered architectures*

In the previous chapters, we discussed how the electronic enterprise operates and navigates in the global event cloud. And we drew some conclusions about the underlying technology of complex event processing that would be needed to manage the operation of its processes. Now we look at the first step in developing electronic enterprises—*process design.*

The electronic enterprise's business processes, taken together with all their interactions, will constitute a very complex system. In fact, as we discuss in this chapter, this system of processes will be as complex as any of today's operating systems. It is also a mission-critical system for the electronic enterprise. Errors—especially early design errors, which are always the most costly in the long run—must be uncovered as quickly as possible.

We need to reduce errors at every stage in the lifecycle of mission-critical business processes. Furthermore, we need to rapidly modify operational processes to meet the Internet-speed variations in the electronic business environment. In fact, the electronic enterprise process system will be almost completely automated—no humans in the loop. But we must be able to keep the human informed and in control. Personalized viewing of enterprise operations must be treated as just another part of the process architecture. All these requirements call for a process development technology that goes beyond what is currently practiced today—a technology that can be employed end to end across the lifecycle, from design time to deployment and runtime management.

This chapter describes a complete lifecycle technology for event-driven process systems. It is based upon a very precise concept of *process architecture*. Process architecture has two primary goals: to enable us to rapidly modify individual processes in a system of processes and speed up the activity of designing systems of processes; and to reduce the risk of errors throughout the lifecycle. We describe the concepts of process architecture and *what* it enables us to do. The *how* is dealt with in later chapters.

This is a high-level introduction. Our objective in this chapter is to explore the concepts and the underlying technology foundation needed to support these concepts and their applications. Later chapters go into detailed examples.

4.1   Process Architectures

Remember, we are dealing with event-driven process systems—systems whose operation depends upon receiving and sending events.

Processes can be classified into two general categories: *processes* that react when input events are received by executing activities that may make database entries, compute values, and create new events, and *connectors* whose role is to transport events between activity processes. There are many different types of processes within each category. Both categories are equally important in the electronic enterprise.

Processes and connectors can be composed together to form process systems. Each process and connector is a *component* of a process system.

A *process architecture* is a precise, high-level specification of the behavior of each process in a system of processes and the dependencies and communication between the processes in the system. It is used as a standard to guide and constrain the development of a process system, end to end, throughout its entire lifecycle, from design to implementation, deployment, and modification.

Now we need to go into more detail. In what sense is an architecture "precise" and "high-level"? And, *how* is an architecture used to "guide and constrain"? The answers lie in what an architecture contains—its constituents.

A process architecture has three constituents:

- A graphical constituent, called the *architecture diagram*
- A behavioral constituent, called the *behavior specification*
- A constraint constituent, called the *design constraints*

An architecture diagram graphically shows the processes in the system and the connectors between the processes. Events flow along connectors and effect communication between processes. A diagram depicts the components of a process system and their communication structure. An architecture diagram can in fact consist of several architecture diagrams showing different layers in the system (see Section 4.6).

A behavior specification augments the diagram with a set of precise rules specifying how each process and connector behaves—that is, how a process or connector reacts when it receives events by creating new events and data.

The design constraints augment the diagram with a set of constraints that specify limitations on the process behaviors and interprocess communication via connectors in the architecture. A constraint can, for example, define a protocol by which processes communicate with one another, or access rights of processes to shared data, or time bounds on process activities.

4.2 Roles of Architecture in the Process Lifecycle

Processes are in continuous evolution. In the electronic enterprise, the system of operational-level management processes change daily, if not hourly. "*Lifecycle*" describes all the activities that go on in the life of a system of processes.

There are four major roles in which architecture can be applied to reduce errors during the lifecycle of mission-critical processes:

- Precise design of processes,
- Early simulation of processes during the design or redesign phases,

- Automated runtime checking of process implementations for consistency with process architectures,

- Component-based techniques for replacement of process components, with guaranteed freedom from the common kinds of errors that frequently happen during system modification.

Each of these roles applies to multiple activities during the lifecycle of a process. The roles are made possible because a process architecture has the precise mathematical or programming constituents described earlier that provide information to application tools such as simulators, constraint checkers, and runtime monitors. These tools are critical elements needed to automate the lifecycle applications of architecture.

Architecture constituents are described in Section 4.3. The following example illustrates the roles of architecture as facilitated by these constituents and the support tools that they enable.

Example: *Lifecycle Stages in Process Development*

Suppose our enterprise has a system of processes in operation, and we need to upgrade the system by adding a new process. Figure 4.1 shows typical steps in the process lifecycle and how architecture enables new interactions between those steps. Here's a scenario describing how our upgrade might proceed.

1. *Design a new process.* The major role of architecture is to express the design—to capture it for use in all the other lifecycle activities. So this step involves creating a graphical design showing how the new process interacts with other processes in the existing system, together with a behavior constituent specifying how it reacts to their inputs, and a constraint constituent specifying bounds on its behavior.

   This step is sometimes called *authoring.* The process is designed to achieve business goals. The behavior rules must specify how the process reaches the goals. The design constraints express business rules and policies that the process must conform to.

   The practice of precision in design is enforced by the need to provide behavioral rules and constraints in a precise mathematical language as constituents of the design. Although this makes technical demands on the architect, it enables automated architecture-checking tools to uncover many kinds of common errors, akin to type checking in programming languages. Behavior rules also enable event-based simulation (see step 3).

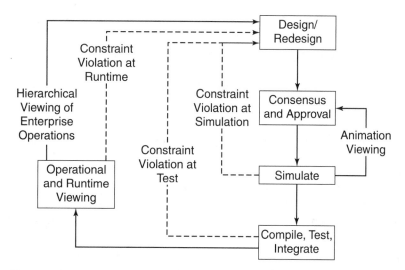

Figure 4.1: Activities in the architecture-based process lifecycle

2. *Convey the process design to all stakeholders. Form consensus on its acceptability in the enterprise.* For this purpose, architecture must be intuitively understandable by humans with different skills. This role of architecture usually depends in large measure upon a graphical constituent together with accompanying documentation in a non-mathematical language and style. Simulation of a design, and particularly animation of the simulation, is also a powerful conveyor of design issues—see the next step.

3. *Simulate the new process on event streams expected when it communicates with other processes in the system. Correct the design according to simulation results.* The behavior and constraint constituents make simulation possible. Reactive behavior rules can be executed on event streams. The rules react to input events by creating new output events. This reactive behavior can be executed by interpreters or compilers for the rules. Similarly, event streams can be checked for violations of constraints.

   The role of simulation is to catch design errors as early as possible. This step is itself a multistep activity. An architecture's behavior constituent consists of high-level executable rules that enable the new process design to be executed on test data consisting of event streams. The event streams represent communication between the new process and other processes in the system. This kind of test data is called a *communication scenario*. Execution of architecture rules on communication scenarios is called *event-based simulation*. The output of an event-based simulation is usually another event stream. The input scenario and the output event stream can be fed in real time to an animation of activity in the processes. This illustrates graphically how the proposed new process reacts to a scenario of inputs from other processes.

An architecture's constraint constituent contains design constraints on the runtime behavior of the process. Design constraints can be automatically checked to see if simulation results conform to them. By using architecture, we automate two activities: simulating the architectural design on communication scenarios, and checking the simulation output for conformance to design constraints.

Developing a complete set of design constraints is an ongoing activity throughout the lifetime of a process. Animation is useful in enabling humans to see errors and exceptional situations that have been overlooked at design.

4. *Implement, compile, and integrate the new process into the system, and test. Correct its design accordingly.*   To implement the new process, we must supply efficient programs that can be used in place of the behavior rules. They must process events received from other processes in the system via connectors to conform with the behavior rules and constraints. Implementation can use an off-the-shelf component from a process components library. A component might, for example, consist of another, lower-level architecture of processes that deal with the detailed workings of our new process. Or else we can resort to writing code and integrating it with event adapters that can read and write events from the connectors.

The design constraints on the process runtime behavior serve as a standard to which the process's test behavior is compared. Discrepancies are automatically reported by the constraint-checking tools. The constraints can be applied to monitor the process both in testing and in production.

5. *Continuously monitor the runtime operation of the upgraded system.* Similar to the test activity, runtime monitoring compares the process's behavior with its architectural design constraints. Discrepancies are automatically reported.

But equally important, runtime monitoring provides personalized business and management views of how the process system is performing in the ever-changing electronic business context. This aspect goes well beyond reporting inconsistencies with design constraints and imposes new technology demands—to be discussed.

6. *Modify the process system as dictated either by the results of runtime design constraint monitoring or personalized viewing or changes in the business environment.*   This step takes us back to step 1 of the cycle,

to modify the architecture design. However, a redesign can often be avoided by component substitution. This is possible when the desired modification can be made by replacing an existing process component in the system with a library component that has already been designed, tested, and entered into a process library.

The existing process occupies a position, or "slot," in the architecture called a *process interface*. A process interface contains the behavior rules and constraints that apply to that process. A library component can be correctly substituted into the process architecture if it is compatible with the interface of the existing process.

Testing the compatibility of a process with an interface uses the behavior rules and constraints in that process interface. The runtime behavior of the new library process must be consistent with the behavior rules and constraints in the interface. This guarantees that the substitution will not introduce the kinds of errors that commonly happen when components are swapped.

Process interfaces and their role in process architectures are described later. Component substitution as described here is often called *"plug-and-play,"* but it is seldom supported by rigorous interface compatibility checking.

As we said earlier, these roles in the lifecycle depend upon process architecture containing three constituents. Although we are all familiar with examples of the first constituent, graphical depictions of systems, the other two constituents demand much more precision in their specification. These include executable rules specifying runtime behavior, and design constraints restricting runtime behavior. These latter two constituents are intended to provide the information needed by simulators, constraint checkers, and many other kinds of analysis tools to automate analysis activities throughout the lifecycle. They imply some new technology demands. So, next we look at these constituents in more detail.

4.3 Constituents of Process Architectures

In this section we describe the constituents of a process architecture.

4.3.1 Annotations

Behavior specifications and design constraints are associated with, or linked to, various processes and connectors in the architecture diagram. Generally, any behavior or constraint that is associated with an architecture component is called an *annotation* of the component. Behaviors and constraints are called annotations.

An annotation is a mathematical or programming condition that either defines or constrains an activity of a process, or the communication on a connector between processes. The kinds of formal languages needed to express annotations are discussed in later chapters.

Annotations are precise, formal statements that can be used by supporting tools. They are meta-level documentation to be used by tools, as opposed to our normal informal notion of documentation for humans.

4.3.2   Architectural Structure

Structure is a means of organizing the components of an architecture and the annotations that apply to them. The two structuring elements, or "building blocks," are

- *Process interfaces.*   A process interface specifies a class of processes. A process interface defines the events that a process of the class can receive as input or generate as output, and the behavior rules and the constraints that apply to that process.
- *Connector interfaces.*   A connector interface specifies a class of connectors. A connector interface specifies the events a connector can receive as input and deliver as output, and the behavior rules and the constraints that apply to the event flow carried by that class of connectors.

Since connectors are processes too, there really is only one kind of structuring element—the process interface. But it is convenient to separate them into two kinds, depending upon whether they specify *activity* components or *connector* components. Usually, the two kinds are represented by very different graphics in architecture diagrams, which helps convey an important architectural feature—communication dependencies between activity processes.

More than one process may satisfy the behavior rules and constraints in an interface. So, in general, an interface defines a class of processes: A *process class* contains all the processes whose behaviors satisfy the rules and constraints in an interface.

4.3.3   Interface Communication Architectures

Architectures are constructed out of the two kinds of interfaces. Interfaces are used to specify the processes and connectors in the architecture. They are linked together so that output events of processes are received as input events

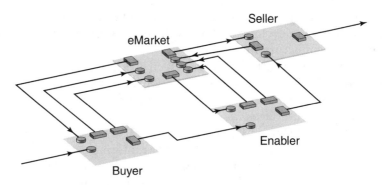

Figure 4.2: An interface connection architecture

of connectors and conversely. The resulting kind of architecture is called an *interface communication architecture* because it specifies the communication structure between interfaces.

There is an analogy between interface communication architectures for process systems and hardware architectures, as illustrated in Figures 4.2 and 4.7 (as shown in Section 4.6).

Figure 4.2 shows an interface communication architecture for financial transactions involving communication between the processes of various enterprises. The enterprises are buyers, sellers, an eMarketplace, and an enabler that provides insurance, legal services, and so on. Imagine that the events, behavior rules, and constraints for the processes of each enterprise are defined in the interface of that enterprise in Figure 4.2.

All the communication between processes is specified at the level of the interfaces in Figure 4.2. The behavior rules in the process and connector interfaces express the transaction protocols between the enterprises and give us the ability to simulate the behavior of the system—early in the lifecycle, before we commit to implementations of each of the components. This is one of the strategies for using architectures to reduce the risk of design errors early in the lifecycle.

The use of interfaces instead of particular processes gives architecture a degree of generality. To build a process system that implements the architecture, we can use any process in the class of processes specified by an interface at the position of the interface in the communication structure. This means that the architecture leaves open implementation decisions—for example, the choice of whether a connector is implemented on top of an ORB or publish/subscribe middleware. There may be many different systems that implement an architecture. This generality is what we mean by "high level." An interface communication architecture is a template for a class of process systems.

Interfaces play a pivotal role in layered architectures and plug-and-play techniques of system development. We will see how Figure 4.2 is developed into a layered architecture in Section 4.6.

In this book, "architecture" means *layered interface communication architecture.* We will deal with layers later. So, when we talk about "process architecture," we mean an interface communication architecture with process and connector interfaces.

Notice one other thing: "High level" as applied to architecture refers to its generality—that is, its use of process class interfaces to separate behavioral concerns, which are properly specified in architectures, from implementation concerns. "High level" does not refer to the level in the enterprise. We can design architectures for networks or architectures for business processes.

4.3.4   Architecture Diagrams

Architecture diagrams are the primary means of communicating process architectures to humans simply because they are usually easy to understand. A diagram provides a visualization of the kinds of processes in the system and their dependencies and interactions.

There is a spectrum of different commercial tools that give us various ways to construct architecture diagrams. These vary from drawing tools such as Visio[1] on one hand to comprehensive modeling formalisms such as UML[2] on the other hand. It is not our purpose to choose any particular graphical methodology. We are interested in what we can do when we have a graphical architecture and its associated behavior and constraint constituents. For our purpose, to illustrate architecture concepts, "boxes and arrows" diagrams will do fine.

A useful diagram of a simple architecture is a boxes and arrows picture such as Figure 4.3. This is a rather simple workflow version of an interface connection architecture with special icons and connectors that flow forward only—no communication loops.

In Figure 4.3 each icon depicts a process class interface. An icon represents a process of that class but does not specify which one. So, for example, there may be many different processes that can be used for CD Fulfillment provided they satisfy the interface represented by that icon.

Similarly, connector class interfaces are depicted by arrows in a boxes and arrows diagram. Communication between activity processes is accomplished by events flowing along connectors between the processes, in the directions of the arrows (one or both directions). The direction of the arrow indicates which processes generate events and which processes receive

---

[1]Web search on "Microsoft Visio."
[2]Web search on "unified modeling language."

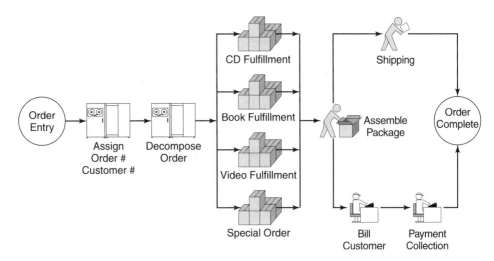

Figure 4.3: A diagram showing interfaces and connectors in
a process architecture

them. Usually, connectors are bidirectional, so we must look to the interface annotations to tell us which events are flowing in which directions. Connector interfaces can also be implemented in different ways. For example, different arrows in Figure 4.3 might depict connector classes that can be implemented using different IT layer components—for example, pipelines, buses, databases, ORBs, or publish/subscribe middleware.

Figure 4.3 shows the processes that are invoked by a customer's order and the directional sequences in which they are invoked. It also shows which processes do not communicate with one another. This is an example of an *architecture diagram* showing some features of an architecture. It is a widely used and familiar graphical form. But we must remember that it is only one constituent of an architecture, not a "complete picture."

The purpose of an architectural diagram is to give us useful information in an easily understandable form. Looking at Figure 4.3, we can tell how many processes there are in any system having that architecture, which ones communicate with each other, and which processes execute independently of one another by not having an arrow, or a sequence of arrows, between them. For example, Figure 4.3 shows the various fulfillment processes executing in parallel. It also shows no connector allowing Shipping to communicate with Billing or Collection. This might be a design error so obvious that it is evident by just looking at the diagram.

Diagrams, however, are usually very incomplete. They often do not show any of the interprocess communications that take place in exceptional situations where the normal or expected events fail to happen. If diagrams showed all that, they would become very messy and hard to draw or understand.

Visualizations do not scale well for depicting detailed behavior. For example, Figure 4.3 doesn't show what happens when one of the fulfillment processes fails. What do the other processes do if only part of an order can be filled?

Moreover, a diagram cannot provide precise specifications of behavior. That is very difficult to do by purely graphical techniques. We can't tell from the diagram whether Assemble Package has enough information to do its job effectively because we don't know what data is passed to it from the DecomposeOrder process. How does it know which parts of orders go together? There must be a detailed specification, which augments the diagram, of the data structures of documents flowing between the processes.

4.3.5 Behavior Specification

The purpose of a *behavior specification* is to define in the process interface *how* a process or connector reacts to various inputs. Given input events, it can be executed to create output events and change the values of variables.

A behavior specification consists of annotations of the architecture diagram. They are added to interfaces for both processes and connectors.

Annotations are expressed in a mathematical or computer language. Mathematical precision is needed because these annotations are used by various analysis tools that help automate the use of architecture to guide the lifecycle process.

A behavior specification consists of annotations of

- *A process interface.* The interface is depicted by a box or an icon. Annotations of an interface specify
  - The types of events that a process can receive as input and generate as output.
  - The event pattern behavior of a process. A process's behavior is specified in terms of its reactions to the events it receives. A behavior annotation defines how a process will react to various sets of input events by generating output events and changing its state. Annotations that specify the behavior of cyclical or continually executing processes draw heavily upon a language for specifying patterns of events.
- *A connector interface.* The interface is depicted by an arrow or multiple arrows in the diagram. Annotations of a connector interface specify
  - The types of events that a connector can receive as input and deliver as output.
  - The patterns of events that flow along the connector, including protocols of event flow.

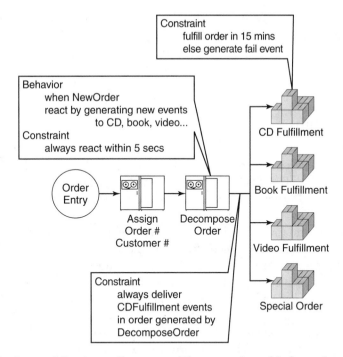

Figure 4.4: An architecture diagram with examples of informal annotations

To see informal examples of annotations, look ahead to Section 4.4 and Figure 4.4.

A process's interface is also often called its *type* or its *class*. The behavior annotations tell us *what* the process does, but not *how* it does it. This applies to connector interfaces too. The connector class interface depicted by the arrow can be given behavior annotations to specify the event flow in detail. In this case, the role of a behavior is to specify exactly what type of connector an arrow is depicting. It specifies the types of events that can flow along the connector and the protocols governing the order in which events flow along that connector. A connector interface can be implemented on different IT layer components—for example, pipes, buses, databases, ORBs, or message-oriented middleware.

When supported by appropriate tools, interface annotations have several key applications in the lifecycle.

First, process interfaces play a similar role to object-oriented programming language types or classes in automatically eliminating some kinds of errors. Interfaces allow automatic detection of architecture errors, such as mismatches of event types and data types between processes and connectors.

Second, reactive behavior rules allow event-based simulation of architectures on communication scenarios. Simulation can be used at early stages of the lifecycle to investigate both the correctness and the performance of systems having that architecture, before a system is built.

Third, the use of components whose behavior conforms to the rules and constraints of their class interface allow us to use plug-and-play techniques to rapidly modify process systems. More about all these roles in later chapters.

4.3.6 Design Constraints

Design constraints are annotations that place bounds on various aspects of the behavior of a system of processes. Constraints are intended to express limitations on behavior, while behaviors express what a process does. Constraints can annotate a single interface of a process or connector, or a group of processes and connectors in an architecture.

A time bound within which a process must react to input events is a very common constraint. See, for example, the constraint in Figure 4.4 on the CDFulfillment process. Access rights are another example, specifying conditions on when a process may communicate with another process within the system—for example, a process that represents a resource such as a database.

Constraints can be checked whenever a process is executed at any stage in the lifecycle, from simulation to production, by constraint-checking tools. During production operations, the event traffic of the process system is automatically monitored for violations of constraints.

4.4 Examples of Informal Annotations

Here are examples of behavior rules and design constraints. Some of them are shown in Figure 4.4 as annotations of interfaces in Figure 4.3. These examples are described in English because we haven't decided yet what kind of mathematical or programming language would be adequate for expressing the full range of architecture annotations. So we call them "informal annotations."

A behavior rule is a reactive rule containing a trigger and a body. The trigger is a pattern of one or more events that specifies the input events that the process reacts to. The body is a set of instructions that may contain another event pattern that specifies the events that the process creates and outputs in response. For example, in Figure 4.4, the behavior rule for DecomposeOrder triggers whenever a single input event, NewOrder, is received and creates new output events.

Connector interfaces define the events they transport between activity processes. Their annotations define how the output events of one process interface are transported to the input events of another process interface. So, as shown in Figure 4.4, a one-directional connector rule might, for example, trigger on output events from a DecomposeOrder interface and create input events of the CDFulfillment interface or the BookFulfillment interface, depending upon data in the triggering event.

Example 1: *Behavior annotation of DecomposeOrder process*

We might annotate the DecomposeOrder process interface, as shown in Figure 4.4, with a rule that specifies how it reacts to new order events. Such a rule, informally in English, might be

> Whenever a new order event is received with order number N,
> **if** it contains CD items, then **generate** a CD-Request event with order number N, a description of CD items, and an indicator that there are other components in the order;
> **if** it contains Book items, then **generate** a Book-Request event with order number N, a description of Book items, and another components indicator;
> ...

So the result of a new order event is that the process will output a number of Request events, each for a component of the order and describing that component of the order, the order number, and what other components are in the order. These events should provide enough information for all the processes downstream to do their jobs, particularly the AssemblePackage process in Figure 4.3.

Example 2: *Constraint on the DecomposeOrder process*

DecomposeOrder must generate all its output events within five seconds of receiving a new order event.

This is an example of a timing constraint specifying a time window within which the process must respond to a new input order. It will also annotate the DecomposeOrder process interface, as shown in Figure 4.4.

Notice, however, that the constraint is as important for what it omits as for what it constrains. Namely, it does not specify that DecomposeOrder must complete its reaction to one input before commencing another, which would be the standard semantics of a workflow activity. Multiprocessing of new orders is consistent with this constraint.

Example 3: *Behavior annotation of the connector between the DecomposeOrder process and the four order fulfillment processes*

This connector must take as input any type of event that is a product request event. It must deliver CD-Request events to the CDFulfillment process, Book-Request events to the BookFulfillment process, and so on.

This example of a behavior rule annotates the interface of the connector between DecomposeOrder and all the fulfillment processes. For simplicity, we don't show it in Figure 4.4. The connector must behave as a distributor of the events it transports to specific processes, depending upon the data in the event. The rule does not specify *how* it distributes events. It might, for example, randomly choose which fulfillment process to deliver events to first. When the connector behavior rule is triggered by a product request input event (an output from DecomposeOrder), it reacts by calling the event input feature of the fulfillment process interface that deals with the type of product named in the product request event. So the rule is "content based." It must access the data contained in the triggering event to choose the correct fulfillment process.

Example 4: *A constraint annotation of the connector between the DecomposeOrder process and the order fulfillment processes*

This connector must always deliver CD-Request events in the order generated by the DecomposeOrder process.

This constraint annotation of the connector is shown in Figure 4.4. The connector is a *fan-out* connector between one output process and four input processes. The constraint specifies "no overtaking" of CD-Request events. They must be delivered to CDFulfillment in the order in which they are sent by DecomposeOrder. The "order generated" would be specified precisely using timestamps from the DecomposeOrder process.

Other examples of constraint annotations of this connector might be, for example, a specification of priorities between events constraining some types of events to be delivered before others, or "no overtaking" of events from different orders.

Example 5: *Early lifecycle applications*

Type correctness.   Annotations of processes and connectors enable us to select a variety of automated type-correctness tests for architectures. These tests use the class interfaces of processes and connectors to help us avoid simple kinds of errors.

For example, suppose we try to connect DecomposeOrder to one of the fulfillment processes. We choose a connector to connect the two processes. When we try to make the connection, say, by graphically linking the ends of an arrow representing the connector to the icons for the two processes, some type-correctness tests will be made automatically. One type-correctness test would require our connector interface to accept at least one of the output event types in the DecomposeOrder interface and to deliver at least one of the input event types in the fulfillment process interface. Several different correctness tests might be applied to a connection that we try to make. We can choose between them. A stronger test might require our connector interface to accept all the outputs from DecomposeOrder and to deliver all the inputs of the fulfillment process. That test might be too strong for our particular design, which is why we need the ability to select the tests.

This kind of compatibility testing between the interfaces of processes and connectors is also called *interface compatibility.*

Simulation. An interface communication architecture can be simulated before we make any decisions about implementing the process and connector interfaces. This is done by feeding communication scenarios to an interpreter for the behavior rules.

For example, suppose a scenario is a single NewOrder event with data fields giving the types of products and quantities. Figure 4.4 shows a rule in the interface of DecomposeOrder that will be triggered by this event. This rule reacts by generating a set of new Request events, one for each type of product in the order. It will add other data to these new events too—for example, an order ID number. These new product request events are output events from the DecomposeOrder interface. They will be sent to an appropriate interface that is connected to its output events. Suppose there is a connector interface that connects the outputs of the Decompose-Order interface to the input events of the various fulfillment processes. And the connector interface has a behavior rule described earlier. The rule will trigger on each of these Request events and react by inputting them to the appropriate fulfillment interface. Behavior rules in the fulfillment process interfaces will be triggered and result in more events being output to other connectors. And so on.

We can also simulate how an architecture will behave in exceptional situations. For example, suppose we want to simulate the behavior of a process when it does not receive an event that it should receive in normal conditions. That process should have behavior rules specifying what it does if the event does not arrive, say, within some time bound. We can set up the scenario so that the expected event does not arrive—for example, by changing a connector's behavior to drop that specific event. The simulation will show us what happens following the timeout behavior.

Example 6: *Behavior annotations of AssemblePackage in Figure 4.3*

Keep customer happy. Whenever part of an order is received, commence assembling and sending to shipping whatever parts of that order have been received at one-hour intervals.

Ship complete orders only. "Whenever the first part of an order to arrive is received, wait for all other parts to arrive before assembling a package for shipping. If all parts have not arrived within one hour of the first part, send queries to the fulfillment processes involved in the order. If all parts have not arrived within one further hour, or if a failure message arrives from a fulfillment process, send a 'contact customer' message to shipping. Whenever all parts of an order are received, assemble a package and send it to shipping unless a 'contact customer' message has been sent."

These behavior rules are a little more complex than the previous examples. They are not shown in Figure 4.4. Also, they are not consistent with each other, so we can't have both of them in the AssemblePackage process interface.

The "keep customer happy" rule uses the time of arrival of the first part of an order to decide when to assemble packages of parts for shipping. When parts arrive, it has to know if it has already packed some parts of the order. So this rule requires recognizing events in the context of their time of arrival and what has been done previously with the relevant order.

The "ship complete orders only" rule involves different types of events in its decision making. Also, it assumes that event flow on the connector between AssemblePackage and the fulfillment processes is two-way because it may send them queries. A two-way connection would be a change to the architecture shown in Figure 4.3. There must be enough data about an order in a parts-arrival event for this rule to know which other parts to expect. It is a complex rule, generally involving several events and updating the context of which events have been received and sent, to successfully complete packaging an order.

4.5 Dynamic Process Architectures

An architecture is *static* if

- It consists of a fixed number of interfaces.
- No behavior rule creates a new process or connector, or destroys a process or connector.
- The process interfaces connected by a connector do not depend upon runtime parameters.

In a system with a static architecture, the actual processes and connectors in the system and their communication structure are all known before the system becomes operational and remain the same when the system is running.

Notice that according to this definition, architectures with simple runtime-dependent behavior by a connector, such as routing of events depending upon their contents, are *static*. The architecture in Figure 4.3 is static even though the connector between DecomposeOrder and the fulfillment processes does content-based delivery.

The process architectures of the electronic enterprise will be *dynamic*. We saw a simple example of this, the asynchronous RFQ process, in the last chapter. This kind of asynchronous auction process is typical of what we can expect to take place when an enterprise enters into time-bounded supply chain agreements with partners using large trading hubs as the infrastructure. Process architectures will become far more dynamic as enterprises struggle to deal with the global event cloud that results from these activities.

In a *dynamic architecture,* certain aspects can vary at runtime.

1. The types of processes and the actual numbers of processes of each type in the system can depend upon runtime parameters. At runtime, processes may come and go, depending upon the system's demand for their services.
2. The interprocess communication—that is, who is talking to whom—can depend upon runtime parameters. The number of connectors can vary. The behavior of connectors can depend upon runtime parameters.

Figure 4.5 is an example of a diagram for a dynamic architecture. It is a detailed view of the architecture of the SpecialOrder process in Figure 4.3—that is, it depicts a lower-level architecture for that process. The central part of this architecture is the connector called *negotiation protocol,* which we can imagine might be carrying the communication between the enterprise and booksellers over a trading Web site for rare books. It is depicted in the figure by a varying number of arrows in both directions. The number

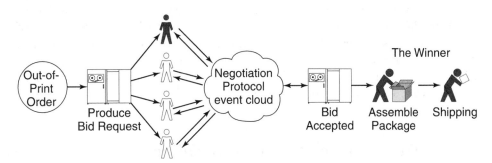

Figure 4.5: Architecture diagram of a parallel, asynchronous auction process

of rare booksellers can vary during the execution of the negotiation protocol to fill an order. This protocol may depend upon the number of booksellers entering the negotiation, their prices, and the time for which their offers are guaranteed. The diagram shows that the selected bookseller (shaded) executes the assembly and shipping processes, so now more of those processes are in the architecture temporarily whenever there is a rare-book special order.

Another example of a dynamic architecture is an FAA terminal control area (TCA). Air traffic control is a complex management process system with a dynamic architecture of communicating processes. Suppose we were architecting the processes at a TCA. Aircraft can be represented as types of processes that alter position, have operational states that include fuel levels and so on, and communicate by specified protocols. The control tower is also a set of processes. The number of aircraft in the architecture and the number of processes in the control tower vary at runtime. Processes are continually being created and killed. TCAs communicate with other systems as well, weather systems and FAA en route centers, for example. Within a TCA, the number and types of aircraft, together with other parameters such as the aircraft states, weather conditions, and so on, affect the management protocol. Also, the communication (event flow) between aircraft and control tower processes depends upon runtime parameters such as distance and stage in the management protocol.

This is an example of a dynamic architecture with a large number of behavioral constraints, especially safety constraints such as distance separation between aircraft. Consequently, many ad hoc tools and devices have been introduced to check the most critical subsets of these constraints—for example, aircraft transponders and many different special radar warning systems. But there is a large amount of unused and uncoordinated information in the system. In other words, much of the global event cloud goes unnoticed. Flight monitoring, conflict prediction, and airspace scheduling are all issues that need to utilize much more of the operational state information than is currently possible. Furthermore, the human is still very much in the loop and performing the most critical tasks. The net effect of this situation is decreased efficiency and capacity of the system in the face of rising demands. A much more comprehensive and accurate technology is needed for real-time monitoring of architectural policies and safety constraints that can effectively deal with the global event cloud of air traffic operations.

4.5.1   Diagrams for Dynamic Architectures?

How well do graphical paradigms deal with dynamic architecture? Not very well. What tends to happen is a proliferation of separate architectural diagrams, leading to a problem keeping the diagrams consistent with each other. Graphics don't scale in any natural way to deal with dynamic architectures. The most promising approach is to annotate easy-to-understand diagrams that do not try to depict dynamic aspects, but simply depict a typical "snapshot" instance of a dynamic architecture. The annotations capture the runtime variations with precise mathematical specifications, which give us capabilities to simulate dynamic architectures and check their operations for conformance to constraints. However, these annotations need to be rich enough to express patterns consisting of many events that must happen in specified contexts that include the runtime state. More about this later.

4.6 Layered Architectures and Plug-and-Play

Layering is a technique for controlling complexity. Architectures are layered—just like enterprises. At the highest level, we see a simple architecture—a workflow, for example, as in Figure 4.3. As we unfold the layers, we see details, more complicated architectures, such as in Figure 4.5.

A process at one level in an architecture is represented by behavior rules and constraints. That is the highest-level view of that process, called the *process interface* or *class*. It tells us *what* the process does—and what it must not do. Figure 4.2 depicts the idea of a high-level interface connection architecture—just the details contained in the behavior rules and constraints in process and connector interfaces.

When we ask for "more detail" as to *how* the process carries out those rules, we go down a level in the architecture to a lower-level, more detailed view. This is like "opening the interface" and looking inside the process. What we see is called the *implementation* of the process. Figure 4.6 shows two layers, the interfaces and the implementations of the interfaces as boxes with events flowing between the boxes and the interfaces. The boxes contain a lot more detail.

In a layered architecture, an implementation can be a lower-level architecture of processes. In this case, the lower-level architecture implements the process interface. The lower-level processes are called *subprocesses* of that process. Figures 4.6 and 4.7 show two kinds of layered architectures where the top layer is an interface connection architecture and the lower layer consists of architectures of subprocesses for each interface. Subprocesses for connectors aren't shown in these figures because the graphics would get too complicated. We discuss differences between the figures later. At the lowest level of a layered architecture, an implementation can be code of some kind.

For example, suppose we want more detail about the SpecialOrder process in Figure 4.3. The SpecialOrder process has an interface that specifies that it will accept input events that are special orders and will output

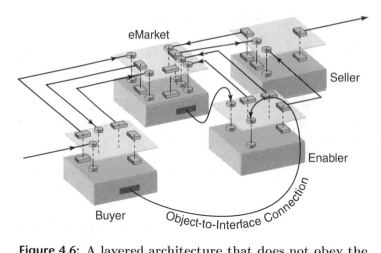

Figure 4.6: A layered architecture that does not obey the abstraction principle

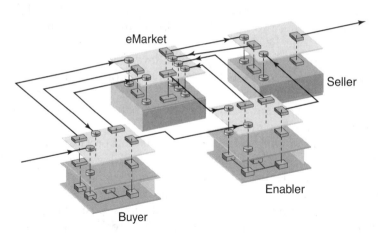

Figure 4.7: A layered architecture conforming to the abstraction principle

events that are fulfillments of orders. Maybe there are some timing constraints and failure conditions too. So far, there is just enough detail to understand what the process does. Now we can open the interface of the SpecialOrder process to see the implementation. Then we get to view a lower-level architecture diagram showing how the SpecialOrder process is implemented by subprocesses. Part of that architecture may be the negotiation process with any number of rare book sellers, shown in Figure 4.5. This gives us a lot more detail.

Another way of describing the layering relationship is that the process interface is an *abstraction* of the lower-level architecture of subprocesses that implements it.

Now we come to the issue of how the levels in a layered architecture are related to one another.

4.6.1 Abstraction Principle

The *abstraction principle* governs the relationship between architectures of subprocesses and the process interfaces that they implement.

Architectures of subprocesses that implement a process interface must obey two rules.

- *Interface conformance:* The architecture of subprocesses must conform to the behavior rules and constraints in the process interface.
- *Communication conformance:* Subprocesses can communicate with processes outside their sub-architecture only by receiving input events or creating output events that are defined in the process's interface.

Interface conformance means that we should not be able to distinguish by monitoring the runtime behavior at the interface, consisting of input and output events at the process's interface, whether the behavior rules in the interface are being executed or the architecture of subprocesses is being executed. Also, design constraints in the interface should not be violated.

Communication conformance means that all communication between the subprocesses implementing a process and processes that are not part of the subarchitecture takes place by means of input and output events declared in the process's interface. In Figure 4.7, the communication between subprocesses in different boxes is through the interfaces of those boxes.

Typical object-oriented programming languages such as Java do not enforce the second rule of the abstraction principle but allow a class that implements an interface to make method calls to other interfaces at the same level. This is illustrated in Figure 4.6. Boxes represent implementations of interfaces. Figure 4.6 shows "object-to-interface" communication between the boxes and methods declared in other process interfaces. This means that communication between processes at the same level is not always defined by the connectors, rules, and constraints at that level. As Figure 4.6 shows, there is communication between process implementations where there are no connectors between their interfaces.

If, as in Figure 4.6, interprocess communication is dependent upon the implementations, we cannot interchange different implementations for the same interface. When one subarchitecture implementing an interface is replaced by another one, new interprocess communication may be introduced, or old communications upon which the system depended may be broken. Either way, the system may not behave the same way after the interchange. Plug-and-play is likely to result in errors.

We would like to achieve the layered architecture discipline depicted in Figure 4.7. Here, all communication between processes is specified by connectors at the same layer as the process interfaces. Any subprocess in an implementation communicates with processes outside of its sub-architecture through the interface of the process it implements. This gives us two important capabilities.

- *Simulation before implementation:* The ability to simulate the processes and their communications using only the behavior rules specified in the interfaces of the processes and connectors at that level.
- *Plug-and-play with reduced risk of errors:* The two rules of the abstraction principle ensure that any two implementations for the same process interface conform to the rules and constraints in the interface, and that they communicate with outside processes only by means of connectors between their interfaces. This greatly improves our chances of being able to interchange different implementations for a process interface without disturbing the functioning of the system as it is specified.

The abstraction principle is a basic rule of component-based systems. Building systems that conform to it is encouraged by industry standards for software component interfaces (so-called APIs) and component-based software techniques. Hardware architectures adhere strictly to the abstraction principle. Communication to a chip or board is through the pins at the interface. We don't put a chip on a board and stick a wire from the middle of the chip out to someplace else on the board.

The abstraction principle allows us to swap implementations for the same process interface without changing the conformance of the process system to its architecture specifications—provided the components conform to the interface behavior specifications. This plug-and-play feature is critical in controlling the effects of lifecycle modifications and enabling rapid, correct modifications to processes at any level.

4.7   Summary: Technology to Support Process Architecture

The concept of layered, event-driven, interface connection architecture that we have outlined in this chapter was published in [14] and later, in comparison with other kinds of software architecture, in [16]. The use of complex event patterns to specify and track the runtime changes in dynamic software system architectures is described in [24]. Many other concepts of software architecture can be found in the literature.[3]

Process architectures as described here have applications across the entire lifecycle. These applications go beyond design to include simulation, interface conformance testing, and monitoring for design constraint violations during operation, all of which require sophisticated event processing technology. So we can expect that the technologies needed to support process architecting will have a large overlap with our discussion in the previous chapter. The technologies needed to enable enterprise process monitoring and management in the global event cloud are part of the foundation for process architecture.

The technology demands of process architecture are heavily weighted toward a new generation of architect's aids—tools to enable the lifecycle applications.

1. Annotation languages that are rich enough to express event-driven behaviors and constraints associated with complex processes. They must enable the architect to specify patterns of multiple events, including the timing and causal relationships between the events.

2. Architecting tools that enable the process architect to easily navigate between graphics for architectural components and their annotations, and to navigate between levels of architecture. These tools must be capable of checking annotations for various properties, such as mutual consistency, and checking components for conformance to the rules of abstraction.

3. Event-based simulators capable of interpreting behaviors involving multievent patterns expressed in the annotation languages. Analytic tools may also be placed in this class of tools. They enable the architect to explore logical consequences of the annotations of an architecture, within a level and across levels.

4. Design constraint checkers that can detect violations of constraints involving patterns of multiple events and contexts in which the constraints apply. Checkers must have performance that permits them to be used in all lifecycle stages, including runtime operations.

5. Diagnostic tools that can track the causal history of events back through the stages of a process system and down through the layers of a layered architecture.

---

[3]Web search on "software architecture."

6. Underlying event processing infrastructure to enable simulation and checking tools. Such infrastructure would interface with the IT layers by means of event adapters and would supply event sources, event notification, event databases, and so on. It would also be capable of computing causal relations and aggregation relations, and storing events to enable rapid retrieval of related events.

Chapter 5

Events, Timing, and Causality

- *What events are*
- *How events are created*
- *The form, significance, and relativity of an event*
- *Timing, causality, and aggregation*
- *Genetic parameters of events*
- *Partial orderings of events*
- *Timing requirements expressed as patterns of events*
- *Examples of causal tracking of interprocess activity*

This chapter discusses the basic concepts: what events are, and the timing and causal relationships between events. The two chapters following this one discuss concepts related to applying complex event processing (CEP). The goal of these three chapters is to give a simple overview of CEP. Later chapters go into details of how to build actual applications of CEP to solve the issues that we have discussed in the first four chapters.

The basic concepts of CEP are very familiar to us because they crop up over and over in our dealings with computers and the Internet. But CEP defines the concepts more precisely than everyday usage. In this chapter we cross the boundary from everyday usage to CEP. For example, in everyday usage an "event" is something that happens.[1] In CEP an "event" is an object that can be subjected to computer processing. It signifies, or is a record of, an activity that has happened.

5.1 What Events Are

An event is an object that is a record of an activity in a system. The event *signifies* the activity. An event may be related to other events.

An event has three *aspects*.

- *Form:* The form of an event is an object. It may have particular attributes or data components. A form can be something as simple as a string or more often a tuple of data components. Data components of an event can include, for example, the time period of the activity, where it happened, who did it, and other data, including a description of its significance and relativities.

- *Significance:* An event *signifies* an activity. We call this activity the *significance* of the event. An event's form usually contains data describing the activity it signifies.

- *Relativity:* An activity is related to other activities by *time, causality,* and *aggregation.* Events have the same relationships to one another as the activities they signify. The relationships between an event and other events are together called its *relativity.* An event's form usually encodes its relativities—that is, contains methods that can be invoked to reconstruct the relationships with other events.

We often talk about "an attribute of an event" as a short way of saying, "a data component of an event's form." This is a useful abbreviation, so we'll use it from time to time.

Here are some examples of events giving their forms, significance, and relativities. These examples show events signifying the message activity coming into and going out of the DecomposeOrder process in Section 4.4, Example 1. See also Figure 4.3.

Example 1: *Input events in the DecomposeOrder process*

An input event signifies the activity of a NewOrder message being received by the DecomposeOrder process. The message would be in some

---

[1]The *Oxford English Dictionary* defines "event" as "something that happens or is thought of as happening."

standard format such as XML, containing data fields for the order number, customer, types of goods and quantities, and so on. The event's form would be similar to the message but would contain extra data fields, for example, giving its time of generation, time of arrival, and relation to other events. So the form of an input event would be an object of a Java class called InputEvent:

```
Class   InputEvent {Name        NewOrder;
                     Event_Id    E_Id;
                     Customer    Id;
                     OrderNo     O_Id;
                     Order       (CD  X,  Book ...);
                     Time        T;
                     Causality   (Id1,  Id2, ...);
                    }
```

Every event has a unique identifier field, Event_Id. The Time field is the timestamp, or in many cases the time interval, when the activity happened—according to a reading from a system clock. The Causality attribute of the event provides a way of tracing its causal history. Here we show it as a list of the Ids of events that are immediate causes of this event. This list can be empty if the events that caused this one are not known. In this example, the Name field describes the kind of activity signified by the event. In conjunction with other fields—for example, the Time field—the actual activity can be determined. Other data elements are the data in the message.

Example 2: *Output events in the DecomposeOrder process*

DecomposeOrder creates and outputs new messages in response to inputs. These activities are signified by new events, which we call output events. Each of the output events contains the input event's Id, E_Id, in its *causality* list. For example:

```
Class  OutputEvent {Name:        CDOrder;
                     Event_Id     E_Id1;
                     Customer     Id;
                     OrderNo      O_Id;
                     SubOrder     O_Id1;
                     Order        CD: X;
                     SubOrders    (O_Id2, ...);
                     Time         T1;
                     Causality    (E_Id);
                    }
```

This output event signifies the sending of a message to the CDFulfillment process in response to the input event. The input activity *caused* the output activity. So the Id of the input event, E_Id, is placed in the list of immediate causes of this output event. In fact, it's the only immediate cause. The causes of the input event are now one step further down the causal chain. They are not immediate causes of this output event. The timestamp, T1, of this output event is greater than the timestamp of the input event, representing the time that DecomposeOrder took to react.

There are two confusions between everyday usage and CEP that we want to avoid. The first is confusing the everyday usage of "event" as "something that happens" with the CEP concept of an event as an object signifying an activity. In event processing, we are processing event objects and not activities.

Another confusion happens often in computer science: It is quite common to confuse an event with its form, such as "An event is just a message." This happens because generating a message is a common way of generating an event that signifies an activity. This confusion ignores the other aspects of events. The forms of events may be messages, but the events also have significance and relativity.

Event processing is different from message processing because it must deal with the relationships between events.

5.2 How Events Are Created

To apply CEP to a target enterprise system, we must be able to create events that signify the activities that are happening in the system. There are two steps.

1. *Observation step:* First, we must be able to access and observe the activities at any level of a hierarchical system. Observation must be *benign*—that is, it must not change the system's behavior.

2. *Adaptation step:* Second, observations must be transformed into event objects that can be processed by CEP. Generally, this is done by tools called *adapters*.

There are three principal sources of events in modern enterprise systems.

1. *IT layer:* Communication between the components at every level of the system is observable, generally speaking, from the IT layer of the system. The IT layer may contain a variety of components—for example, message-oriented middleware ORBs, and databases. The messages in middleware or method calls in ORBs or databases can be observed and transformed into CEP events.

2. *Instrumentation:* Components of the target system are instrumented to create events signifying activities and situations resulting from activities. This includes, for example, at a low level, heartbeats and alerts generated by network management systems, status probes in operating systems, and at higher levels, instrumentation of applications.

3. *CEP:* Events are created by CEP in the course of processing events observed in the system.

Here are examples of events from each of these sources.

Example 1: *Observing message-oriented middleware*

The use of message-oriented middleware for integrating distributed applications is becoming more and more commonplace. Messages are used as the primary way of communicating between the applications in an enterprise. The most common form of message communication falls in the category of *publish/subscribe* middleware. Messages can be created and published by one application, called a sender, without the sender's having to block or wait for a reply. In this form of communication, the sender doesn't know who receives its messages and it doesn't need to wait to see what happens. This is *asynchronous communication.* Clients (receivers of the messages) subscribe to message categories. Messages are categorized by subject. A client subscribes by a special subscription message saying, "I want to receive messages on a given subject." Various middleware products use a variety of strategies for transporting messages between senders and clients, the commonest being simple broadcast.

CEP observes message activity by subscribing to messages in the IT layer. CEP is simply a benign client, subscribing to all message subjects, but not interfering with system operations. For example, the In Adapter in Figure 5.1 would be a client that subscribes to all subjects. When messages arrive at the CEP client, they are fed to an adapter that transforms them into events that contain data that indicates both their significance and relativity.

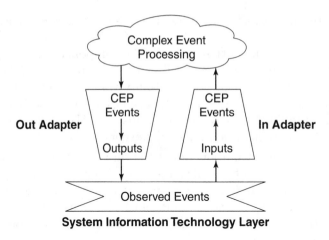

Figure 5.1: Observation of events from an IT layer

Example 2: *Object Request Brokers*

Another kind of IT layer that uses object-based middleware such as Common Object Request Broker Architecture (CORBA) ORBs is also popular in enterprise systems. Communication between component applications is achieved by calling the methods provided by the ORB, which acts as a broker between the methods of various applications. This is a *synchronous* communication paradigm, in which the client application waits for a server application's response to its method call. The method call and return can be observed benignly at the ORB by clients such as CEP. An adapter is applied to these observations to convert them to CEP events.

Example 3: *Adapting events*

Observed events may be in any format—for example, a popular format such as XML. We might observe an event such as a book order with a form such as the following:

```
<bookorder>
<id> Id </id>
<isbn> Isbn_No </isbn>
<qnty> Integer_No </qnty>
<customerId> CuId </customerId>
</bookorder>
```

An adapter will transform the event into a CEP form. If, in fact, the CEP internal form is also XML, there is not much for the adapter to do except add CEP attribute fields, such as causality and timing. If the CEP form is the Java class form described in Section 5.1, the event will be translated into a form such as the following:

```
Class   InputEvent {Name        BookOrder;
                    ExtFormat    XML
                    Event_Id     Id;
                    Customer     CuId;
                    Isbn         Isbn_No;
                    Qnty         Integer_No;
                    Time         T;
                    Causality    (Id1, Id2, ...);
                   }
```

Example 4: *Events created as instrumentation*

Instrumentation is a second source of events. There are many examples of instrumentation at all levels in a target system, the effect of which is to generate events signifying activities and their results. In the past, instrumentation has been a feature of operating systems, message protocols, and network management systems. Examples of network-level instrumentation include alerts signifying various network activities (traffic overloads, node failures), status information on nodes (CPU consumption, disk usage), and heartbeats for failure monitoring. Operating systems also provide such information as process status and disk usage. The intended use of this instrumentation was monitoring and management of the system, particularly safety-critical systems in which continuous operation is required.

Now we are also seeing increasing use of higher-level instrumentation in enterprise systems. Applications are instrumented for monitoring and continuous testing during the normal system operation. The code in applications is *preprocessed* to generate events as a side effect of the normal behavior. An example of application-level instrumentation is the use of tools that add assertions to the source code—Java, for example. These source code assertions allow observers to specify two things: what events are of interest and when those events should be generated. The source code with event assertions is run through a preprocessor that converts the event assertions into event generation code. Generation of instrumentation events has no effect on the normal operation of the applications—except perhaps a minor performance penalty.

The event-driven process engines that drive enterprise processes, as described in Chapters 2 and 4, operate by communicating messages back and forth with the applications that execute the process activities. The process engines can be instrumented to send these messages (or copies of them) directly to CEP adapters.

The point for CEP is that events resulting from instrumentation at any level in enterprise systems can be transformed into CEP event objects.

Example 5: *Events generated by CEP applications*

The third and final source of events is CEP itself. Events are generated by CEP. A typical example is when an event processing agent (more about these objects later) has detected a set of low-level events on an IT layer that signifies some activity. The event processing agent then communicates this observation to another agent. Communication between CEP agents is done by the first agent generating a new event containing data that signifies the activity that has been detected. This new event contains data that summarizes the aspects of the lower-level events. It aggregates the set of lower-level events. The second agent processes aggregate events. The second agent can be viewed as working at a higher level relative to the system's activity than the first agent. And the aggregated events that it uses may signify higher-level activities in the system. So, as we shall see, CEP can be used to piece together (aggregate) new information about the system from events that can be observed.

5.3   Time, Causality, and Aggregation

The three most common and important relationships between events are the following.

- *Time.*   Time is a relationship that orders events—for example, event A *happened before* event B.

  A time relationship between events depends upon a clock. Typically, when the event's activity happens, the event is created and a reading from a clock is entered into the event as its *timestamp*. The timestamp is taken at the time at which the activity (and the event) happened according to that clock.

  The order of their timestamps defines the time relationship between the events. Events may have more than one time relationship. A system may contain several clocks. This means that events associated with that system may have several time relationships, one for each of the clocks. Timing relationships due to different clocks may or may not be comparable, depending upon what is known about how the clocks are related—for example, are the clocks synchronized or independent?

- *Cause.* If the activity signified by event A *had to happen* in order for the activity signified by event B to happen, then A *caused* B.

  Causality, as defined here, is a *dependence* relationship between activities in a system. It is critical in understanding distributed behavior. An event *depends* upon other events if it happened only because the other events happened. In this sense, we say that if event B depends upon event A, then A *caused* B.[2] Conversely, we say events A and B are *independent* if neither caused the other.

- *Aggregation.* If event A signifies an activity that consists of the activities of a set of events, $B_1, B_2, B_3, \ldots$, then A is an *aggregation* of all the events B_i. Conversely, the events, B_i, are *members* of A.

  Aggregation is an abstraction relationship. Usually, event A is created when a set of events, $\{B_i\}$, happens. A is a higher-level event. It signifies a complex activity that consists of all the activities in the system that the aggregated events signify. We call A a *complex event*. Its members, $B_1, B_2, B_3, \ldots$, are the events that *caused* it. A is a different event from any of the B_i events.

  A complex event signifies an activity that takes place over a time interval. Examples will be discussed in the next chapter on event hierarchies. The timing of a complex event starts when the earliest activities of its member events start, and ends when the latest activities of its members end. So, instead of a single timestamp, we will usually see a time interval attribute of a complex event.

All these relationships between events have some simple mathematical properties. They are *transitive* and *asymmetric*.

For example, time orderings according to the same clock are transitive: *If A is earlier than B, and B is earlier than C, then A is earlier than C.* Causality and aggregation are also transitive relationships.

As an example of asymmetry: *If A caused B and A $\neq$ B, then B did not cause A.* Time and aggregation are also asymmetric.

Each of these relationships is called a *partial ordering* rather than a total ordering because there can be events that are not ordered by the relationship. That is, events A and B can exist such that neither A **R** B nor B **R** A is true, where **R** is any of our three relationships.

---

[2]This is *computational causality*, which depends only upon properties of the target system. It is a much more limited concept than philosophical or statistical notions of cause and effect.

5.3.1   The Cause-Time Axiom

In most systems, causality and time always have a very simple consistency relationship, which is stated in the following law.

Cause-time axiom: *If event A caused event B in system S, then no clock in S gives B an earlier timestamp than it gives A.*

Systems that satisfy the cause-time axiom have clocks that all agree in the sense that they do not "see" pairs of causally related events in different orders. Our discussion of CEP is simplified if the target system obeys the cause-time axiom.

5.4   Genetic Parameters in Events

In CEP an event's relationships to other events are encoded as data in the event.[3] Special data parameters are added to an event to encode its timing and its causal relationships to other events. They are often referred to as *genetic parameters* because they tell us an event's timing and causal history—that is, when it was created and which events caused the event.

The genetic parameters include the following.

- *Timestamps,* which give the readings of various clocks in the system defining the time interval when the event's activity started and ended. Often, there is just one timestamp giving a single point in time when the activity happened.

- A *causal vector,* which is the set of event indentifiers of the events that are the causes of the event.

5.4.1   Timestamps

Timestamps are a common way to represent the timing of an event. Many systems use timestamps—for example, in log files and simulator histories. An event contains timestamps indicating when the activity it signifies happened. We say "timestamps," plural, because there are many situations relating an event to time. The activity may happen over a time interval, in which case the event contains timestamps for its *start time* and *end time* according to the reading of a clock in the system. An event can have timestamps indicating readings from different clocks. A third kind of timestamp can indicate when the event was observed at some observer in the system—

---

[3]Remember, when we talk about an event containing data, we are really talking about its form.

called the *arrival time* at that observer. An observer can be, for example, a log file or a database.

5.4.2   Causal Vectors

The causal genetic parameters in an event, A, are the unique identifiers of the events that caused A. They define the causal attribute of A.

A *causal vector* is a parameter of an event that contains the identifiers of the set of events that caused the event. Placing causal vectors in the events gives us a practical way to trace causal relationships in complex systems. The information needed to locate the events that caused an event is in the event—not, for example, to be extracted from some database. This makes easier the task of building tools to do the causal tracking.

There are other ways to track causality, but most of them work only in simple systems such as workflow processes where the causes of an event are known in advance of its creation.

For example, to identify the transactions in a transaction system, transaction identifiers are often used. A unique transaction identifier is placed in each event participating in a transaction. This serves to identify the events within the event cloud that are part of the same transaction and to separate them from other transactions going on at the same time. Although this is useful, it does not provide sufficient information to enable tracking the causal relationship between events in all cases.

For example, events happening in each transaction may have varying numbers of causes, differing depending upon the business context. That is, the causes of an event are dynamic, known only when the event is created. Transaction identifiers do not indicate which events are causally related within a transaction. We need additional information. If, for example, there is a precise transaction protocol defining the order in which events are created in response to other events, and there is a global clock that is used to timestamp all events, we can infer causal relationships.

Next-generation electronic eBusiness transaction systems will not be simple workflows. The ability to easily build tools to do causal tracking in these kinds of systems is the important practical application of genetic parameters. Later chapters on *causal modeling* will describe how genetic parameters are constructed.

5.5   Time

A timing relationship between events created by a system tells how the system is performing. Timing is also an important filter in debugging. For example, if we are trying to diagnose why a system is not performing properly, knowing which events happened earlier than the event we are investigating tells us where we should start looking—here time is used as a gross filter to narrow the search space to the earlier events.

Example 1: *A timing requirement on message routing*

A typical example is a publish/subscribe middleware system. Suppose the system has to be set up as the IT layer of some enterprise to meet a timing requirement. A requirement could be that whenever a message is published, any client subscribing to the subject of that message would get it within some deadline. So, assume that we can observe events signifying the publishing and receiving activities, and that they are timestamped by the same clock and have forms like the following:

```
Publish(Subject, TransactionId, Message, Time...)
Receive(Subject, TransactionId, Message, Time...)
```

Examples of these events, coming off the IT layer and entered into a log file as they arrive (that is, order of observation) might be the following:

```
Publish(StockTrade, A05643094, IBM, 09.51EST...)
Publish(StockTrade, A05643302, CSCO, 09.52EST...)
Receive(StockTrade, A05643309, CSCO, 10.02EST...)
Publish(StockTrade, A05650309, JWEB, 09.53EST...)
Receive(StockTrade, A05643094, IBM, 09.55EST...)
     ...
```

The events shown here all have the same subject, "StockTrade," and hey have a transaction Id, message, timestamp giving the time they happened, and other data indicating the publishers and subscribers, the kind of trade, price, and so on. Notice that the order of observation is not necessarily their time order of execution.

The events are related by time of execution. They have timestamps from an eastern standard time clock giving the time they were created. The transaction Ids tell us which Publish and Receive events signify activities in the same transaction—there can be several Receives for each Publish. The timestamps give us the information we need to check whether the deadline requirement is being met.

In this example, the Publish and Receive events related to transaction Id A05643094 have a time difference of 4 seconds. If the timing deadline is 30 seconds, this meets the requirement. But what about every other publish/subscribe transaction?

Notice that the Publish and Receive events on CSCO have different Id numbers. Receive events for Id A05643302 are not in this segment of the log file. Because the log file is ordered by time of arrival at the log file and not by time of execution of the activity (publishing or receiving), we can't tell anything about the time differences between the Publish and Receive events with Id A05643302 from this segment. All Receives might have been executed by 09.55EST but haven't been entered into the log file yet. Obviously, it would be useful to have a watchdog that checks the time-bound constraint.

If middleware messages contain timestamps, as in this example, we can use CEP to monitor that *all* Publish messages are routed to subscribers and received within a specified time deadline. By using CEP, we can easily deal with the issue that their order of observation might be different from their order of execution. The concept that makes this possible is *event pattern matching*.

Event patterns are a powerful way to state our deadline requirement simply and concisely, as the next example shows.

Example 2: *A rule using an event pattern to test the timing of message delivery*

This example uses a simple pattern language that is described in the next chapter. Patterns and rules are expressed in tables, as shown in Table 5.1. Here's what the table means.

The table defines an example of a CEP rule that reacts to a pattern of two events, a Publish and a Receive, shown in the *pattern* row of the table. The pattern matches any pair of Publish and Receive events that have the subject StockTrade and the same Id and message.

Table 5.1: Rule: Check Timely Delivery

Element	Declarations
Variables	Subject S, Message M, String Id, Time T, Time T1, Time T2
Event types	Publish(Subject S, String Id, Message M, Time T),
	Receive(Subject S, String Id, Message M, Time T),
	Warning(String Id, Time T)
Relational operators	**and**
Pattern	Publish(StockTrade, Id, M, T1) **and**
	Receive(StockTrade, Id, M, T2)
Context test	$T2 - T1 \geq 10$ mins
Action	**create** Warning(Id, $T2 - T1$)

The *variables* row defines the variables in the pattern. The *event types* row defines the types of events in the pattern. The *relational operators* row defines the relational operator between events that is used in the pattern.

In applying CEP rules, the matching takes place in real time as the events arrive at the log file. Whenever a match of the pattern is found, the timestamps T1 and T2 of the Publish and Receive events are tested to see if their difference exceeds a deadline of ten minutes. If so, the rule creates a Warning event giving the Id of the events and their time difference.

For example, if this event

```
Receive(StockTrade, A05643302, CISCO, 10.22EST...)
```

is entered into the log file in the previous example, the pattern in the *Check Timely Delivery* rule will match with this event and one of the previous Publish events. The context test on their timestamps will be satisfied, and a warning event will be created:

```
Warning(A05643302, 20 mins)
```

CEP rules like this example are called *constraints* because their purpose is to check a system's performance for violation of requirements.

This is a typical illustration of the importance of timing relationships between events and how event patterns enable us to monitor timing requirements on a target system. Making this concept practical requires developing powerful event pattern languages and pattern matching that can scale to many thousands of transactions per second.

5.6   Causality and Posets

Events in a distributed system (or more precisely, the activities they signify) happen in a relationship of dependence or independence, as we explained in Section 5.3. This relationship, called *causality,* plays an important role in any kind of analysis of what happened in a system, either online or postmortem.

As discussed in Section 5.3, the causal relationship between events is transitive and asymmetric. It is a partial ordering of events. A set of events together with their causal relationship is called a *poset,* an abbreviation for a *partially ordered set of events.* Posets are often represented graphically by DAGs, *directed acyclic graphs.* We can see examples of DAG representations of posets consisting of events from different kinds of systems in Figures 5.2, 5.4, and 5.6 later in this chapter.

When the causal relationship is represented explicitly as in a DAG, it is much easier to build tools to trace back through the causal ancestors of an event or to search for patterns of causally related events.

The essential role of causality is to focus the search space for the causes of some activity. Each event in a poset has a *causal history* consisting of the events that caused it (its immediate ancestors), their causes, and so on. We search the causal history of events leading up to the event in question. If we do not know the causal relationships between events, our searches are often dependent upon what happened earlier in time, which includes a lot of events that are unrelated to what we are looking for.

Example 1: *Tracking causally related events in banking systems*

CEP enables tools to use causality. Some useful ones are graphical browsers that let us look at the causal relationship. The simplest way to graphically depict a causal event history is as a directed acyclic graph. A node represents an event (and its data) and a directed arc (or arrow) represents a dependency relationship—that the event at its head is dependent upon the event at its tail. We use this graphical paradigm in this book. Figure 5.2 shows a DAG representation of causality between banking events.

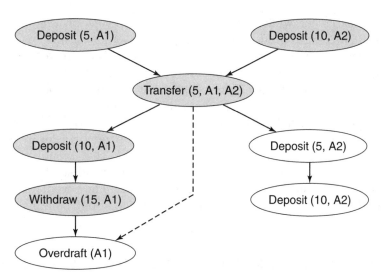

Figure 5.2: Dependencies in a banking system's causal event history

Here the events are Deposit money to an account, Withdraw money from an account, and Transfer money from one account to another account. There's an Overdraft event too.

The figure shows that events on any one account are all dependent in a single sequence. This is the result of an account's being a critical region allowing only one operation at a time. Because an earlier operation on an account has to happen before a later operation can happen, all the events dealing with any single account are causally related in a single sequence. On the other hand, events involving different accounts are usually independent because the banking system allows different accounts to be processed independently—in most cases. Transfers between accounts, however, involve operations on both accounts. They act like a communication between the two accounts. They depend upon previous events in both accounts (simply because accounts are critical regions) and contribute to the causal history of events that follow in both accounts.

The causality graph in Figure 5.2 shows the dependencies between events and also shows events that happened independently. For example, Deposit (10, A1) causes Withdraw (15, A1) because operations on the same account are sequentialy ordered, and Deposit (10, A1) is independent of Deposit (5, A2).

Figure 5.2 is a reduced graph that shows only a subset of dependencies. All other dependencies between events can be seen by transitivity. So the dotted arc between Transfer and Overdraft is not shown in a reduced graph but is the result of transitivity combining the path of arcs from Transfer to Overdraft.

If we search for what caused the Overdraft event on account A1, we will look at its causal predecessors in the graph—that is, its causal history, which is shaded in the figure. This shows that the Overdraft on account A1 depends upon a Transfer from A1 to A2. This event will be chosen as the probable real cause. The figure shows that a causal history can contain irrelevent events, such as the first deposit on account A2.

Suppose we did not have causal tracking and had only timestamps. If the Deposit events on A2 that come causally after the Transfer in the graph had earlier timestamps than the Overdraft on A1, they would be included in the initial search space of all earlier events. We would start with a larger search space that included those Deposit events. They would have to be eliminated from consideration by using knowledge about banking.

5.7   Causal Event Executions—Real-Time Posets

A *causal event execution* is a poset consisting of the events generated by a system and their relationships. We use "causal event execution" to emphasize that we are dealing with events and their relativities online in real time.

Example 1: *Augmenting time with causality*

Events are transmitted between pairs of nodes in a network according to a protocol. Figure 5.3 shows a log file of events in the time order in which they happened. Events that have the same timestamp are arranged vertically.

The protocol is called *alternating bit*. The log file in Figure 5.3 shows attempts to Send three messages, M, M1, and M2, at times 1, 2, and 3, respectively. Each message is accompanied by a bit, b, either 0 or 1. Ideally, a Send(M, b) should be followed by a Receive(M, b), an Ack(M, b), and RecAck(M, b).

Figure 5.3 shows that the ideal transmission, without timeouts, happened in the transmission of message M1. But what about the first message to be sent, M? It was received twice at time 5, but only after a TimeOut and a ReSend. Was the ReSend necessary? If the TimeOut had been delayed, does the log file show that the message would have been received anyway? Reducing the number of ReSends is important in optimizing the network traffic. The next Send from that node contains the alternate bit.

An easy way to answer these questions is to check the causal relationships between the events. Figure 5.4 shows the causal relationships as well as the timing. Now it is clear that the ReSend of M is part of the complete transmission with an acknowledgment from the receiver and a final receipt by the sender, RecAck.

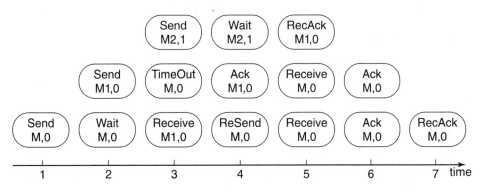

Figure 5.3: An event log of network protocol events ordered by time

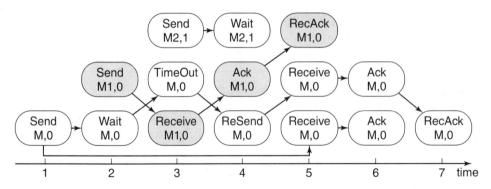

Figure 5.4: The same event log with causal relationships added explicitly

---

Example 2: *Causality in network management*

The need for knowledge of causal relationships between events is well illustrated by some present-day "network management" tools. Such tools allow a user to view the events in a widely distributed network, such as the IT layer of an international banking system. The tool displays the events, their data, and timing. Looking at the tool's GUI, we might see an event in its display that tells us, "The server in Hong Kong is very slow in responding." The tool might even give us an alert message when the event arrives. But we can't ask the tool questions like "What events contributed to that?" Network management tools have a hard time answering questions about causality because the answers depend in part upon the topology of the network, which can be continuously changing. We have to figure out the answer manually by inspecting the events. We are forced to try to reconstruct the causal relationships manually from our knowledge of the system. This is tedious, to say the least, and difficult to do in a timely manner, and we often won't be able to do it because the necessary information is lacking.

Example 3: *Causality in inter-enterprise commerce*

The ability to track causality between business events will become essential in the developing area of B2B Internet commerce. Here, different enterprises perform complicated multistep transactions in collaborating with one another across one or more eMarketplaces. We will want to answer questions such as "How did this electronic buy order get triggered?" This requires tracing the events in the buy order's causal ancestry. It may involve discovering events that should have been in the causal ancestry but are missing.

We may also want monitor conformance to policies such as "An order confirmation must not cause both an order allocation event and a request

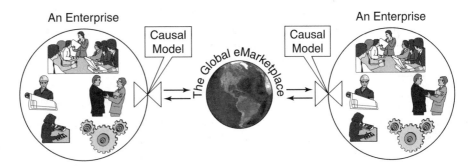

Figure 5.5: Causal modeling across collaborating electronic processes

to cancel an order, unless a time bound has been violated." This requires detecting patterns of several events that are causally related and monitoring their timing.

A solution amounts to tracking causality in a general way that supersedes the conventions of any one standard or legacy transaction system. We can piggyback CEP causal tracking techniques on top of different transaction systems, using genetic data parameters in the events (see Section 5.4). Figure 5.5 shows conceptually how causal tracking across collaborating processes might be done. The "bow ties" represent causal models positioned at the gateways or firewalls of enterprises. They are essentially rule-based event transformers, rather like Electronic Data Interchange (EDI) data format transformers. Their purpose is to add causal data to outgoing events and to observe and remember incoming events. The rules express knowledge about how an enterprise's internal transaction system works—for example, "When we get these types of messages, we respond with those types of messages." The rules take account of the events flowing in and out, across the IT boundaries of the enterprise. The internal policies of the enterprise, whereby decisions are made and events are ouput, don't need to be exposed in the causal models. Those policies are applied to input events and, in due course, result in output events. The causal rules simply express that there is a causal relationship between the input events with such and such data and the resulting output events containing related data. This is called *causal modeling* of a transaction system. Causal models don't have to be "complete" to be useful; they may simply document some of the known or understood processes. More about causal models and their applications in Chapter 11.

This use of CEP will add value to multi-enterprise transaction systems.

- It will add diagnostics and predictive capabilities spanning the multiple process systems based upon causal event histories.
- It will provide efficient diagnostics for exceptional situations arising during a transaction.

- It will enable causal analysis to predict exceptions—for example, by analyzing the expected causal history of a desired event to find what is missing in the actual monitored activity.

Example 4: *Causal modeling of activity between collaborating processes*

Figure 5.6 shows a causal history of events generated by financial trading processes such as those in the system in Figure 3.1. These processes collabo-

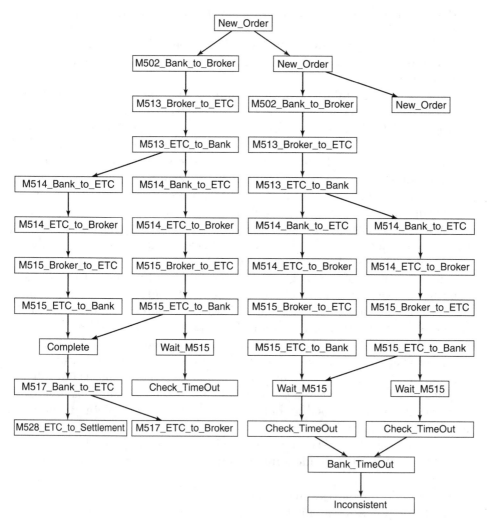

Figure 5.6: A poset showing events in two concurrent financial transactions

rate over an ISO 15022 financial transaction network.[4] This causal history is created by a *causal model* of the processes. The model transforms the message activity of the processes by adding the genetic parameters that express the causal relationship between messages.

The enterprises in Figure 3.1 agree to a protocol for collaboration using the ISO 15022 network. The network provides standard messaging facilities and makes services such as Electronic Trade Confirmation (ETC) and settlement of transactions available to clients. A collaborative aggreement could include the rules that follow.

Each transaction is initiated by the bank's sending an MT502 message with a new order to the brokerage house. It is agreed that each transaction will involve a sequence of messages of ISO 15022 types, flowing to and from the bank to the trading house via an ETC system.

1. *Initiate a trade:* A message of type MT502 can be sent from the bank to the trading house to initiate a new order, which is defined by the values of its data fields.

2. *Confirm execution of a trade:* A message of type MT513 must be sent from the trading house in response to an MT502 new order, via the ETC, to the bank, confirming the execution of an order.

3. *Allocate portions of a trade:* One or more messages of type MT514 in response to an MT513 must be sent by the bank, via the ETC, to the trading house. Each message allocates all or part of a confirmed trade to the bank's accounts. There may be several MT514 messages in response to one MT513, together covering completely the allocation of a trade to the bank's various accounts.

4. *Confirm an allocation:* A message of type MT515 in response to each MT514 message must be sent from the trading house, via the ETC, to the bank, confirming receipt of the MT514.

5. *Finalize a trade:* A message of type MT517 in response to a complete set of MT515 messages confirming all MT514 allocations must be sent from the bank, via the ETC, to the trading house, finalizing settlement of an order.

Details of the data contents of the messages would be spelled out as part of the agreement.

A causal model captures the agreement by rules that enable it to add genetic parameters to the events generated by the collaborating processes.

---

[4]Web search on "ISO15022."

Figure 5.6 shows the progress of two separate transactions as tracked by a causal model. Each event signifies the sending of a message conforming to an ISO 15022 message type, called MT502, MT513, and so on.[5]

The event traffic is visible on the financial network, outside the enterprises. It represents their collaborative activity. Their internal decision making remains hidden. For example, MT502 events flow from the bank to the trading house and initiate new transactions. MT513 events flow in response to MT502 events, from the trading house to the ETC, and from the ETC to the bank. The internal processing of the trading house, whereby it responds to an MT502 by sending an MT513, is hidden. Similarly, the bank responds to an MT513 by sending one or more MT514 messages, which allocate portions of a trade to various accounts. The bank's internal processes are also hidden from view.

Obviously, since many of these transactions can be in progress simultaneously, tracking the causal relationships between these collaborative events is important. Sometimes, this may be as simple as using a unique identifier for each transaction throughout all the internal processes as well as the collaboration across the ISO 15022 network.[6] But the various internal legacy processes may not be equipped to handle a new kind of identifier. For example, an MT502 to the trading house may be broken down and distributed internally to various agents or brokers. The distribution system may be set up to give each order a different order number. And it may totally fail to handle multiple replies with the same order number. Upgrading the legacy systems may not be easy. Instead, it may be quicker and easier to express the relationships between external messages received and sent by rules in a high-level language. Such a set of rules is a *causal model.*

The objective of causal modeling of a collaboration is to create an event execution in which the causal relationships between events are explicitly represented by adding genetic parameters to the events. This makes the analysis of event histories easier, particularly tracking problems such as whether the transactions correctly follow the collaboration agreement. Tools that are designed to trace causal histories can be applied to the problems of how transactions failed to complete or deviated from the agreement.

A causal model at the interface of the trading house (see example 3 and Figure 5.5) tracks the causal relationships between the incoming MT502s and the outgoing MT513s. Similarly, it tracks relationships between incoming MT514s and outgoing MT515s. There is also a causal model at the interface of the bank that tracks how the bank responds to incoming MT513s by sending MT514s, to incoming MT515s by sending MT517s, and so on.

---

[5]Note that in the figure, messages of types MT502, MT513, and so on are signified by events named M502, M513, and so on.

[6]See the discussion in Section 5.4.2.

The causal models at each enterprise interface enable us to separate the events that belong to one transaction from those of another, as shown in Figure 5.6, and to track causal relationships between events within a transaction. Integration of the causal model with the processes of each enterprise is not needed. The causal models work separately from the processes by observing the message traffic on the network and adding genetic parameters.

Figure 5.6 shows differences in the progress of two transactions. Causal tracking provides an easy way to analyze how these differences happened. The leftmost transaction goes through a normal progress to completion. It commences with an M502 event from the bank to the broker initiating a new trade, and finally completes with an M517 event from the bank to the ETC and on to the broker finalizing the trade. Along the way, we can see an M513 confirming execution of the trade, from the broker to the ETC and on to the bank. This causes two M514 events from the bank, each allocating part of an order to an account and each caused by the same M513 event. Subsequent M515 events from the broker cause a completion of the transaction by the bank issuing the M517.

The right-hand transaction, however, shows a transaction that times out before it is completed. The two M515 events generated by the ETC are checked by an assistant at the bank's interface in parallel with their delivery to the bank. The constraint check is initiated by a watchdog process sending a Wait_M515 event to a transaction timing checker. In this case, the transaction violated the time constraint and caused a Bank_timeout event.

The point to be made in this example is that causal models at the interfaces of enteprises are a powerful method of tracking and analyzing the activity of collaborative processes. They present an alternative to upgrading internal processes to achieve causal tracking of collaborations between process systems.

5.8   Orderly Observation

Events can arrive at the CEP adapters from the target system, as shown in Figure 5.1, in an order that may or may not be consistent with their causal order. If their time of arrival is consistent with their causal relationship in the target system, we say that the *observation is orderly*. That is:

> **Orderly observation:** for any pair of events A and B,
> if A $\longrightarrow$ B then ArrivalTime(A) $\leq$ ArrivalTime(B).

where A $\longrightarrow$ B means "A causes B," and the ArrivalTime of an event is its time of arrival at a CEP adapter, assuming adapters have synchronized clocks. Note that if events A and B are causally independent of one another, they can arrive in any order.

Orderly observation is not necessary for CEP to apply to a system. But it is convenient and makes some applications of CEP simpler and easier to implement.

5.9   Observation and Uncertainty

In the course of processing the events adapted from the target system's IT layers, as described in Section 5.2, CEP may also create new events signifying activities in the system. The events created by CEP can be thought of as *event inferences* drawn from observed events. CEP may also process these event inferences and use them to create more inferences.

Event inferences can signify activities within the system that were not signified by events observed in the system itself. Using knowledge about the system, CEP can give us a more comprehensive picture of what is going on in the system than what events in the system actually tell us. The totality of what we can observe, together with what we can infer, is called the *observable system.*

- *The Observable System*   The set of all events that can be observed from a target system, or inferred from observations, is called *the observable system.*

  As in the physical universe, in the computer universe, we must also live with uncertainty for a multitude of reasons. For example, our observations may be incomplete in that they cannot observe sufficiently many system activities, or we do not know enough about the target system to make event inferences, or there may be failures that result in activities not being observed at observation points.

- *Uncertainty Principle*   An activity within a target system may not have any signifying event in the observable system.

  The *uncertainty principle* applies to the application of CEP to a target system. It covers not only the events we can observe from a target system, but also the inferences we can draw from them by CEP. The uncertainty principle does *not* apply to all systems. It says that for some systems we won't be able to achieve total observability. That is, sometimes it will be true that there are activities of interest to us in the target system for which no signifying event is created in the observable system. We must not expect total observability no matter how clever we are at extracting events and applying CEP.

CEP gives us the tools to make maximal use of the information that is available. But we must always bear in mind that there may be activities going on in the system that we cannot know about.

5.10   Summary

We have introduced the first group of primary concepts of CEP: *event, time, cause, aggregation,* and *poset.*

The idea of using partial ordering relationships between events to understand the behavior of distributed systems goes back to a few publications in the 1980s and early 1990s. The relationship between time and event orderings in distributed systems was the subject of several early publications, including [10], [4], [3], [17], and [2]. Perhaps the earliest proponent of developing a theory of partial orders of events to model concurrency was V. Pratt [21]. Strategies for ensuring orderly observation were studied in [18].

The incorporation of causal orderings of events into computer simulation languages was first described in [15]. The first practical applications of causal orderings of events to improve event-based simulation results were reported in [5], [15], and [13]. The wider application of these ideas, beyond simulation, to event-driven systems in general, led to CEP.[7] Application of causal orderings of events to analysis of computer programs in languages such as Java is described in [23].

---

[7]http://pavg.stanford.edu/cep/

Chapter $\boxed{6}$

Event Patterns, Rules, and Constraints

- *Familiar kinds of pattern searching*
- *Event patterns*
- *A strawman event pattern language*
- *Event pattern rules*
- *Event pattern constraints*
- *Capturing business rules as event patterns*

This chapter explains concepts that form the foundation for applications of CEP: *event patterns, reactive event pattern rules,* and *event pattern constraints.*

6.1   Common Kinds of Pattern Searching

An ability to pick out sets of events of interest as they happen from large event executions is fundamental to viewing and controlling an event-driven system. We need to be able to describe a pattern of events that we are interested in and quickly find the sets of events that match the pattern. To do this, we first need a precise method to describe event patterns. One way is to write the pattern in a computer language called an *event pattern language* (EPL). Another way, which many of us are familiar with, is to use a graphical user interface (GUI) such as those provided in popular Web search engines. A graphical interface lets us write basic parts of the pattern in a search box and combine them into a complete pattern using search options. Unfortunately, search GUIs usually allow only very simple patterns to be described.

Pattern matching applied to other kinds of objects than events, such as strings and files, has been around a lot longer than the Internet. Operating systems give us pattern languages that help us find files that contain strings we are looking for. We must specify the string in a pattern language, say grep or awk. These pattern languages let us specify variable parts in our patterns. So we can search for all the strings that have certain parts in common. For example, using grep, which does searches for strings that are specified using regular expression patterns, the following statement

grep　Bas.ba.*　AFileName

will find all strings in the file AFileName that start with "Bas" followed by any single character, and then "ba", and ending with one or more characters. Our string specification, "Bas.ba.*", is a *template,* in which the "." and the ".*" are variables. The "." can match any character, and the ".*" can match any sequence of one or more characters. So among the matches we'll get are "Baseball", "Bashballs", "Bassbaite", and so on.

In CEP we need to specify sets of events that have certain common data in some of the events and also have specific timing, causal, and aggregation relationships between the events. The need to specify sets of events that have parts in common and specific relativities is a step beyond string searching. A pattern language in which we can express such patterns will necessarily be more complex than string searching languages.

6.2　Event Patterns

An *event pattern* is a template that matches certain sets of events—the sets you want to find. It describes precisely not only the events but also their causal dependencies, timing, data parameters, and context. So an event pattern is a template for *posets.*

Some examples of event patterns are the following:

1. All orders from customer C in the last month
2. All orders from frequent customers in the last month
3. All orders from customers in response to a discount announcement

4. All orders from customers at the regular price that have led to the customer requesting a reduced price in response to the discount announcement

The first pattern matches all the order events from a particular customer, C, that happened during a one-month period. To see if an order matches this pattern, we must look at the data in the order to see if the customer is C and the time bound is met. This is called a *content-sensitive* pattern.

The second pattern is similar to the first one, except that instead of searching the data in an order to see if the customer is C, we must evaluate the *context* of the customer—for example, by searching a database to see if the customer is frequent. This is a context-sensitive pattern where the context is part of the state in which the matching takes place.

The third pattern matches all order events that are related to the discount announcement event. We interpret "in response to" as a causal relationship (see Figure 6.1). To find these events, we must have a method of determining if there is a causal relationship between an order event and the discount announcement. For example, one method could be to search the contents of the order to see if it refers to the announcement. So the pattern "picks out" from the set of all order events those orders that are caused by the announcement—shown as shaded events in Figure 6.1. It acts as a *filter*, using the causal relationship between an order event and the announcement event to reduce the space of events to a small part of the incoming events.

The fourth pattern is more complicated. It matches a set of order events that happened independently of the announcement (since they quote the regular price) and caused a request event when the announcement was made

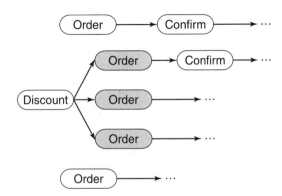

Figure 6.1: Order events caused by a discount announcement event

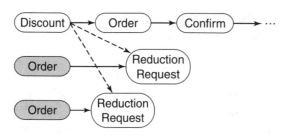

Figure 6.2: Reduction requests caused by a discount announcement

(see Figure 6.2). Matching this pattern uses relationships between three events: the order, the announcement, and the request in the poset of incoming events. This kind of pattern is beyond the power of expression of most event pattern languages.

6.3   A Strawman Pattern Language

Here we describe a strawman event pattern language. Let's call it STRAW-EPL. This is not a powerful event pattern language. But it serves as an introduction to pattern languages and allows us to give examples of some complex event patterns. STRAW-EPL can be used to specify patterns with three relational operators: **and, or,** $\longrightarrow$ (causes).

Some examples are as follows:

- A **and** B **and** C: Matches a set of three events, A, B, C
- A **or** B **or** C: Matches any one of A, B, or C
- A $\longrightarrow$ B: Matches pairs of events A, B where A causes B

A pattern in STRAW-EPL must declare the following four elements:

1. A list of variables. Variables are declared with their types:
   - *A variable M of type Message:* Message M;
   - *A variable T of type Time:* Time T;
2. A list of types of events. Event types have a name and a parameter list of variables and their types:
   - *A Send event:* Send(Message M, Bit B, Time T);
   - *A ReSend event:* ReSend(Message M, Bit B, Time T);
3. A pattern. A pattern is a set of event templates together with relationships between the event templates. An event template is an

event with variables or constants as parameters. Each template must belong to one of the event types:

- *A Send and a ReSend with the same message and bit, and possibly different timestamps:* Send(M, B, T1) **and** ReSend(M, B, T2);

4. A condition on the context of any match. A context condition is a test that must be true when the pattern is matched:

- *The time between the Send and ReSend events must be less than a bound:* $0 < T2 - T1 < Bnd$;

6.3.1 Pattern Matching

Each *match* of a pattern is a poset that is an instance of the pattern constructed by replacing variables in the pattern with values. A variable must be replaced by the same value wherever it occurs in the pattern.

The process of replacing variables in a pattern with values is called *matching*.

6.3.2 Writing Patterns in STRAW-EPL

Patterns in STRAW-EPL are written in a tabular format, as shown in Table 6.1. The table gives the name of the pattern and each of its elements.

Example 1: *A pattern of events signifying a successful network data transfer*

The tabular format declares the variables (also called *placeholders*) in the pattern together with their types, the types of events in the pattern, and the relational operators used in the pattern. In this case, one operator, $\longrightarrow$, is used in the pattern.

The Data Transfer pattern matches posets consisting of a sequence of four events, each being a cause of the next one. The first event is a Send of

Table 6.1: Pattern: Data Transfer

Element	Declarations
Variables	Data D, Bit B, Time T, Time T1, Time T2
Event types	Send(Data D, Bit B, Time T), Receive(Data D, Bit B, Time T), Ack(Bit B, Time T), RecAck(Bit B, Time T)
Relational operators	$\rightarrow$ (causes)
Pattern	Send(D, B, T1) $\rightarrow$ Receive(D, B) $\rightarrow$ Ack(B) $\rightarrow$ RecAck(B, T2)
Context test	$T2 - T1 < 10$ secs.

data D and a Bit B at time T1. D can be any data, and B can be either 0 or 1. The Send must cause the second event, a Receive with the same data D and bit B. Its time is not mentioned, so it can happen at any time—but no sooner than T1.[1] The Receive must in turn cause an Ack with the same Bit, which finally causes a RecAck with the same Bit at time T2. The times of the intermediate events are not mentioned. The context test restricts the matches, so that the four events match the Data Transfer pattern only if the time difference between the last and the first events is less than ten seconds.

```
-- This poset is a match of the Data Transfer pattern:
Send("hello", 0, 12:00EST) → Receive("hello", 0, 12:01EST) → Ack(0, 12:02EST) →
RecAck(0, 12:03EST)
-- where D = "hello", B = 0, T1 = 12:00EST, and T2 = 12:03EST.

-- This poset is not a match of the Data Transfer pattern:
Send("hello", 0, 12:00EST) → Receive("goodbye", 0, 12:01EST) → Ack(0, 12:02EST) →
RecAck(0, 12:03EST)
-- because the Send and Receive events contain different data.
```

Example 2: *A pattern for completed message delivery on messaging middleware*

The StockTrade Message Test pattern, as shown in Table 6.2, matches any pair of events consisting of a Publish and a Receive that have the same Id and message, provided the subject of the events is "StockTrade" and the time difference between the two events is less than 35 minutes.

In Section 5.5 there is an example of events created by publish/subscribe middleware. The StockTrade Message Test pattern matches pairs of middleware events that indicate completed Publish/Receive message delivery on

Table 6.2: Pattern: StockTrade Message Test

Element	Declarations
Variables	Subject S, Message M, String Id, Time T, Time T1, Time T2
Event types	Publish(Subject S, String Id, Message M, Time T), Receive(Subject S, String Id, Message M, Time T)
Relational operators	**and**
Pattern	Publish(S, Id, M, T1) **and** Receive(S, Id, M, T2)
Context test	$T2 - T1 < 35$ mins **and** S = "StockTrade"

---

[1]See the cause-time axiom, Section 5.3.1.

the subject "StockTrade". So, let's go through these events and see which pairs match.

Example 3: *Recognizing corresponding pairs of Publish/Receive events*

```
-- Events generated by the middleware
Publish(StockTrade, A05643094, IBM, 09:51EST...)
Publish(StockTrade, A05643302, CISCO, 09:52EST...)
Receive(StockTrade, A05643309,  CISCO, 10:02EST...)
Publish(StockTrade, A05650309, JWEB, 09:53EST...)
Receive(StockTrade, A05643094, IBM, 09:55EST...)
Receive(StockTrade, A05643302, CISCO, 10:22EST...)
  ...


-- Examples of  pairs of middleware events  that match the
-- StockTrade Message Test pattern are:
Publish(StockTrade, A05643094, IBM, 09:51EST...)
Receive(StockTrade, A05643094, IBM, 09:55EST...)

Publish(StockTrade, A05643302, CISCO, 09:52EST...)
Receive(StockTrade, A05643302, CISCO, 10:22EST...)

-- But not a pair like:
Publish(StockTrade, A05643302, CISCO, 09:52EST...)
Receive(StockTrade, A05643309, CISCO, 10:02EST...)
-- because the Ids in the two events are different.
```

6.4 Event Pattern Rules

An event pattern rule is a *reactive rule* that specifies an action to be taken whenever an event pattern is matched. An event pattern rule implies a causal relationship between the events that trigger it by matching its pattern and the events that are created when the rule executes its actions.

Here we describe a strawman rule language in which the patterns are written in STRAW-EPL and the only action is to create a new event.

A reactive rule has two parts:

- *A trigger,* which is an event pattern
- *An action,* which is an event that is created whenever the trigger matches

The *causal implication* is, whenever an event pattern rule is triggered by a poset of events, the event it creates is *caused by* the triggering events. The triggering events are *causal ancestors* of the new event.

A typical example is a rule that expresses a management policy requiring an action to be taken whenever a situation arises—for example: "Always respond to a message of type MT502 containing a stock trade order by issuing a message of type MT513 either confirming or denying the order."

Here the situation is receiving a financial trade order message of type MT502. The action is to respond with a trade confirmation message of type MT513. In each instance, the triggering MT502 message is the immediate causal ancestor of the resulting MT513 message.

Reactive rules can be either *sequential* or *parallel*. A sequential rule implies that all its triggerings take place in a sequence, one after the other. As a consequence, all the events it creates are causally ordered in a sequence (see Figure 6.3).

A parallel rule implies that its triggerings take place independently, as if executed by new threads of control. As a consequence, none of the events it creates depend causally upon one another (see Figure 6.4) unless the events created on one triggering are part of the match in another triggering of the rule. The events created by a parallel rule depend only upon the triggering events.

Both kinds of rules are useful in modeling the causal behavior of systems. Most of our examples are illustrated with sequential reactive rules.

We can write event pattern rules in a tabular format similar to STRAW-EPL. A rule table is a pattern table with an additional row specifying an action. A sequential rule uses **create** to indicate its action, whereas a parallel rule uses **create parallel**.

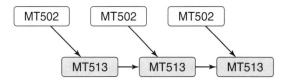

Figure 6.3: Causal ordering of events created by a sequential reactive rule

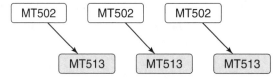

Figure 6.4: Causal ordering of events created by a parallel reactive rule

Example 1: *A sequential rule to confirm execution of trade orders*

Tabular format (see Table 6.3) declares the variables and the types of events used in the rule. The pattern is the rule's trigger. In this example, it is a single MT502 event. The context test must be true when an event matches the pattern for the rule to trigger. In this case, the test involves a function call for a price quotation, and the value returned must be below the MT502 order limit. When the rule triggers, the action to create an MT513 event is executed. All the variables in the create action must have values as a result of the pattern match so that an instance of the MT513 event type is specified. This event is created.

Figure 6.3 shows the causal ordering of MT502 events that trigger the rule and MT513 events it creates. Each MT502 event causes the resulting MT513 event. In addition, all the MT513 events are causally ordered in the sequence in which they were created. This kind of reactive rule models the semantics of a single thread of control. That is, the rule is always executed by the same thread. Therefore, all its executions are linearly ordered by causality, one after the other.

Table 6.3: **Rule: Respond to an MT502 Order with an MT513 Confirmation**

Element	Declarations
Variables	TransactionId Id, OrderType O, StockSym S, Quantity Q, Accnt A, Dollars Limit, Time Date, Time Bnd;
Event types	MT502(TransactionId Id, OrderType O, StockSym S, Quantity Q, Accnt A, Dollars Limit, Time Date, Time Bound) MT513(TransactionId Id, OrderType O, StockSym S, Quantity Q, Accnt A, Dollars Price)
Relational operators	none
Pattern	MT502(Id, O, S, Q, A, Limit, Date, Bound);
Context test	MarketQuote(S, Q) < Limit
Action	**create** MT513(Id, O, S, Q, A, MarketQuote(S, Q))

If we changed the rule to be a **create parallel** rule, the events it creates would have the causal order shown in Figure 6.4.

Example 2: *Warning of late network data transfer*

The *Late Data Transfer Warning* rule expresses a management rule: "Whenever a data transfer takes more than one hour, send a warning event."

A completed data transfer consists of four events, as in the Data Transfer pattern in Section 6.3. The trigger is a pattern that matches completed data transfers. In this example in Table 6.4, however, additional variables are used to match the network nodes, contained as parameters of the events, where the data is being sent from and to. The context test is true only if the time bound for data transfer is violated.

Table 6.4: Rule: Late Data Transfer Warning

Element	Declarations
Variables	Node N1, Node N2, Data D, Bit B, Time T1, Time T2, Time T3, Time T4;
Event types	Send(Node N1, Node N2, Data D, Bit B, Time T1), Receive(Node N1, Node N2, Data D, Bit B, Time T1), Ack(Node N1, Node N2, Bit B, Time T1), RecAck(Node N1, Node N2, Bit B, Time T1), Warning(Node N1, Node N2, Time T1, Time T2);
Relational operators	→ (causes)
Pattern	Send(N1, N2 D, B, T1) → Receive(N2, N1, D, B, T2) → Ack(N2, N1, B, T3) → RecAck(N1, N2, B, T4);
Context test	$T4 - T1 \geq 1$ hour
Action	**create** Warning(N1, N2, T1, T4)

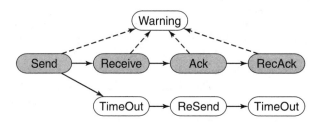

Figure 6.5: Immediate causal ancestors of a Warning event

The rule also declares a new event type, Warning. A Warning event is created by the rule when its trigger matches. It contains the nodes involved in the data transfer, and the times of the Send and the final RecAck. This Warning event has the triggering events as its immediate causal ancestors, as shown in Figure 6.5.

Note that we might want our Warning events to be more informative. For example, it would be nice to have them include a *count* of the number of previous warnings between the pair of nodes in a specified time period. Owing to the very limited capability of our strawman rule language to express actions, we can't do this.

Example 3: *Recognizing priority orders caused by a discount price announcement*

The *Create Priority Orders* rule (see Table 6.5) triggers on customer orders that respond to a discount price announcement on an item. The context test

Table 6.5: Rule: Create Priority Orders

Element	Declarations
Variables	Customer Id, Item I, Dollars Price, Dollars Total, Quantity Q1, Quantity Q2, Time Until, Time T1, Time T2;
Event types	Discount(Item I, Dollars Price, Quantity Q1, Time Until, Time T1), Order(Customer Id, Item I, Quantity Q, Dollars Total, Time T1), PriorityOrder(Customer Id, Item I, Quantity Q1, Dollars Total)
Relational operators	$\rightarrow$ (causes)
Pattern	Discount(I, Price, Q1, Until, T1) $\rightarrow$ Order(Id, I, Q2, Total, T2);
Context test	CreditRating(Id) ≥ 7 **and** $Q2 \leq Q1$ **and** Total $\geq \$1000$ **and** $T2 \leq T1 +$ Until
Action	**create** PriorityOrder(Id, I, Q2, Total)

requires the customer's credit rating to be at least 7, the quantity ordered (Q2) to be not more than the limit (Q1), the total value of the order (Total) to be at least $1,000, and finally, the order to be within the time limit (Until) of the time of the offer. If the context test is passed, a PriorityOrder event is created with the relevant data. The triggering events are its immediate causal ancestors.

The use of $\longrightarrow$ in the rule's trigger distinguishes between orders that simply happened after the announcement and those that are specifically in response to the announcement.

We might want to create two actions, a PriorityOrder and a SpecialOffer to be sent to this customer. Because of the limited action capabilities of our strawman rules, we would need two rules with this trigger, each of which takes one of these actions.

The causal ordering between triggering events and the created Priority-Order event is shown in Figure 6.6.

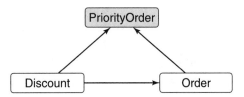

Figure 6.6: Causal ordering between triggering and created events

6.5   Constraints

A constraint expresses a condition that must be satisfied by the events observed in a system. Constraints can be used to specify not only how a target system should behave, but also how its users should use it.

Our strawman constraints express a very simple form of condition called **never** constraints.

A **never** constraint consists of the following:

- The temporal operator **never**
- A STRAW-EPL pattern

The pattern may contain a context test.

Essentially, a constraint tests that its pattern of events never happens in the system. It is a *watchdog*. These constraints do not enforce behavior or guarantee that the behavior will not happen. They simply test for the behavior.

never constraints are used to express business or management policies, such as the absence of inconsistent behavior or quality of service requirements that must always be met.

Example 1: *Simple constraint against an inconsistent behavior*

The constraint in Table 6.6 expresses a policy that an order from a customer must never be first confirmed and then, at the same or a later time, denied. The pattern matches an **and** of a Confirm and a Deny with the same

Table 6.6: Constraint: Never Confirm and Then Cancel an Order

Element	Declarations
Variables	Customer Id, Item I, OrderNo N, Dollars Price, Time T1, Time T2;
Event types	Confirm(Customer Id, OrderNo N, Item I, Dollars Price, Time T1) Deny(Customer Id, OrderNo N, Item I, Dollars Price, Time T1)
Relational operators	**and**
Temporal operator	**never**
Pattern	Confirm(Id, N, I, Price, T1) **and** Deny(Id, N, I, Price, T2);
Context test	T1 $\leq$ T2

parameters and tests their timing. The constraint does allow an order to be first denied and later on to be confirmed.

Example 2: *Level of service check*

The *Level of Service Check* constraint in Table 6.7 is expressed in terms of messaging priorities. Its pattern matches two pairs of causally related Send/Receive events. Each pair sends and receives a message on a subject over a period of time. The pairs can have different subjects and messages, but the Send events must happen at the same time. The context test is that the priority (Lvl1) of one of the Send events is higher than the other (Lvl2) (that is, numerically lower, priority 1 being higher than priority 2), and the Receive event that it causes has a later timestamp (T1) than the other Receive event (T2). The constraint expresses that this pattern must never match.

Table 6.7: **Constraint: Level of Service Check**

Element	Declarations
Variables	Subject S, Subject S1, Message M, Message M1, Priority Lvl1, Priority Lvl2, Time T, Time, T1, Time T2
Event types	Send(Subject S, Message M, Priority Lvl1, Time T), Receive(Subject S, Message M, Time T)
Relational operators	$\longrightarrow$, **and**
Temporal operator	**never**
Pattern	(Send(S, M, Lvl1, T) $\longrightarrow$ Receive(S, M, T1)) **and** (Send(S1, M1, Lvl2, T) $\longrightarrow$ Receive(S, M, T2))
Context test	Lvl1 < Lvl2 **and** T1 > T2

Notice that *Level of Service Check* does not check that messages sent at different times have delivery times in accordance with their priority levels, because, for example, the network load could vary with time.

This kind of constraint can be expressed in terms of types of events associated with any kind of event-driven system—application service providers, for example. Its function is to monitor a level of service policy or agreement.

Constraints are essentially runtime checks. They are a simple kind of rule in which the only action is to produce a result, *violated* or *satisfied*. A violation event is created whenever there is a violation, whereas a satisfied result happens when some time limit elapses or when the target system ceases operations.

The purpose of a rule is to create new events in response to situations. The purpose of a constraint is different, simply to monitor for a situation. Typically, a constraint is used to express a requirement on system behavior that is not guaranteed by the system. This might happen for these reasons.

- Handling the situation is dependent upon runtime conditions, so exception handling code cannot be applied.
- The situation was not foreseen in the system design but arose in later experience when the system was fielded.
- The situation concerns a particular application of the system and not all applications.

Constraints can easily be converted to rules that create Warning events (see Table 6.4).

6.6 Summary

This chapter has explained the second set of primary concepts of CEP: *event pattern* (involving relationships between events), *event pattern reactive rule,* and *event pattern constraint.*

A high-level language for rules and constraints facilitates the capture of business rules and policies in a format suitable for computer processing and automation.

We have introduced a simple strawman event pattern language and used it to build rules and constraints. Our purpose is to give simple examples of event pattern rules and constraints without going into a lot of language design details.

Some of our examples point out weaknesses of the strawman rules language. However, even this rules language is beyond the current "state of the art" for commercial applications. No commercial rules language deals with a causal relation between events. Also, our context test in STRAW-EPL may contain any number of Boolean conditions. The Boolean conditions can refer to a system state, such as in databases (for example, credit ratings)—that is, the *context* in which matching takes place. Many commercial rules languages allow only tests that refer to the parameters of the events. These are called *content* tests because the content of the events is tested. The use of content tests versus context tests affects the efficiency of rules engines that execute rules. We discuss systems that enable application of CEP in a later chapter.

Chapter 7

Complex Events and Event Hierarchies

- *Event aggregation*
- *Complex events*
- *Event abstraction hierarchies*
- *Personalized and role-based views of hierarchical systems*

This chapter explains two of the most important concepts that form the basis for applications of event pattern rules and constraints: *event aggregation* and *event abstraction hierarchies*. We will continue to use STRAW-EPL and strawman rules to give examples.

7.1   Aggregation and Complex Events

A complex event is an *aggregation* of other events, called its *members,* as defined in Section 5.3. The relationship between a complex event and its members is called *aggregation*.

The member events of a complex event can signify activities that happen at different times and perhaps in widely separate components of a system. So a complex event can signify an activity that consists of several activities in different parts of a distributed system. Conceptually, we think of a complex event as an event at a higher level than the levels of its members.

Here are some examples of complex events from different kinds of systems: hardware design, network protocols, business transactions, security, and message routing.

Example 1: *A CPU instruction, Add(X, Y)*

An Add instruction of a processor is a complex event made up of a set of events generated by the registers, asynchronous logic units, control units, and the clock of a processor. These member events must happen in a particular order over, say, three or four clock cycles. The Add event is thought of as being an event at the instruction level, and its member events are thought of as being at a lower level, the register transfer level of the processor.

Example 2: *Customer C's order has been fulfilled.*

This is an event that aggregates a sequence of events at the level of the architecture shown in Chapter 4, Figure 4.3. It aggregates events that include the initial order entry, order decomposition, the separate fulfillments of the order's components, assembly, billing, collection, and shipping. It takes place over a time interval, from the time of the initial order entry to the completion of the shipping event.

Example 3: *An intrusion has been attempted on subnet N.*

An event like this may be an aggregation of many different sets of network-level events, each corresponding to a particular method of searching a network for a weakness. For example, it could signify an IP address scan consisting of several thousand network-level events attempting to find an operating system with a known weakness.

Example 4: *Message M has been routed to client C based upon C's message content filter.*

Clients running applications on messaging middleware can request the contents of messages to be tested before receiving them. Such tests are called content filters. An example is, "Send me stock-trade messages on IBM only if the price differs by five points from the previous trade."

This event signifies a successful content-based routing activity carried out on a publish/subscribe middleware. It is an event at a level above the middleware activities. It aggregates several middleware events and rules engine events. For example, its members might be a Publish event in which M is published on a subject, followed by events in which M is received by, and processed by, a rules engine that tests the content of M to see if it satisfies the message filters of various clients, followed by client C receiving M.

Example 5: *Message M is routed to client C depending upon the context when it was received.*

If we continue Example 4, clients might request not only that IBM stock-trade messages pass a content test, but also that they be forwarded only if certain other stocks have recently traded above specified values—for example, "Send me stock trade messages on IBM only if the price differs by five points from the previous trade and MSFT has dropped two points in the previous hour."

This event is an aggregation of middleware events, as in Example 4, but includes other events concerning Microsoft's stock trades. This aggregation test goes beyond the content of the IBM stock-trade messages and includes the *context* of MSFT stock-trade messages in the past hour.

7.2   Creating Complex Events

Event pattern rules are used in CEP to create complex events signifying the activities of sets of events. We refer to rules used to create complex events as *aggregation rules.* This use of event pattern rules gives us a powerful method of recognizing significant high-level events from among a cloud of low-level events.

Example 1: *Using event pattern rules to create complex events*

For example, suppose we are monitoring events in the alternating bit protocol for transmitting data over a network (see Section 5.7). There may be many TimeOuts and ReSends. We want to recognize in the cloud of protocol events when attempts to transmit data are successfully completed. In CEP we write a reactive rule, as shown in Table 7.1.

The pattern matches a causal sequence of protocol events: Send, Receive, Ack, and RecAck. The Send and Receive must contain all the same parameters; the Ack and RecAck omit the Data. There can be TimeOuts and ReSends in between that are part of the data transfer (see Figure 5.4). The pattern picks out a subset of events that signifies that a data transfer has

Table 7.1: Rule: Completed Data Transfer

Element	Declarations
Variables	Node N1, Node N2, Data D, Bit B, Time T1, Time T2, Time T3, Time T4;
Event types	Send(Node N1, Node N2, Data D, Bit B, Time T1), Receive(Node N1, Node N2, Data D, Bit B, Time T1), Ack(Node N1, Node N2, Bit B, Time T1), RecAck(Node N1, Node N2, Bit B, Time T1), CompletedTrans(Node N1, Node N2, Data D, Time T1, Time T2);
Relational operators	$\rightarrow$ (causes)
Pattern	Send(N1, N2, D, B, T1) $\rightarrow$ Receive(N2, N1, D, B, T2) $\rightarrow$ Ack(N2, N1, B, T3) $\rightarrow$ RecAck(N1, N2, B, T4);
Context test	T4 $-$ T1 $\leq$ TimeBound
Action	**create** CompletedTran(N1, N2, D, T1, T4)

been completed. If the Send and the RecAck events happen within the time bound, the pattern matches and the rule creates a CompletedTran event with parameters summarizing the data transfer.

The CompletedTran event is a higher-level event. Lower-level details, such as the value of the bit used in the transfer, are abstracted away. The complex event gives only the data, nodes, and duration.

CEP treats CompletedTran just as any other event. And if needed, the lower-level events can be traced back from the complex event. Backtracking from a complex event to its members in CEP is called *drill down*.

Aggregation is a tool for making the activities in a complex system understandable to humans. Aggregation rules allow us to define any complex events we want to. This lets us monitor a system from many different points of view. When a complex event is created by an aggregation rule, genetic parameters containing the Ids of member events are placed in the data parameters of the complex event. This makes it easy to build tools to drill down.

One of the reasons we need event patterns to create complex events is that a complex event can happen in more than one way—more than one set of lower-level events, related in the right way, can signify the activity of the complex event. For example, in an Add instruction, it does not matter which registers from the bank of registers in a CPU generated the member events, but only that those events were generated at the right times in the right order. So an Add can happen when different sets of member events happen.

Also, we need more powerful pattern languages than STRAW-EPL. For example, an aggregation rule to construct the intrusion-warning events described in Example 3, Section 7.1, cannot be expressed using our STRAW-EPL. A more powerful pattern language is needed, and the actions taken by a rule need to include operations on variables—for example, to count the number of times an event happens.

Finally, aggregation is a causal relationship. The lower-level events that are aggregated by a complex event can be thought of as causing the complex event. They have to happen for the complex event to happen. However, our primary use of complex events is to view the activities in the system as happening at a series of abstraction levels. Hence we distinguish between causality, which is a relationship between events at the same level of abstraction, and aggregation, which is an abstraction relationship. We sometimes refer to aggregation later on as *vertical causality.*

7.3 Event Abstraction Hierarchies

Hierarchical structure is ubiquitous in everyday life. Our societies are hierarchical, our business and military organizations are hierarchical, and our computer systems are hierarchical. So it is only natural that this very familiar idea should form a foundation for organizing how CEP is applied to systems.

In CEP an *event abstraction hierarchy* consists of the following elements.

1. *A sequence of levels of activities.* Each level consists of a set of descriptions of system activities and, for each activity, a specification of the types of events that signify instances of that activity. Level 1 is the lowest level.

2. *A set of event aggregation rules for each level.* For each level (except level 1), there must be a rule for creating each type of event at that level as an aggregation of events at levels below.

The crucial aspect of this definition is the set of rules specifying how each event at a higher level is an aggregation of events at levels below it. This is where the CEP event hierarchy goes beyond prior uses of hierarchy in system organization. This requirement allows CEP to infer higher-level events from whatever events can be monitored in the system. Of course, there is an assumption that level 1 events can be observed from the target system.

As we described in Section 3.7, event abstraction hierarchies are a powerful way of organizing how we view a system. Aggregation rules create complex events that abstract large numbers of low-level events. This technique helps us understand the activities that take place in a system. All the events created by the system, or by the rules that are organized hierarchically.

7.3.1   Viewing a Fabrication Line

As an example, look at Figure 7.1. It shows a structuring of events in a chip fabrication facility into three levels. At each level, events are shown as boxes, and causal relationships between them by arrows. An event at a higher level has a shadow of events at the next level down. These are the events that are aggregated from the lower level to create the higher-level event.

At the lowest level, *equipment monitoring,* are events signifying communication between the controllers on the fabline. The controllers control the processing stages in each of the chip fabrication machines. They communicate with one another and with centralized databases that contain the manufacturing recipes, machine status and performance, and the tests that

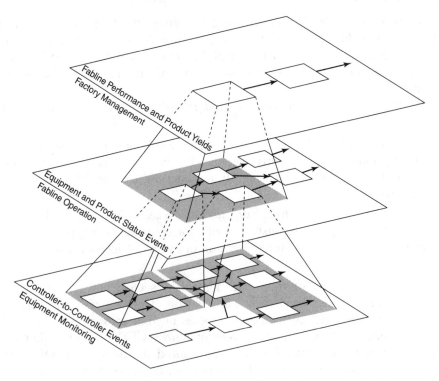

Figure 7.1: A hierarchy of levels of computations in a manufacturing system

must be made at each stage. We can monitor the messages between the controllers because they are usually carried on some standard middleware.

At level 1, equipment monitoring, the events signify messages from the fabline process controllers to the controllers of individual fabrication machines, and messages from controllers to central databases. At this level, events signify steps in the process of individual machines (load, unload, start, and so on), movements of cassettes by robots from one stage to the next in the fabline, and test results and diagnostics from monitoring the process of each machine. It is very detailed information of interest to operators of the fabline.

At level 2 in Figure 7.1, *fabline operation,* we see complex events that aggregate sets of level 1 events according to predefined aggregation rules. An aggregation rule specifies a pattern of level 1 events and how they must be related (by time and causality), and creates the level 2 event that signifies that pattern. In the figure, the shadow of a level 2 event on the cloud of level 1 events shows an instance of a pattern of level 1 events that signifies the level 2 event. When the pattern of an aggregation rule matches events in the flow of level 1 controller communication, the corresponding level 2 event is created. The hierarchical aggregation process takes place in real time. As a result, we can imagine events flowing through each of the levels in Figure 7.1. Normally, the higher the level, the fewer the number of events.

Level 2 events signify the performance of fabrication machines (processing time, idle time, success rate), the status of each fabrication machine (online, down, ready, in process), and the status of each cassette (stage in the manufacturing process, cumulative test results) on the fabline. The details of processing steps and tests have been abstracted away. This is higher-level information that gives a manager of the fabline a view of how the fabline is operating.

At level 3, *factory management,* are even higher-level events that aggregate sets of level 2 events. Aggregation rules are applied to level 2 events to create level 3 events. Level 3 events contain information about the performance of the fabline as a complete production entity. Level 3 events signify chip yields, aggregate machine downtime, complete end-to-end processing time, and information that would be of concern to a factory manager.

7.4 Building Personalized Concept Abstraction Hierarchies

We use event abstraction hierarchies to specify and implement *personalized views* of a target system for each stakeholder in the system. This is a two-step process following the definition in Section 7.3. Aggregation rules are the key to the second step.

1. The types of events that we choose to view at each hierarchical level must be specified as types of CEP events (as in the previous examples of patterns and rules). This is the step where "personalization" of views takes place. It requires sensible organization, because if we jumble up low- and high-level events into the same level, we won't be able to achieve step 2.

2. An aggregation rule must be defined for each type of event at each level above level 1. The rule must contain a pattern of lower-level event types that specifies both the events and their relationships. The rule must also specify the instance (event object) of the higher-level event type that corresponds to a match of the pattern.

In the fabline example, if we can specify the hierarchy depicted in Figure 7.1, together with aggregation rules, CEP will automatically create the higher-level complex events as the fabline is running. The equipment operators, the fabline managers, and the factory managers (the stakeholders) see the information of interest to them. And the individual views are all coordinated in real time.

Monitoring refers to observing and analyzing level 1 events. *Viewing* refers to computing higher-level complex events using aggregation rules, and analyzing them by graphical and drill-down techniques.

CEP allows us to change our hierarchy definition and introduce new aggregation rules on the fly, while the target system is running. Viewing should always be flexible, allowing changes to meet shifts of interest in what the target system is doing. CEP lets us choose our types of complex events to suit our roles and needs. In other words, we can *personalize* our views.

A word of caution. The set of events that can be observed from the target system is not always under our control (see Section 5.9). We have to take what we can get at level 1. The complex events at every other level are entirely for us to choose. The only caveat is that we must be able to define aggregation rules for them.

7.4.1   Viewing Network Activity

This section is an example of the two-step process of building an event abstraction hierarchy to specify the higher-level events for a personalized view.

Step 1: Define an Event Abstraction Hierarchy

Table 7.2 shows how we might carry out step 1 to organize an event abstraction hierarchy. We revisit the alternating bit network protocol in a little more detail than in previous examples. Our goal is to show how an abstraction hierarchy is used to define monitoring and viewing. The table has two levels.

Table 7.2: A Concept Hierarchy for a Network Protocol

Level	Activities	Event Types
Level 2	Completed transmission	CompletedTran(Node N1, Node N2, Data D, Time T1, Time T2, . . .)
	Degraded performance	DegPerf(Node N1, Node N2, Time T, Time T1)
Level 1	Send data with bit	Send(Node N1, Node N2, Data D, Bit B, Time T)
	Wait for acknowledge	Wait(Node N, Data D, Bit B, Time T)
	Time out	TimeOut(Node N, Time Delta, Time T)
	Resend data	ReSend(Node N1, Node N2, Data D, Bit B, Time T)
	Acknowledge data with bit	Ack(Node N1, Node N2, Data D, Bit B, Time T)
	Receive data	Receive(Node N1, Node N2, Bit B, Time T)
	Receive an acknowledge	ReceiveAck(Node N1, Node N2, Bit B, Time T)

Level 1 activities are those of the alternating bit protocol itself. A sender can perform the activities *send data, wait for an acknowledgment, time out,* and *resend* the same data. After receiving an acknowledge (Ack) with the current bit, a sender can start sending new data. Each time it initiates a new transmission to send new data, it changes the bit, either from 0 to 1 or from 1 to 0. A receiver must *acknowledge* receiving data. When a receiver acknowledges data, it uses the bit that came with the data. When the sender gets an acknowledge, it checks that the bit is the one sent with the current data. Only when this is true does the sender consider the transmission completed.

Each level 1 activity has a corresponding event type that signifies that activity. The parameters in events give us data about the activity such as the sender and receiver (Nodes), Data, the current transmission Bit, and Time. We assume these level 1 events are observable in the network and servers that are sending, transmitting, and delivering data. Wait and TimeOut events must be observed in the sender process, say, by instrumentation.

Level 2 defines the activities that are significant to us in our view of the network protocol activity. We are not interested in seeing TimeOuts and ReSends. In this example, we choose two views: *completed transmission* as a measure of good performance and *degraded performance* as a measure of bad performance. Each level 2 event is an aggregation of level 1 events.

A CompletedTran event can result from many different sequences of events. Here is a typical transmission:

1. Send(Node1, Node2, Data, Bit, Timestamp1), *the initiation of a transmission*
2. Wait(Node1, Data, Bit, Timestamp2), *sender waits*

3. TimeOut(Node1, Delta, TimestampX), *sender does X TimeOuts*

4. ReSend(Node1, Node2, Data, Bit, TimestampXX), *sender resends the same data and bit X times*

5. Receive(Node2, Node1, Data, Bit, Timestamp3), *receiver gets the data*

6. Ack(Node2, Node1, Bit, TimestampY), *receiver acknowledges each receipt with the transmission Id (Bit)—say Y times in all*

7. ReceiveAck(Node1, Node2, Bit, Timestamp4), *sender gets an acknowledge with current Bit*

The events in any completed transmission are all causally related. The aggregation rule uses causality in its pattern to ensure matching correctly a sequence of events that corresponds to a single transmission.

Step 2: Define Aggregation Rules

Completed Transmissions: A rule for CompletedTran events has already been defined in Section 7.2, Example 1, Table 7.1, the Completed Data Transfer rule.

Figure 7.2 shows the same poset of level 1 events as Figure 5.4, and also the level 2 CompletedTran events created by this rule. Note that for clarity, the Ack and RecAck events in Figure 7.2 show the messages being acknolwedged; network node parameters are omitted for simplicity.

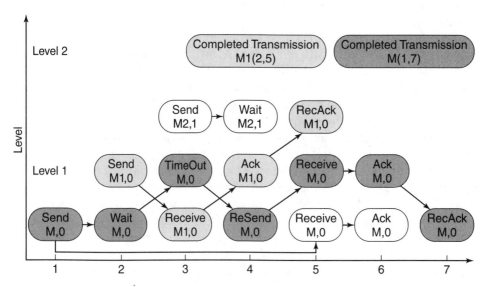

Figure 7.2: Level 1 network events and corresponding level 2 complex events

At level 2, the light-shaded CompletedTran event with data M1 corresponds to a causal sequence of four light-shaded events at level 1. This CompletedTran event is shown as taking place over a time interval from time 2 to time 5. This corresponds to the timestamp of the initial level 1 Send event, which is time 2, and the timestamp of the final RecAck event, which is time 5.

The dark-shaded CompletedTran event with data M and time intervals 1 through 7 corresponds to a longer transmission sequence between different nodes at level 1 that contains TimeOut and ReSend events.

It is much easier to view how the protocol is performing at level 2 than at level 1. By viewing the level 2 CompletedTran events, we can "see" how the protocol is performing without having to look at all the low-level TimeOut and ReSend events. Very simple CEP rules applied to events at level 2 will, for example, count the number of completed transaction events in a time window or compare the times for completed transactions between different pairs of network nodes.

Drill Down: Drill down is a process of going from a level 2 event to the level 1 events that caused it by triggering an aggregation rule.

Figure 7.2 shows by shading the corresponding level 1 events that caused each level 2 event. These are the events that matched the Completed Data Transfer rule's pattern, causing it to create the level 2 event. By viewing level 2 first, we can see the significant events (for us) that happened in the level 1 event cloud. By drilling down from level 2 to level 1, we can see which events caused them.

If we want to go into the details of level 1, we see two causal sequences of level 1 events that match the pattern in the rule. Both sequences cause a CompletedTran event to be created at level 2. The first CompletedTran event begins at time 2 and consists of a minimal causal sequence of events needed to match the rule's pattern. The second CompletedTran event begins at time 1 but contains TimeOut and ReSend events, which increase its transmission time, so it ends at time 7. The rule's pattern matches a subset of the events that must be part of a successful transmission.

Degraded Performance: The rule for degraded performance in Table 7.3 is similar to the Late Data Transfer Warning rule in Example 2, Section 6.4. We can imagine that an entirely different person would be interested in viewing the transmission activity this way, looking for performance degradation rather than completed transmissions.

This rule defines a level 2 event, degraded performance, as an aggregation of level 1 events. The pattern detects an attempted transmission in which the send/receive side is greater or equal to the time bound minus a δ, or the Ack/RecAck side is greater or equal to the time bound minus a δ.

Table 7.3: Rule: Degraded Performance

Element	Declarations
Variables	Node N1, Node N2, Data D, Bit B, Time T1, Time T2, Time T3, Time T4;
Event types	Send(Node N1, Node N2, Data D, Bit B, Time T1), Receive(Node N1, Node N2, Data D, Bit B, Time T1), Ack(Node N1, Node N2, Bit B, Time T1), RecAck(Node N1, Node N2, Bit B, Time T1), DegPerf(Node N1, Node N2);
Relational operators	→, **or**
Pattern	(Send(N1, N2, D, B, T1) → Receive(N2, N1, D, B, T2)) **or** (Ack(N2, N1, B, T3) → RecAck(N1, N2, B, T4))
Context test	$T2 - T1 \geq$ TimeBound $-\delta$ **or** $T4 - T3 \geq$ TimeBound $-\delta$
Action	**create** DegPerf(N1, N2)

For example, in Figure 7.2, if the time bound is 7, CompletedTran(M, (1,7)) is within the time bound. But if the δ is 3, the two pairs of Send(M, 0) $\longrightarrow$ Receive(M, 0) events would each cause a degraded performance event.

   We could define degraded performance in many ways. One definition that comes to mind is that a sender tries to initiate a transmission and times out more than X times. This rule however, involves counting a number of events, which requires a more powerful rules language than our strawman. Rules should be able to process local variables as part of their actions.

Drill Down: Degraded performance events give us a second view at level 2 of the protocol system. For example, by viewing level 2, we can keep statistics on the most frequent nodes to have degraded performance. Also, the aggregation relation lets us apply drill-down diagnostics. For example, we can drill down from any DegPerf event to track the ReSend events that failed to reach the receiver or were superflous in that they didnt play a role in completing the transmission. This may be useful in reducing unnecessary network traffic by adjusting TimeOuts.

7.4.2   Viewing Stock-Trading Activity

An event abstraction hierarchy can be defined at any level in an enterprise system. As long as we can observe events at some level, we can build a hierarchy of concepts from that level upward. The previous network example showed a hierarchy at a rather low level. The next example is at an application level.

Step 1: Event Abstraction Hierarchy

Suppose we are dealing with a financial trading system, and we can observe events signifying messages flowing between customers and brokers in the system. For example, event monitoring could be hosted on an Internet trading site used by customers to interact with brokers who service their requests. The brokers could be completely automated, by the way. Table 7.4 shows a two-level concept hierarchy for monitoring the performance of brokers. At level 1 are the activities of customers and brokers. Customers request services such as stock price quotes or to buy or sell a stock. Brokers try to carry out requests and reply with the results. At any time there can be lots of pending requests from the same customer that have not been answered.

Table 7.4: Concept Hierarchy for Stock-Trading Events

Level	Activities	Events
Level 2	Completed price quote	PriceQuery(Symbol S, Price P, Customer C, Broker B, Time Start, Time End)
	Completed purchase	BuyAction(Symbol S, Price P, Customer C, Broker B, Time Start, Time End)
	Completed sale	SellAction(Symbol S, Price P, Customer C, Broker B, Time Start, Time End)
	Completed stop loss order	StopLoss(Symbol S, Price Limit, Price Exe, Customer C, Broker B)
Level 1	*Customer's activities:*	
	Request a stock price quote	GetPrice(Customer C, Symbol S, Broker B, Time T)
	Request to buy a stock	Buy(Customer C, Symbol S, Number N, Price P, Broker B, Time T)
	Request to sell a stock	Sell(Customer C, Symbol S, Number N, Price P, Broker B, Time T)
	Request stop loss order	StopLoss(Customer C, Symbol S, Number N, Price P, Broker B, Time T)
	Broker's activities:	
	Reply to request	Reply(Customer C, Symbol S, Number N, Price P, Message M, Broker B, Time T)
	Order stock purchase	BuyOrder(Customer C, Symbol S, Number N, Price P, Message M, Broker B, Time T)
	Order stock sale	SellOrder(Customer C, Symbol S, Number N, Price P, Message M, Broker B, Time T)
	Receive confirmation	RecConf(Customer C, Symbol S, Number N, Price P, Message M, Broker B, Time T)

The event hierarchy in Table 7.4 has four types of level 2 events corresponding to completed transactions at level 1. This hierarchy has been defined so that viewing level 2 events allows us to "see" the mix of completed transactions and their time intervals.

For example, each level 2 event signifies a transaction that has been completed between a customer and a broker. Level 2 events include the timing of the transaction, with Start as the time when the customer makes a request and End as the time when the broker replies to that request with a favorable message. In the case of stop loss orders, there is a Limit parameter, which is the price requested by the customer, and an Exe, which is the executed price. So we can also see which stop loss orders were carried out properly by the broker.

Step 2: Defining Aggregation Rules

We can define aggregation rules for the level 2 events. An example is shown in Table 7.5.

The pattern of the rule matches two events that are causally related. The first is the customer's request to buy a stock, and the second is a response from the broker. Because the broker might be responding to one of several requests from this customer to buy the same stock, the pattern requires the response to be causally related to the Buy request. Finally, the message in the response must be "confirmed." Then the pattern matches, and a BuyAction event is created.

Figure 7.3 shows two level 2 events and the events that caused them at level 1. Level 2 events are aggregated from the communication traffic between the applications (customers and brokers) at level 1. From level 2

Table 7.5: Stock-Trading Aggregation Rule: BuyAction

Element	Declarations
Variables	Customer C, Symbol S, Number N, Price P, Message M, Broker B, Time T1, Time T2, Time T3, Time T4;
Event types	Reply(Customer C, Symbol S, Number N, Price P, Message M, Broker B, Time T)
	Buy(Customer C, Symbol S, Number N, Price P, Message M, Broker B, Time T)
	BuyAction(Symbol S, Price P, Customer C, Broker B, Time Start, Time End)
Relational operators	$\rightarrow$ (causes)
Pattern	Buy(C, S, N, P, B, T1) $\rightarrow$ Reply(C, S, N, P, M, B, T2)
Context test	M = "Confirmed"
Action	**create** BuyAction(C, S, N, P, B, T1, T2);

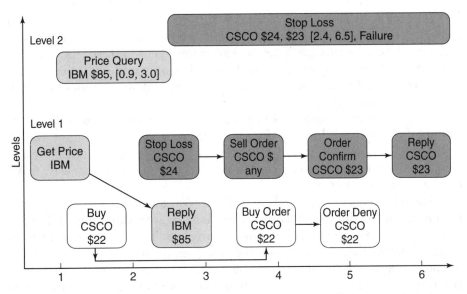

Figure 7.3: Two levels of posets in stock-trading events

events we can easily construct views of how brokers are performing—for example, the average time they take to complete transactions, the number of stop loss orders that are completed below the requested price, and so on. That is, level 2 would be used to give performance views of brokers. As before, drill down allows us to track the level 1 events related to any level 2 event of interest.

7.5   Summary

The earliest application of complex event hierarchies and event aggregation rules was in hardware simulation [5]. This work demonstrated the possibility of creating and viewing events at different levels of abstraction simultaneously during simulation of hardware designs. It was applied to a VHDL [8] simulator.[1] This work demonstrated that errors in designs were often easily detected by viewing higher-level events and that drill-down techniques could be used to locate the cause of an error in a low-level design. The presence of an error would often go undetected if only low-level events were monitored during simulation.

In this chapter, we have seen how a simple strawman event pattern language can be used to define reactive rules that allow us to create complex events. This capability can be applied to provide personalized views of the activity in event-based distributed systems.

---

[1]Web search on "VHDL."

The key to personalized viewing is the use of event abstraction hierarchies to precisely specify the complex events we want to view, and to organize them in a layered structure. Then we can define event pattern rules to create those events from the system's event traffic. The only underlying assumption is that the level 1 events of the abstraction hierarchy are events that can be monitored in the target system.

We can apply personalized viewing to any level of system activity—for example, the network level or the application level. Typical target systems could be eMarketplaces, global enterprises, or the Internet. Multiple views of a target system's activity can be constructed to run simultaneously, driven by the same level 1 events.

The set of views never needs to be fixed. We can always modify a concept hierarchy and define the corresponding new aggregation rules. Often, we cannot predict the most useful views in advance. The views we want to see at any moment may depend upon the activities in the target system at that moment. Views can be changed on the fly to focus on different situations in the target system or to satisfy changing concerns on the part of the user. We continue this discussion of event hierarchies and personalized viewing in Chapter 13.

Building Solutions with CEP

Highlights in Part II:

- *The fundamental elements:*
    - *Event patterns and pattern languages*
    - *Reactive event pattern rules and constraints*
    - *Event causality and event hierarchies*
- *The building blocks of CEP applications:*
    - *Event processing agents*
    - *Architectures of agents*
- *Case studies of CEP applications*
- *Steps towards developing an infrastructure to support CEP applications*

Chapter 8

The RAPIDE *Pattern Language*

- *Designing event pattern languages*
- *The* RAPIDE *event pattern language* (RAPIDE-EPL)
- *Classes of events*
- *Pattern matching—the fundamental operation in CEP*
- *Single event patterns*
- *Complex event patterns*
- *Repetitive and recursive event patterns*
- *Event pattern macros*
- *Building libraries of patterns*

So far we have explored the concepts of CEP using a simple event pattern language, STRAW-EPL. We chose the tabular format because it lays out all the elements of an event pattern in a way similar to a graphical user interface. STRAW-EPL is fine for explaining easy examples. But when we deal with how to build real applications of CEP, we need a more powerful event pattern language.

In this chapter, we describe in some detail the features of a particular event pattern language that formed the basis for early research into CEP.

This is the RAPIDE-EPL for specifying patterns of events in causal event executions (posets). The RAPIDE-EPL contains a core of features that are needed to support CEP. We use it extensively in later chapters to illustrate example applications of CEP because it is a more powerful and succinct notation than the tabular format of STRAW-EPL. As the complexity of CEP applications develops over time, we expect that EPLs will include many more features.

8.1   Event Pattern Languages—Basic Requirements

First, we discuss some general requirements that an event pattern language should meet in order to adequately support CEP.

An event pattern language is a computer language in which we can precisely describe patterns of events. It is similar to mathematical language for logical expressions or a Web search language with more than the usual options and some other bells and whistles. It lets us describe, without any ambiguity, exactly the patterns in which we are interested.

A *pattern matcher* for an EPL is a program that processes one or more event executions in real time and picks out all, and only, posets that match a pattern.

An EPL must have the following properties.

- *Power of expression:* It must be powerful enough to specify the kinds of complex patterns that are needed in order to apply CEP to the problems described in Chapters 1 through 4. To do this, it must provide relational operators corresponding to relationships between events (for example, "and," "or," "causes," and "is independent of"), temporal operators (for example, "during," "at," "within") that refer to time bounds and time intervals, and ways to refer to data inside events and to context.

- *Notational simplicity:* It must let us write patterns easily and succinctly. The tabular format of our STRAW-EPL is too lengthy and restrictive for "heavy-duty" use. Some powerful pattern language constructs would be difficult to express in tabular format.

- *Precise semantics:* It must have a mathematically precise concept of *match* so that when we specify a pattern, we know the posets of events that can match it.

- *Scalable pattern matching:* It must have an efficient pattern matcher that can scale to matching large numbers of patterns over high volumes of events in real time. This issue will inevitably influence language design.

When it comes to designing EPLs, we have a "tension" between our requirements: *simplicity, ease of use,* and *efficiency of pattern matching* versus *power of expression.*

There is a fact-of-life reason for this. If an EPL is simple and easy to use, we won't be able to specify some kinds of complex patterns in it. On the other hand, if it is powerful and lets us specify complex patterns, it will contain "advanced" features or options that take time to learn how to use. And pattern matching for complex patterns is computationally demanding and difficult to implement efficiently.

8.2   Features of RAPIDE

The RAPIDE event pattern language is a declarative computer language for writing patterns of events. The patterns can specify sets of events together with their parameters, timestamps, and causal dependencies, and which events are causally independent of each other.

Declarative means that RAPIDE-EPL consists of mathematical expressions that "declare" (or describe) patterns. It does not include any algorithmic programming features like assignment or conditional branches. It is as simple a language as can meet the basic requirements for CEP.

Here is a summary of its main features.

- *Strong typing* to avoid common errors in writing patterns.
- *Basic data types* for specifying the data parameters of events and contexts.
- *Event types* for expressing the types of events in a pattern.
- *Basic event patterns* that allow us to express patterns that match single events—for example, any order from any customer.
- *Pattern operators* for expressing relationships between events. Pattern operators are used to specify complex patterns of many events in precise relationships.
- *Context* that lets us restrict matches of patterns to specific contexts in which events are observed.
- *Temporal operators* that allow us to specify the timing of events that match a pattern, or when a pattern should or should not match.
- *Pattern macros* that let us express complex patterns succinctly and build libraries of patterns.
- *Mathematical semantics.* RAPIDE-EPL has a simple one-page definition of matching that provides a specification for any pattern matcher.

The syntax is easy to understand and is similar to the syntax of object-oriented languages such as Java or C#, with a few small variations. In fact,

Rᴀᴘɪᴅᴇ-EPL can be viewed as an "add-on" or extension of expressions in these languages.

In the following sections, we describe Rᴀᴘɪᴅᴇ-EPL and the semantics of pattern matching. We want to tell you, the reader, as simply as possible how to write event patterns in Rᴀᴘɪᴅᴇ-EPL. This is done with informal, intuitive descriptions of matching. We don't give a mathematical definition of matching here. There are precise formal definitions of matching in other documents about Rᴀᴘɪᴅᴇ.

8.3   Types

Rᴀᴘɪᴅᴇ-EPL is strongly typed, much like most modern object-oriented languages. It may seem odd to impose strong typing on patterns, but it turns out to help users avoid all kinds of silly errors in patterns, such as typos. Such errors show up as type mismatches in the pattern. Types also play a powerful role in restricting the context in which a pattern can match. This makes pattern matching more efficient.

There are three kinds of types: *data types, event types,* and *execution types.*

When we write a pattern, we must first declare the types of data in the pattern and the types of events we expect to match the pattern against. A set of type declarations is called a *type context.*

Example 1: *Defining Warning events*

If we want to write patterns that will match Warning events, either about the loads on routes in a network or about the distance between aircraft, we first define the types of these Warning events:

```
// type declarations preceding a pattern.
typedef   Network_Path ...;            -- data type
typedef   Aircraft ...:                -- data type
action  Warning(Network_Path P1, Real P2); -- event type
action  Warning(Aircraft P1, Feet P2);    -- event type
```

This type context declares two types of Warning events. It defines a *global type context* for patterns that follow it. Following these type declarations (that is, in the scope of the global type context), we can write a pattern such as this:

```
// pattern that matches network Warning events.
(Network_Path Route; Real Load) Warning(Route, Load);
```

This a basic event pattern that can match single events. It consists of declarations of the types of parameters in the pattern followed by an event template. The type declarations of the parameters are a *local type context* for the pattern that restricts the types of parameters only in this pattern.

As the example shows, a pattern consists of two parts: first a list in parentheses of the variables in the pattern together with their types, and then the pattern part—the part that describes the events to be matched. Events have names called *action names* followed by a list of parameters. The name of an event is in fact a parameter of the event that we give a special syntactic emphasis by putting it first. It is similar to the subject of a message. The name of an event must match the action name in the event pattern in order for a match to be possible. So, for example, a Warning(...) pattern cannot match a ConnectTime event.

Here, the pattern matches events with the action name, Warning, and parameters Route (which is of type Network_Path) and Load (which is a Real number).

Patterns are checked for type consistency before they are compiled for matching. This is where typos and other errors are caught.

Matching must be consistent with the types of the parameters in the pattern, and this restricts the events that can match the pattern. Our Warning pattern will match events like Warning(London–NewYork, 0.75), which is the kind of event we are looking for. London–NewYork is a Route and 0.75 is a Real number giving a measure of urgency.

If we omitted the typed parameter list from the pattern and just wrote the pattern part, we might get matches of Warning events from a different type of Warning event, like Warning(UA51, 5000), a warning of an aircraft within 5,000 feet. Although this may be an interesting match, it isn't a network warning, which is the kind of event our pattern is intended to match.

A pattern has both a *global type context*, where the types of events it can match are declared, and a *local type context*, where its variables and their types are declared. Because different types of events can have the same action name, the local context is important in disambiguating action names and specifying the types of events a pattern is intended to match. The data types in the local context must be subtypes of data types in the global context.

8.3.1 Predefined Types

RAPIDE-EPL has a set of predefined types. These are very common data types that appear in the events generated by many systems.

The predefined types include Boolean, Character, String, Integer, Float, and so on. Each predefined type comes with a set of operations. For example, Integers have the usual operations "+", "−", "=", and so on. Strings have a rich set of predefined operations—for example, comparison operations, such as S < T; selection operations, such as S [2 .. 4], which returns the substring consisting of the second, third, and fourth characters of S; and concatenation, &, which lets us construct a new string, S&T, from strings S and T.

8.3.2 Structured Types

Structured types are composed from other types. They let us define objects that have other objects as components.

Common kinds of structured types that are in many languages are predefined: **record** (record types), **array** (array types), **enum** (enumeration types), and some special types that we will describe later. Each of these structured types has predefined selection operations that let us select out the components of structured objects. To construct a structured object, we can assign objects as its components.

Structured types are defined by using *type definitions*. A type definition lets us define a type and give it a name. We can then use that name in declaring parameters of that type. The form of a type definition is

typedef   *type–expression   name*;

Example 1: *The record type definition*

An example of a record type definition is

typedef record {Node N1; Connection C;   Node N2} Network_Path;

Here we have defined Network_Path to be a record type with three components: two nodes and a connection. We can select components of a record object using the parameters of the type definition and the "." selection operation. So, if Route is an object of type Network_Path, "Route . N1" is the first Node of Route, and so on.

Example 2: *The array type definition*

An example of an array type definition is

typedef array [1, 2, 3] **of** String Triplet;

The *index* type in "[,]" must be an enumeration type, such as Integer. All the components of an array type must be of the same type—in this example, String.

Selection of components is done by applying a value of the index type to an object of the array type using "( )" notation. For example, if ThreeSome is of type Triplet, then ThreeSome(1) is its first string component.

8.3.3 Event Types

Events are objects that are tuples of data. An event contains the values of predefined attributes (such as its action name and its timestamps) as well as additional data parameters.

In RAPIDE-EPL there is a predefined *event type,* Event, which is the type of all events. This is the type of all events with any name, any parameter list (which can be empty), and the predefined attributes (which may have undefined values).

It is useful—for example, for efficient pattern matching—to be able to classify events into subtypes. Subtypes of events are declared by *action declarations.*

An *action declaration* specifies a subtype of events. An action declaration has the format

> **action**   *identifier* (*list of parameter declarations*);

where the *identifier* is the *action name,* and the list of parameters in paraentheses declares the tuple of data in the events. The parameter list is a list of declarations that consist of the type of a parameter followed by the name of the parameter. The predefined attributes are always implied members of the list of parameters and are not explicitly declared. An action declaration specifies the set of those events that have the action's name as their *action name attribute* and contain a tuple of data parameters that conform to the types of the action's parameter declarations.

Example 1: *A Warning event*

A type of **Warning** event is

> **action** Warning(Network_Path Route; Real Load);

Examples of events in this action type are

```
Warning(London—NewYork,  0.75)
Warning(Paris—London,  0.92)
```

However, the following events are not members of this action type:

```
ConnectTime(London—NewYork,  02.56)   —because the action name is not "Warning"
Warning(UA51,  5000)   —because the data parameters are of the wrong types
```

Example 2: *An Order event*

A type of order event in a supply chain system is

    action Order(Cust_Id Customer, Parts_Order Data, Accnt_no Accnt, ...);

Here we specify a subtype of events that contain the customer's Id, the order form in a required Parts_Order format, the account number, and other data. Order events will also contain the attributes they inherit from the RAPIDE-EPL event type, such as timestamps.

Figure 8.1 shows three subtypes of events that can be defined by *action declarations*. Each event subtype defines events from a particular system, or problem domain. The DTP events are the kind of events created by a

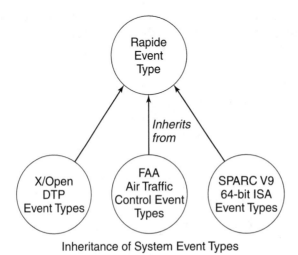

Inheritance of System Event Types

Figure 8.1: Subtypes of the RAPIDE event type

distributed transaction system, the FAA events are the type of events created in air traffic control, and SPARC V9 events are created by a simulation of a CPU architecture. In each subtype, the events inherit the attributes of the basic event type and contain additional data specific to a particular kind of system.

The subtype of XML events—that is, events having an XML format—is another example of an event subtype.

The idea behind actions is very simple. We think of an activity in the target system as leading to the creation of an event. We call such an activity an *action*. We give it a name—its *action name*—and a list of parameter declarations. The action declaration defines the subtype of the forms of events[1] that signify the system activity.

8.3.4 Execution Types

An execution is a poset of events. Its type is called an *execution type*. An execution type is a set of action declarations specifying the types of events that can happen in an execution. We can define execution types using the keyword execution:

typedef **execution** {*list of action declarations* } *Name*;

As we shall see, execution types are useful in ensuring the correct use of event processing agents, particularly connecting them to work together.

Example 1: *The NetMngmt execution type*

If a network monitoring system generates load warnings, connect times, and messages on various topics, we can specify its execution type as consisting of the following event types:

```
typedef   execution {
    action  Warning(Network_Path Route;  Real Load);
    action  Alert(Node_Type Node;  Real CPU_Load, Memory_Allocation;
                             Int 1 .. 5    Severity; Time_Type Time);
    action  ConnectTime(Network_Path Route; Time_Type Time);
    action  Send(Subject_Type Subject;  String Message, Id; Time_Type Time);
    action  Acknowledge(String Id; Time_Type Time)
  }   NetMngmt ;
```

---

[1]See Section 5.1 for a definition of "event."

Suppose NetMngmt is the type of execution a network monitor is expected to deal with. Its events are classified into five subtypes, with the action names Warning, Alert, ConnectTime, Send, and Acknowledge. These are the types of events it expects to deal with and should be programmed to handle.

Example 2: *The ATM-Use execution type*

A similar example is a simple automated bank teller system (ATM). Its execution type might be specified according to three actions that it allows customers to perform at the ATMs:

```
typedef   execution {
    action Deposit(Dollars Amount; Account_Type Accnt);
    action Withdraw(Dollars Amount; Account_Type Accnt);
    action Transfer(Dollars Amount; Account_Type From_Accnt, To_Accnt)
    } ATM–Use;
```

If an ATM's execution type is ATM–Use, we know that its executions can consist only of events with the action names Deposit, Withdraw, and Transfer.

Example 3: *The SupplyChainEvents execution type*

An execution type for a supply chain

```
typedef   execution {
    action RFQ(RFQId Id; ProdSpec Spec; Dollars Price; Quantity Num; Schedule ...);
    action Bid(Vendor VId; BidId Id; ProdSpec Spec; Dollars Price; Quantity Num; ...)
    action Order(OrderId Id; CustId Customer; PartsOrder Data; AccntNo Accnt; ...);
    action Confirm(OrderId Id; PartsOrder Data; AccntNo Accnt; Schedule Dates; ...);
    ...
} SupplyChainEvents;
```

The supply chain execution type defines the types of events that we used in Chapter 2 to illustrate the global event cloud. In real life, of course, it will have many more action types in it. Execution types will eventually be the subject of standardization for particular industries, analogously to the standards for sets of message types today—for example, the ISO 15022 standard for for messaging to execute transactions in financial markets.

8.3.5 Subtyping of Executions

Execution types have a simple subtyping rule:

$$\text{type } T1 \text{ is a } \textit{subtype} \text{ of } T2 \text{ if } T2 \subset T1 \quad —T1 \quad contains \quad T2.$$

This rule means that T1 is a subtype of T2 if the set of actions in T1 contains all the actions in T2.

This is very similar to the object-oriented subtyping rule: type *colored point* is a subtype of type *point*. A colored point contains the X and Y coordinates of a point and the additional color component. The importance in object-oriented programs is that any function that computes on *points* also computes on *colored points* because colored points contain all the data it needs—but not conversely. The O-O rule is that you can always evaluate a function on an object of a subtype of a function's input type.

Execution types turn out to be useful when we build networks of agents. Event processing agents (EPAs) are typed with their input and output execution types. This lets us analyze whether or not it is sensible to feed the output of one agent into the input of another. Here's how we do it. Composition of EPAs follows the same rule as function composition in typed languages. Namely, if EPA1 outputs to EPA2, the execution type of the output of EPA1 must be a subtype of the execution type of input expected by EPA2. So, it's just as if EPA1 is pumping out colored points and EPA2 is computing on points.

It is easy to see that we shouldn't try, for example, to hook up a network monitor agent and an ATM agent, because they process entirely different types of events. Such a hookup would be a complete waste of time.

8.4   Attributes of Events

RAPIDE-EPL events have a set of *predefined attributes* that are common to all events. Not all attributes need to have defined values in an event.

Attributes give basic information about events. This includes, for example, their timestamps, their *origin* (the system component that generated them), their *destinations* (the components that received them), and information about what events caused them. Attributes give us an ability to write patterns that more precisely match the events we want to match, and to trace through event hierarchies.

There are *public* and *private* attributes. Public attributes can be named and used in patterns just like the declared parameters of actions (examples come later). Private attributes cannot be named in patterns—at least, not explicitly. They are used by tools such as the semantic checker to do type

Table 8.1: Predefined Attributes

Attribute Name	Meaning
name	Action name of the event
origin	Object in the target system whose execution created the event
thread	Thread in the target system that created the event
countervalue	Counter value of the thread that created the event
archstamp*	Target architecture information related to the event, such as destinations and connections to destinations traveled by the event
timestamp start, end	Start and end times of the event according to clocks in the target system
causality	References to immediate predecessors in the causal history of the event
point-of-creation*	Method call in the target system that created the event
declaration*	Reference to the action declaration defining the subtype of the event
trigger set*	References to events that were aggregated to create this event

checking or the pattern matcher to compute causal history, or animation tools to display event movements on architectural diagrams.

Table 8.1 shows a complete list of the predefined attributes. The ones that are starred (*) are private and cannot be used to write patterns.

The meaning or interpretation of event attributes must be defined for each target system. Interpretations of most attributes are defined in *adapters,* whose job is to monitor the target system and translate the target system's events into RAPIDE-EPL events (we will discuss adapters in detail later).[2] In some cases, an attribute may not be meaningful for a particular system. Attributes all have default initial values. So, if an attribute isn't defined for some target system, its value in all the events will be its default value.

The interpretation of attributes such as origin and archstamp can vary greatly in different target systems. For example, an origin could be a module in one system, an application in another, and a thread in a third. The timestamp attribute can give an interval consisting of the start and end times of an event with respect to a clock. If there is more than one clock, there may be multiple timestamps, one for each clock, giving a time interval from the reading of one of the clocks together with a reference to the clock.

---

[2]Adapters are sometimes also called *loggers.* This is a historical aberration in CEP.

The causality attribute refers to the events that had to happen in the system for this event to happen. It is often a vector of event Ids. The interpretation of "had to happen" is system dependent and will be incorporated into the adapter for events in that system. The trigger set is a set of references to events that triggered an aggregation rule to create this event. A trigger set encodes hierarchical aggregation (or *vertical causality*, Section 1.3.2) and is available to tools that make drill-down tracking possible.

The interpretation of event attributes may depend upon the programming language in which the target system is written, its components (such as the networking middleware), and its architecture.

8.5   Basic Event Patterns

The simplest event patterns are called *basic patterns*. A basic pattern matches single events. The syntax of a basic pattern is

(list_of_variable_declarations) action_name (list_of_parameter_expressions)

The variables are declared in a list, followed by an action name and a list of parameters, each of which can be either a declared variable or an expression. The parameters must have types corresponding to the formal parameter declarations of the action.

A basic event pattern can match events that have the same action name. To match an event, the variables in the pattern must be replaced by data values in the event to make an instance of the pattern that is identical to the event.

Example 1: *A basic pattern for money transfers*

A basic pattern matching all money transfers from a given account is

(Dollars X, Account_Type A) Transfer (X, Accnt#100, A)

The action name is Transfer, and the variables are X and A. The Transfer action is shown in the ATM–Use example (see Section 8.3.4, Example 2). Accnt#100 is a constant account number for the From_Accnt parameter. To make a match, we can replace X by any dollar amount and A by any account number. This will give us an *instance* of the pattern that must be identical with the event we are trying to match.

For example, the pattern matches Transfer(10, Accnt#100, Accnt#5) if X is replaced by 10 and A is replaced by Accnt#5. Similarly, the pattern matches Transfer(105, Accnt#100, Accnt#21505) if X is replaced by 105 and

A is replaced by Accnt#21505. But the pattern cannot match Transfer(105, Accnt#5, Accnt#21505) because Accnt#100 $\neq$ Accnt#5.

Example 2: *A basic pattern for engine parts*

A basic pattern matching all orders for engine parts is

(OrderId Id, CustId Customer, AccntNo Accnt) Order(Id, Customer, EngineParts, Accnt);

The Order action is shown in the SupplyChainEvents example (Section 8.3.4, Example 3). All parameters in this pattern are variables except the PartsOrder which is a constant called EngineParts. So this pattern has an instance which matches any Order event for engine parts—replace each variable by the corresponding data parameter in the event.

The simplest case of matching is when the pattern does not contain any variables—called a *constant pattern*. In this case, a basic pattern matches an event if it has the same action name as the event, and each expression in its data parameters evaluates to the corresponding value in the event's data parameters.

Example 3: *A constant pattern*

A constant pattern is

Deposit(1000, Accnt#123)

This basic pattern matches any single event in which the name of the action is Deposit, the Dollars amount is 1,000, and the account is Accnt#123. So it matches events like the following:

Deposit(1000, Accnt#123), Deposit(500 + 500, Accnt#123), ...

8.6   Placeholders and Pattern Matching

The variables in patterns are called *placeholders* because they occupy the places in a pattern that are "open." Matching is a game of trying to fill the open places in a pattern with values (also called "objects") so that the instance of the pattern is identical to the event or poset that we are trying to match.

8.6.1 Matching Basic Event Patterns

A basic event pattern *matches* an event if when its placeholders are replaced by objects, the resulting instance of the pattern is identical to the event. Replacing placeholders with objects to make a match is subject to two conditions.

- The type of object that replaces a placeholder must be the same as, or a subtype of, the type of the placeholder.
- A placeholder must be replaced by the same object at all of its positions in a pattern in any one match.

For a basic pattern to match an event, it must have the same action name.

8.6.2 Placeholder Bindings

The result of a successful match of a pattern to an event (or more generally, a poset) is an association of placeholders with objects that replaced them in the instance that matched the event. This is called a *binding* of placeholders to objects.

A binding is usually represented as a set of pairs consisting of a placeholder and an object, <placeholder ← value>, meaning "replace the placeholder by the value."

Example 1: *Matching bids in an RFQ process*

```
// basic pattern
(Vendor VId, BidId Offer) Bid(VId, Offer, EngineSpec#10, $2,000, 5000)

// event
Bid(Vendor#5, RF#20, EngineSpec#10, $2,000, 5000)

// binding that results in a match
{<VId ← Vendor#5>, <Offer ← RF#20>}
```

The pattern has the action name Bid in our supply chain events (see the declaration of Bid line in Section 8.3.4, Example 3). It has a placeholder, VId, for the Vendor parameter and a placeholder, Offer, for the BidId parameter of the Bid action. The other parameters have constant values for the ProdSpec, Price, and Quantity, so the pattern will match Bid events that have those constant values. The example shows an event and the placeholder binding that results in a match. If we replace VId by Vendor#5 and Bid by RF#20, we get an instance of the pattern that is identical the event.

Notice in this example that constants in patterns are very restrictive. Often we want to match a range of values, say, for price or quantity, rather than one value. We will see how to do this with context guards later.

Example 2: *Using a predefined attribute in a pattern*

```
// pattern
   (ATM_Machine M; Dollars D) Deposit(origin is M, D, Accnt#123)

// event
   Deposit(origin is ATM3, 1000, Accnt#123)

// binding resulting in a match
   {<M ← ATM3>, <D ← 1000>}
```

This pattern matches **Deposit** events from our ATM–Use actions (see Section 8.3.4, Example 2). The pattern contains a placeholder, M, for the prefedined attribute, **origin**. It uses a parameter-naming notation (**is**), which we will discuss later.

We are assuming that in the ATM–Use system, the actual ATM can be an origin recorded in the predefined origin attribute in the events it creates. This pattern will match events from any ATM that deposit any amount to a fixed account, Accnt#123. The event in the example is a deposit orginating at ATM3 of $1,000 to Accnt#123. The binding shows that M must be replaced by ATM3 and D by $1,000 to make the pattern match the event.

The golden rule about matching is that in order to match a pattern, a placeholder can be bound to only one object in all its occurrences in the pattern. So, if a placeholder occurs more than once in a pattern, a matching event or poset must have the same data at those positions.

Different matches of a pattern usually (but need not) result in different placeholder bindings.

Here are some examples of basic patterns using placeholders.

Example 3: *Placeholders in basic patterns*

```
// 1.  Any transfer of any amount from and to the same account
   (Dollars D, Account_Type A) Transfer(D, A, A);

// 2.  Any event originating from ATM3
   (event E) E(origin is ATM3);
```

The first pattern has the same placeholder, A, as both the From_Accnt and To_Accnt parameters of a Transfer action in ATM–Use (see Section 8.3.4, Example 2). So, it will match events in which some unspecified amount of money is transfered from any account to the same account. It will match events such as the following:

```
Transfer(10, Accnt#123, Accnt#123),
    if the binding is {<D ← $10>, <A ← Accnt#123>},

Transfer(25, Accnt#47, Accnt#47),
    if the binding is {<D ← $25>, <A ← Accnt#47>},
```

The second pattern shows a powerful use of a placeholder of the predefined **event** type. It matches any event generated by ATM3. E will be bound to the event, whether it is a Deposit, Transfer, or Withdraw. This is a succinct way to write a pattern to monitor a particular ATM. If the event is

```
Transfer(origin   is ATM3, 10, Accnt#47, Accnt#123),
```

the binding is

```
{<E ← Transfer(origin   is ATM3, 10, Accnt#47, Accnt#123)>}
```

8.6.3   Notation to Aid in Writing Patterns

To emphasize the role of placeholders, RAPIDE-EPL allows a "?" as a prefix to a placeholder. The use of "?" is optional. It helps distinguish the variable parts of a pattern from the constant parts. Some of the previous examples of basic patterns can be written as follows:

```
(Dollars ?D, Account_Type ?A) Transfer(?D, ?A, ?A);
(Vendor ?VId, BidId ?Offer) Bid(?VId, ?Offer, EngineSpec#10, $2,000, 5000)
```

Naming Parameters

A common error in writing a basic pattern is misordering the placeholders in the list of parameters of the action name. That is, the order of the placeholder parameters in the pattern is not consistent with the order of the parameters in the action declaration. To prevent this kind of error, each parameter in a basic pattern can be explicitly associated with the name of an action's formal parameter. You just use the parameter from the action declaration to name the parameter in the pattern. The notation for doing this is

> *action parameter name* **is** *pattern parameter*

This is called *naming* the parameters in the pattern and is an optional notation.

Example 1: *A basic pattern written in named parameter form*

> (Dollars ?D, Account_Type ?A, ?B) Transfer(To_Accnt **is** ?A, Amount **is** ?D,
> From_Accnt **is** ?B);

Look at the Transfer action declaration in ATM–Use (see Section 8.3.4, Example 2). The placeholder parameters in the pattern here are written in a different order from the order in which the action's parameters are declared. But it doesn't matter because we have associated each placeholder with the action's parameter that it corresponds to. So in this pattern, the To_Accnt is ?A, the Amount is ?D, and the From_Accnt is ?B.

Omitting Parameters

A useful feature in writing patterns is to omit a parameter whose binding is irrelevant to the matches you want. That means that you don't care about the omitted parameters, so any value will match them. But to do this without ambiguity, you must name the parameters you do use in the pattern so that it is obvious which of an action's parameters you want to include.

Example 2: *Omitting action parameters*

> Deposit(account **is** Accnt#123);
> (Account_Type ?A) Transfer(From_Accnt **is** ?A, To_Accnt **is** ?A);

Here the Deposit pattern matches any Deposit event to account Accnt#123. We are not interested in the amount. The Transfer pattern matches any transfer from and to the same account. We are not interested in the amount of the transfer, but only the accounts where such a transfer happens.

Using an Event's Public Attributes

The public attributes of events (see Section 8.4) can be used to write more precise patterns. The attribute name is used in the named parameter form. For example, there's an attribute called the origin of an event. It denotes the component in the target system that generated the event. That component may be an object or a module or a thread, depending upon the system. The origin attribute's value can be either a name or a reference to that component.

Example 3: *Monitoring all **withdrawals** generated at a particular ATM*

Withdraw(origin **is** ATM3)

Another useful public attribute is the timestamp of an event. Because timestamps are used frequently in patterns, there are special notations such as **at** and **after**, for referring to timestamps that are described later in Section 8.8.3.

Example 4: *Filtering out supply chain events according to their timing*

(OrderId ?Order) Order(Id **is** ?Order, end **is** 12:00)
(RFQ ?R) RFQ(Id **is** ?R, Spec **is** EngineSpec) **after** 12:00

The Order pattern will match those order events that happen over a time interval that ends at 12:00. The binding will contain the OrderId of those events.

The RFQ pattern will match those RFQ events for engine specifications that happen after 12:00 and will bind the Id of the RFQ.

8.7   Relational Operators and Complex Patterns

Relational operators let us write patterns that specify two or more events and a relationship between them. Relational operators are needed to write patterns that match complex behavior in a system.

In the simplest case, relational operators specify how two events are related—for example, whether the events must happen independently or one must cause the other, whether they must happen one before the other or at the same time, and so on. In general, we can use relational operators to specify how two posets are related. So we can start with basic patterns and build more and more complex patterns.

Relational operators are binary operators. A binary relational operator expresses a relationship between two posets. Patterns written with relational operators are called *complex patterns* to distinguish them from *basic patterns,* which specify single events.

Example 1: *Complex patterns illustrating use of relational operators*

1. (Dollars X) Withdraw(X, Accnt#123) $\longrightarrow$ Deposit(X);

2.   Withdraw $\|$ Withdraw;

3. (Event E, E') E(origin **is** "Bonnie") $\sim$ E'(origin **is** "Clyde");

The first pattern uses the causal operator, $\longrightarrow$. It matches whenever a Withdraw event from account Accnt#123 causes a Deposit of the same Dollar amount (to any account). So the pattern matches posets consisting of two causally related events, a Withdraw from Accnt#123 and a Deposit of the same sum of money. Whenever the pattern matches, X is bound to the Dollar amount. Figure 8.2 shows a poset that contains exactly one match of this pattern.

The second pattern uses the parallel operator, $\|$. It matches any two independent Withdraw events. The parameter values in the events do not matter; only their independence determines whether they match the pattern. Figure 8.2 shows a poset that contains two matches of this pattern. If the relational operator in pattern 2 was $\sim$ instead of $\|$, there would be three matches (see the third example).

The third pattern uses the "any" relationship operator, $\sim$, and placeholders that have the most general type, the Event type. This pattern matches any two events, provided "Bonnie" performs one of them (is its origin) and "Clyde" performs the other. Since we don't know what these desperadoes might do, looking for any action rather than specific actions is the best strategy. The events may be in any relation to one another. This means that the pattern can match events that are causally related or that are independent. Whenever the pattern matches, E and E' will be bound to the events. There are six matches in Figure 8.2. The poset shows "Bonnie" and "Clyde" as separate threads of control that generate events and synchronize at two points.

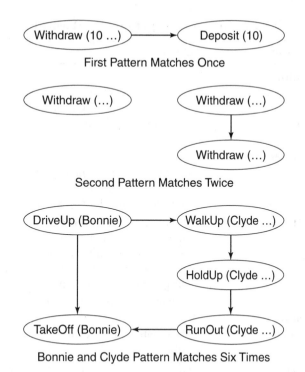

Figure 8.2: Examples of matches of complex patterns

8.7.1 Relational Operators

There are three categories of relational operators: *structural, logical,* and *set* operators. Table 8.2 shows a complete list of the relational operators in RAPIDE-EPL and what they mean. P and Q are patterns, either basic patterns that match single events or complex patterns that match posets.

Structural operators specify the causal structure and timing of matching posets. For example, P $\longrightarrow$ Q tells us that the events matching P must all be in the causal history of all the events in the match for Q. Note, by the way, that the events matching P don't have to immediately precede those matching Q. For example, a grandfather is a causal ancestor of a grandchild.

The independence operator, P $\parallel$ Q, requires that all the events matching P must be independent of all the events matching Q.

The timing operator, P $<$ Q, specifies that all the events matching P must have timestamps less than any timestamp of an event in the match for Q. So it specifies a similar structure as $\longrightarrow$ but for timing instead of

Table 8.2: Relational Operators in R<small>APIDE</small>-EPL

Operator	Name	Description
Structural operators		
$P \longrightarrow Q$	causes	A matching poset consists of two subposets, one matching P and one matching Q so that all events in the match of Q are caused by all the events in the match of P.
$P \parallel Q$	independent	A matching poset consists of two subposets, one matching P and one matching Q so that each event in the match of P is independent of every event in the match of Q, and conversely.
$P < Q$	before	Timing: a matching poset consists of two subposets, one matching P and one matching Q so that any event in the match for P has an earlier timestamp than all events in the match for Q. If there are multiple clocks, a particular clock, C, can be referenced as a parameter of $<$.
Logical operators		
P **and** Q	and	The events in a matching poset must match both P and Q.
P **or** Q	or	The events in a matching poset match P or Q.
P **not** Q	not	A matching poset must match P and not contain any subposet that matches Q.
Set operators		
$P \cup Q$	union	A matching poset consists of two subposets, one matching P and the other matching Q.
$P \sim Q$	disjoint union	A matching poset consists of two disjoint subposets; one matches P and one matches Q.

causality. If events have timestamps from more than one clock, the relevant clock is an explicit parameter of the $<$ operator, written as $<_C$.

Logical operators require a poset to match a logical combination of two patterns. It must match *both* patterns, *either* pattern, or one pattern and *not* the other.

The *set* operators, *union* ($\cup$) and *disjoint union* ($\sim$), require a poset to consist of subposets that each match one of two patterns but don't require any causal or timing relationship between the events in the subposets (that is, no structure). For example, P **and** Q requires the poset to match both patterns, whereas $P \cup Q$ requires the poset to consist of two subposets, each matching one of the patterns.

RAPIDE-EPL contains a rich set of relational operators because it was developed for research into CEP. It is unclear which of the logical and set operators are the most useful. Implementation of efficient pattern matching for some of these operators is challenging and demands smart algorithms.

8.8 Guarded Patterns

We can rarely write a pattern without wanting to restrict the parameters of the events. As we saw in STRAW-EPL context tests, in Chapter 6, we might want to deliver messages according to the data they contain or whether the sender passes a credit check. We can do this with a feature of RAPIDE-EPL called *guards*.

A guarded pattern has this syntax:

pattern **where** *Boolean_ test*

The guard is a Boolean valued test following **where**. Its meaning is that it restricts the matches of the *pattern* to those matches for which the Boolean test is true. We often call the guard in a pattern the *where clause*.

8.8.1 Content-Based Pattern Matching

Guards can refer to data in events (the *content* of the events). This is called *content-based matching*.

Example 1: *Testing the content of messages*

```
(Dollars ?LatestPrice, ?LastQuote)
    StockQuote(IBM, ?LatestPrice, ?LastQuote) where ?LatestPrice > ?LastQuote + $5;
```

This pattern will match stock quotes for IBM stock only if the latest price is $5 more than the last quote. The guard uses the content of the StockQuote event to make the test. Typically, these kinds of tests are used in content-driven message delivery.

Example 2: *Good banking behavior*

```
(Dollars ?X ,?Y; Account ?A)
    (Deposit(?X, ?A) ⟶ Withdraw(?Y, ?A)) where ?Y < ?X ;
```

The pattern, Deposit(?X, ?A) $\longrightarrow$ Withdraw(?Y, ?A), will match any pair of causally related Deposit and Withdraw events on the same account. The guard restricts the matches to those pairs for which the amount withdrawn is less than the amount deposited.

When the pattern matches, the placeholders ?X, ?Y are bound to the data values for the amounts of the deposit and the withdrawal. Those values are then used to evaluate the guard. If its value is true, the guarded pattern matches.

8.8.2   Context-Based Pattern Matching

Guards can also refer to information outside the events, such as database queries or values returned by method calls (that is, the *context* in which the pattern matching happens).

Example 1: *Context-based message filtering*

```
(OrderId ?Id, CustId ?C, AccntNo ?A)
    Order(?Id, ?C, ?A) where CreditCheck(?C) = Pass and Active(?A);
```

This pattern matches Orders from customers if they pass a credit check and their accounts are active. Both of these tests in the guard refer to the *context* in which the Order is received—the status of the customer's credit and the status of their account at that time.

The Boolean test in the guard may refer to the values of placeholders in the pattern and objects from the context in which the pattern is matched. Matching a guarded pattern proceeds in two steps. The first step is to match the unguarded pattern; if there is a match, all the placeholders in the guard must be bound to values by the match. Then the guarded pattern matches if the guard is true when those values are substituted for the placeholders. The guard is evaluated after the unguarded pattern matches. An error results if there is an unmatched placeholder in a guard when it is evaluated—except in some special circumstances, which we mention later.

Context-based pattern matching is more difficult to implement efficiently to allow high throughput of events than content-based matching. Context references in guards make it more difficult to organize large numbers of patterns for sublinear searches for matches. Details are beyond the scope of our discussion here.

8.8.3 Temporal Operators

RAPIDE-EPL provides some operators that simplify writing guards that refer to the timestamps and start and end times of events. They are called *temporal operators*.

- **at**: Applies only to basic event patterns. For example, if P is a basic event pattern, P **at** 3:00pm matches an event E if E matches P and its timestamp is 3:00pm.

  An unbound variable can be a parameter of the **at** operator. If T is a variable of type Time, P **at** T matches an event E that matches P, and a result of the match is to bind T to the timestamp value of E.

- **after**: Applies to complex patterns. For example, P **after** T matches posets that match P and contain events all of whose start times or timestamps are greater than T.

- **during**: Applies to complex patterns. For example, P **during**(T1, T2) matches posets that match P and contain events all of whose start times or timestamps are greater than T1, and all of whose end times or timestamps are less than T2.

Each of these operators is equivalent to writing guards that refer to the timestamps or start and end times of the basic events in the pattern. Normal use of these operators assumes a single global clock in the system. If there are multiple clocks, a particular clock whose readings are to be used can be named as an argument of any of these operators.

8.9 Repetitive Patterns

Many systems repeat the same behavior over and over. A typical example is found in communication protocols that repeat behaviors such as "if no acknowledgement, time out and resend"—lack of success requires the protocol to keep on attempting to send a message. So event patterns must be able to express repetitive behavior.

In RAPIDE-EPL we first express the pattern of the behavior that is repeated. Say this is a pattern, P. Each repetition is another poset that matches P. Next, we need to express *how* P repeats—that is, the causal or timing relationship between one poset that matches P and the next poset that matches P. It can be any of the *structural* relational operators. We do this by writing a prefix to P that specifies the number of repetitions and the relationship between each repetition and the next one—called the *repetition profile*.

So, to express a pattern consisting of repetitions of P, the syntax is:

[*number of repetitions* **rel** *relational operator*] P;

The part inside the square brackets is the repetition profile. It expresses the number of repetitions and the structural relationship between each match of P. P is the body that is being repeated.

The repetition profile can have a counter variable that counts the number of repetitions, and that counter can be used as a parameter of the pattern body—just like a **for** loop.[3]

A repetitive pattern matches a poset if the poset consists of the specified number of subposets, each matching the body, and each of the matches is related by the relational operator in the prefix. The number of repetitions can be specified in various ways: a specific number or any number. We use "*" for any number.

Example 1: *Some repetitive patterns*

1.   [* **rel** ⟶] Deposit

2.   [1..10 **rel** ⟶] Deposit

3.   [I **in** 1..10 **rel** ~] Deposit(I)

4.   [* **rel** ~] (Msg ?M)(Send(?M) ⟶ (Ack(?M.header) **or** Time_Out))

5.   (Msg ?M)([* **rel** ~](Send(?M) ⟶ (Ack(?M.header) **or** Time_Out)))

Each of these examples illustrates a different feature of repetitive patterns.

The body of the first pattern matches any Deposit event. The repetition profile specifies any number (*) of matches related to one another by ⟶. So this repetitive pattern expresses "any number of Deposit events, where each event is causally related to the previous one." A matching poset must be a causally ordered chain of Deposit events.

The (*) repetition pattern has what we call *maximal match* semantics. This means that it will match only the chain of Deposit events that consists of the maximal number of events, not a subchain consisting of some of those events.

---

[3]For this reason, Rapide-EPL specifies the repetition in a prefix profile rather than in postfix notation like regular expressions.

The second pattern differs from the first one only in specifying exactly ten Deposit events. It uses a common range notation, $1..10$, to specify a finite number of matches.

The third pattern uses a repetition counter variable, I, as a parameter of the body. So, the pattern body Deposit(I) changes for each repetition. The repetitive pattern matches a poset consisting of Deposit(1), Deposit(2), ... up to ten, with any relationship between the events. Some could be dependent and some independent.

The fourth pattern is one that is repeated an arbitrary number of times. But it illustrates some "fine points." The pattern body is

$$(\text{Msg } ?M)(\text{Send}(?M) \longrightarrow (\text{Ack}(?M.\text{header}) \textbf{ or } \text{Time\_Out}))$$

which matches a poset consisting of two events, a Send(O) event with a message object, O, that binds to ?M, which causes either an Ack event with the header of O as its parameter or a Time_Out event. The body can be matched repeatedly. Because ?M is declared in the body, it can be bound to a different message O on each of the matches. So the pattern matches a poset consisting of any number of pairs of events, either Send(O) $\longrightarrow$ Ack(O.header), or Send(O) $\longrightarrow$ Time_Out; each pair can be dependent or independent of other pairs (the $\sim$ relation) and can have a different message O.

The fifth pattern matches similar posets to the fourth one, except that the placeholder ?M is declared before the repetition profile. Therefore, it must be common to all the repetitions of the body. So a single binding for M must be common to all the repeated matches.

Example 2: *A pattern that matches a supply chain bidding process*

```
(RFQId ?Id, Time ?T1)(RFQ(?Id) at ?T1 ⟶
    [* rel ~] (Time ?T2) Bid(RFQId is ?Id) at ?T2 where ?T2 < ?T1 + Bnd);
```

This example uses the RFQ and Bid actions in the supply chain example in Section 8.3.4 (Example 3). It matches the kind of electronic bidding process that might be expected in B2B activites of the electronic enterprise (see Chapter 2).

Let's look at the pattern in detail. It matches an RFQ event with an ?Id that happens at time ?T1 and a poset of Bid events that are caused by the RFQ event. There can be any number (*) of Bid events, in any relation ($\sim$) to one another, provided they all occur within a time bound, Bnd, of the RFQ event. The Bid events must all contain the ?Id of the RFQ event.

So this pattern "picks out" from the global event cloud all the Bid events in response to an RFQ that happen within a time limit.

8.10   Pattern Macros

Writing patterns is made much easier by an abstraction feature. An abstraction feature is useful in various ways.

1. First, it lets us abstract commonly used patterns and name them. This lets us shorten the notation for patterns and write readable patterns.

2. Second, we need to build up libraries of patterns for each application domain, say, network protocols, control systems, distributed transaction systems, supply chains for various industries, and so on—each domain has its own common patterns.

3. Third, when we specify hierarchical systems, we need to organize our patterns hierarchically too.

Pattern macros are a simple abstraction feature that helps with all these practical problems.

If we want to define a pattern macro called **PM**, we write:

> **pattern** PM (*parameter list*) {*pattern*};

PM is the name of the macro. It names the part in braces, '{'... '}', which must be a pattern. This is called the *body* of the macro.

The way we use pattern macros is to call them in patterns. So, in some pattern, we can write a call like this:

> ... PM(*actual parameter list*) ...

During pattern matching, a point is reached at which a macro call such as **PM**(...) must be matched. At this point in the matching, the parameters of the call have certain values, either objects or placeholders that haven't been bound yet. The macro call is replaced by an instance of the macro's body. To do this, the parameters in the body are replaced by the corresponding values. The resulting instance of the macro's body replaces the macro call in the pattern. This is called *macro expansion* because the call is "expanded" into an instance of the body, which is usually a lot bigger.

We could do many macro expansions with a text editor except when the macro is recursive—that is, the macro contains a call to itself. So macro expansion takes place at runtime—during pattern matching. And macro expansion is *lazy*—expansion takes place only if a match of the macro call is needed to match the pattern containing the macro call.

Example 1: *A pattern macro to shorten notation*

pattern Reply(Msg X) { Ack(X.header) **or** Time_Out };

[* **rel** ~] (Msg M)(Send(M) ⟶ Reply(M))

We want to shorten the "send causes an acknowledge or time out" pattern in an example in the previous section. So we define the "acknowledge or time out" piece of the pattern to be a macro called Reply. Now we can specify the pattern more succinctly with a macro call to Reply. It is shorter and more readable. The rewritten pattern specifies that each send causes a reply, which happens to be "..." (an instance of the Reply body).

Example 2: *Another pattern macro to shorten notation*

pattern Transaction() { (Msg M)(Send(M) $\longrightarrow$ (Ack(M.header) **or** Time_Out)) };

[∗ **rel** ∼] Transaction();

This second pattern macro shows that if we think of the "send causes an acknowledge or time out" pattern (the part that is being repeated) as a transaction, rather than a send and a reply, we can write the example even more succinctly.

As we said before, we have to be just a little careful about how we define macro expansion of macro calls, because pattern macros can be recursive. If we just dive in and do naive macro expansion, a recursive macro call will keep on being expanded, and we will never stop. This happens in all macro facilities that can be recursive. So, macro expansion is *lazy*. A macro call is expanded during matching of the pattern containing the call, "as needed" to do the match.

Example 3: *A recursive pattern macro*

pattern Saving() **is** Deposit $\longrightarrow$ Saving() **or** Empty() ;

Saving()
-- *matches the same finite posets as:*
[+ **rel** $\longrightarrow$] Deposit

Saving is recursive. It says, "Match a Deposit that causes either another match of the pattern Saving or the empty poset—that is, it causes no events." It matches posets consisting of one or more Deposit events, all in a causal chain.

Empty is a predefined pattern macro that matches the empty poset. Empty is useful for defining other patterns, as here, where it defines the termination case in a recursive macro.

Macros can be used to define other relational operators. Here is an example of a macro defining a new structural operator, $\triangleright$ (*immediate cause*). This expresses a relationship between events P and Q, whereby P is an immediate cause of Q—for example, father and son, but not grandfather and grandson. That is, P causes Q and there is no event, E, such that P causes E and E causes Q.

Example 4: *Immediate cause operator*

pattern P $\triangleright$ Q **is** (P $\longrightarrow$ Q) **not** (P $\longrightarrow$ Any $\longrightarrow$ Q);

A new relational operator, $\triangleright$(P, Q), is defined using the operators $\longrightarrow$ and **not**. It matches a poset if P $\longrightarrow$ Q matches the poset, and there is no nonempty subposet of the matching poset that matches Any and is causally between the matches for P and Q. So, the match for P must be an immediate cause of the match for Q.

8.11   Summary

One of the earliest examples of pattern languages for specifying computer programs is Path Expressions [22], which is conceptually similar to Regular Expressions.[4] Historically, RAPIDE-EPL evolved experimentally from an event pattern language for specifying and monitoring multitasking programs, called Task Sequencing Language [7], which was also rooted in Regular Expressions.

RAPIDE-EPL could be viewed as being designed by taking Regular Expressions of basic event patterns as a basic event pattern language and then adding new features, including the causal ($\longrightarrow$) and independence ($\|$) event pattern operators, predicate guards over complex event patterns, timing operators similar to the ones usually found in simulation languages, strong typing with inheritance, and pattern macros. Today, several pattern languages could be added to in similar ways to be suitable for CEP.

---

[4]Web search on "regular expressions."

Chapter 9

CEP Rules and Agents

- *Event pattern rules—the building blocks for agents*
- *Agents—lightweight rules engines*
- *Filters—agents to reduce event executions to relevant subsets*
- *Maps—agents to aggregate and correlate events*
- *Constraints—agents to detect good and bad behavior*

This chapter introduces the mechanisms for building applications of CEP: *event pattern rules* and *event processing agents* (EPAs). Our strawman tabular rules (see Chapter 6) are designed to illustrate CEP concepts, but they are inadequate for most real-life applications. The CEP rules presented here are more powerful than the strawman rules in Section 6.4 in two ways. First, the triggers of event pattern rules are written in RAPIDE-EPL, a more powerful pattern language. And second, CEP rules can execute a richer set of actions. As before, event pattern rules imply a causal relationship between the events that trigger them and the events they create in the resulting activities. Agents are objects that execute event pattern rules. Agents are the building blocks for CEP applications. We describe three common types of agents.

9.1   Overview

An *event processing agent* is an object that monitors an event execution to detect certain patterns of events. When those patterns occur in its input, it reacts by executing actions. An EPA can monitor an event execution online, in real time as the events are being created, or offline, postmortem, using a log of the execution.

An EPA is really a very simple object (see Figure 9.1). It belongs to a class of objects and consists of event pattern rules and local variables whose values make up its state. Each rule has two parts: a pattern called the *trigger* and a *body* consisting of actions. An EPA monitors its input to detect instances of the rule triggers. Whenever a match of a rule's trigger is detected, the agent executes the actions in the rule's body. As a result of executing a rule, an EPA changes its local state variables and output events. The events that are output can be a newly created poset or a subset of the events in the input, depending upon the kind of rules in the EPA. The output of an EPA can also be an interaction with the target system, such as sending a message or calling a facility in the system.

EPAs can be organized into networks to communicate with one another, as shown in Figure 10.1 in Chapter 10. Each EPA reacts to its input by outputting events that are fed to other EPAs. This kind of monitoring structure is a communication network of EPAs called an *event processing*

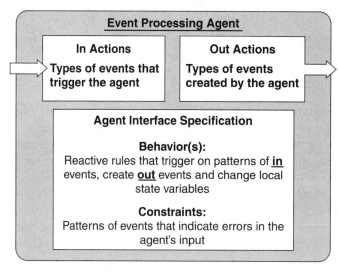

Figure 9.1: Interface of an event processing agent class

network (EPN), discussed in Chapter 10. EPNs are an example of interface communication architectures (see Section 4.3.3).

We begin this chapter by describing the basic building block of EPAs— event pattern rules. Then we describe the basic class of EPAs, from which all other classes of EPAs are derived. We discuss three basic classes of EPAs that have proved useful in CEP applications.

1. *Filters:* A filter uses a pattern to filter out the sets of events in an event execution that are of interest. A filter outputs (or passes on) the posets of events in its input that match its pattern. The other events are not passed on.

2. *Maps:* Maps use event pattern rules to aggregate posets of events into higher-level events. Maps are the basis for defining relationships between sets of system-level events and higher-level abstract events— *event aggregation.* More generally, maps are used to specify hierarchies of events (see Section 7.4).

3. *Constraints:* Constraints use event patterns to check for the presence or absence of posets in an event execution. They output violation notifications.

   Constraints give us a powerful way to define the event sets we expect to observe being generated by the target system as a result of some activity. A typical activity at the system level is correct execution of a communication protocol. At the application level, a constraint might monitor for correct handling of a customer's purchase order. Constraints can also specify event sets that should *never* happen—for example, events that would indicate a system failure or a security violation.

In general, however, an EPA can be viewed as a reactive, multithreaded process with local state that executes concurrently with other EPAs and communicates with them by events. CEP applications require EPAs to be organized into communication architectures (see Chapter 4), often dynamic architectures.

9.2 Event Pattern Rules

An event pattern rule is a reactive rule with two parts: a left side called the *trigger* and a right side called the *body.* The trigger is a RAPIDE-EPL pattern. The body is a list of *statements.* As discussed in Section 6.4, there are two kinds of rules, *sequential* and *parallel,* which differ only in the causal relationships between the events they create.

9.2.1   Definition of Event Pattern Rules

An event pattern rule has the following syntax:

> *pattern* =>   *list-of-statements*;   (sequential rule)
> *pattern* ||>   *list-of-statements*;   (parallel rule)

The symbols "=>" and "|| >" connect the trigger (left side) and body (right side) of the rule. Types and variables declared in the trigger can be used in the body.

Example 1: *A rule to notify network managers of high loads*

(Network_Path ?Route; Real ?Load) Report(?Route, ?Load) **where** ?Load > 7 =>
  generate Notify (Manager_Console, "Warning", Name(?Route),   ?Load, Time);

The trigger of this rule is a RAPIDE-EPL basic event pattern, Report (?Route, ?Load), with a guard, **where** ?Load > 7. The variables ?Route and ?Load are declared in the pattern. The rule reacts when a Report event matches its trigger.

The body is a **generate** statement containing a basic event pattern, Notify(...), with the variables ?Load and ?Route. The result of a match of the trigger is a binding of data values to these variables. The values of ?Route and ?Load and the Time (a function call to a local clock) are used to create a Notify event that is output by the rule.

9.2.2   Rule Bodies

A rule's body is a list of programming statements that are executed in a single thread of control. These statements include familiar programming constructs. There are two new statements called **generate** and **pass** for creating and outputting events. There are timing operators for controlling the time at which events are output. Here are examples of the kinds of statements:

- Assignment

    X =   E;   // *assignment; X is a variable and E is an expression.*

- Conditional

    if *boolean_condition* **then** {*statements*} **else** {*statements*} ;

- While loop

    while *boolean_condition* {*statements*};

- For loop

    for *boolean_condition* {*statements*};

- Return

    return *expression*;

- Function call

    function_name (*parameters*)

- Event creation

    generate *pattern*;

- **pass** statement

    pass ;

- Timing operators

    after *time expression*;
    within *time expression*;

9.2.3   Context and Visibility Laws

A rule is contained in the interface specification of an agent, as shown in Figure 9.1. The agent containing a rule is called the *parent*. A rule can be written using a context of actions, types, functions, and variables that are declared locally in the parent's interface. This context includes the input and output actions declared in the parent's interface; the types, functions, agents, and variables declared in the parent's behavior specification; and the variables declared in the pattern trigger of the rule.

A rule's trigger must be a pattern of events that belong to the actions in the parent's input action set (see Section 8.3.3 on event types) or the **out** actions of EPAs declared locally in the parent's interface specification. A **generate** statement (described later) in a rule's body must create new events that belong either to actions in the parent's output action set, or **in** actions of EPAs declared locally in the parent's interface specification.

A **pass** statement in a rule's body must only refer to events that belong to actions in both the parent's input and output sets of actions.

The context of a rule can also include library items that are *imported* into its parent's class definiton. Whenever this is done, however, rule triggers and bodies should contain guards to ensure the abstraction principle. An example of this is given in Section 4.6.[1]

The types declared locally in the interface specification of a rule's parent may include classes of agents. In this case, the **out** actions of local classes can also be used in the trigger of the rule, and the **in** actions of local classes can also be created by the rule.

Figure 9.1 shows a simple form of EPA. Agents can in fact hide internal activity involving local agents declared inside their interface specification. This is particularly true in the case of architecture classes, as shown in Figure 10.8. Behavior rules described here, and connection rules described in Chapter 10, can trigger on and create events that are part of the local activity of the parent.

The intention of visibility laws governing the writing of CEP rules is to disallow rules from directly triggering on, or creating, events outside their parent. So these laws limit a rule's trigger to events in its parent's input or internal activity, and limit the effect of the rule's execution to the local state of the parent, to the parent's internal activity, and to the parent's output events.

As a consequence, the abstraction principle discussed in Section 4.6 is obeyed when architectures of nested EPAs are constructed. This enables plug-and-play techniques to be applied to nested architectures of EPAs, as discussed in the next chapter.

9.2.4   Semantics of Event Pattern Rules

The semantics of an event pattern rule is that whenever a poset is detected in the input execution to the rule that matches the trigger, the bindings of the match are substituted into the body of the rule, and that instance of the body is executed.

When a rule executes its body, it can do three things:

- Change the state of its parent
- Create new events that its parent outputs or that contribute to the local activity of the parent, or both
- Pass on events from its input that its parent outputs

---

[1]In RAPIDE there are *inheritance* and *import* declarations that apply to EPAs and allow visibility, for example, to functions outside the parent. A full discussion of inheritance, scope, and visibility is beyond this introduction.

A rule changes the state of its parent by executing assignments and function calls. A rule creates new events by executing **generate** statements. A rule passes events from its parent's input to its parent's output by executing **pass** statements.

When a **generate** statement is executed, the rule creates a poset that is an instance of the **generate** pattern. Placeholders in the **generate** pattern must also be in the rule's trigger and must be bound to objects when the trigger is matched. When the rule reacts and executes the **generate** statement, the placeholders are replaced in the **generate** pattern by their bindings. An instance of the **generate** pattern is formed. This instance is the poset that is created by the rule. The triggering events *cause* all the events in the created poset.

A **generate** statement can result in creating a single event or multiple events with specified relationships, depending upon the complexity of the **generate** pattern. If the rule is sequential ($=>$), the posets of events created on different triggerings are causally ordered in a linear sequence. If the rule is parallel ($\| >$), the posets created on different triggerings are independent, unless the created events on one triggering contribute to another triggering of the rule.

A **generate** statement can be modified by a timing operator—for example:

generate A(...) **after** T;

T is an expression whose value is a time at which the event is created. The execution of the rule pauses until the time is T. So, if the **generate** statement begins execution at T_1, its execution terminates by creating the event A(...) at $T_1 + T$.

Similarly,

generate A(...) **within** T;

means that the **generate** statement that begins execution at time T_1 must terminate by creating event A at a time before $T_1 + T$.

A **pass** statement means "pass the events" that matched the trigger of the rule. It does not create new events or copies of the triggering events. Unlike the **generate** statement, a **pass** does not add to the causal relationships between events. A **pass** is like "pass by reference" in programming languages. **pass** statements can only be used in filter agents.

A **pass** statement cannot be used in the same rule body as a **generate** statement. So we sometimes call rules with these statements in them either *generate rules* or *pass rules*.

9.2.5 Examples of Rules

Here are some examples of rules together with the contexts that they use.

Example 1: *A rule that aggregates network node alerts*

```
// actions
in action Alert( Node_Type Node, Real CPU_Load, Real Memory_Allocation,
                             Int 1 .. 5   Severity, Time_Type Time);
out action Notify(Destination_Type C, String M, Network_Path P, Severity S,
                             Time_Type T1, Time_Type T2);
// functions
Boolean      CommonPath(Node N, Node N1);
Time_Type    Clock;
Path_Type    Path(Node N, Node N1);
Int          Max(Int S, Int S');
...
// rule
(Node_Type N, N1; Int 1..5 S, S'; Time_Type T, T')
  (Alert(Node is N, Severity is S) where (S>3 and T=Clock) ~
    Alert(Node is N1, Severity is S') where (N /= N1 and S'>3 and T'=Clock)
⇒
if CommonPath (N, N1)   // nodes are on the same network path.
then {                  // send alert with path, max severity and times.
  generate Notify(Manager_Console, "Path Alert", Path(N, N1),
                             Max(S, S'), T, T');
}
```

This rule is shown in the context of the action declarations, Alert and Notify, of its parent agent. The trigger matches two Alert events in the parent's input, provided they satisfy the guard tests. The Alerts must refer to different nodes in the network and have a Severity level greater than **3**. The Alert events can be either causally dependent or independent (that's the meaning of the $\sim$ operator). Notice the use of named parameters in the pattern (see Section 8.6.3).

The first guard tests the value of $S > 3$ (Severity level) and $T = $ Clock. When T is an unbound variable, the effect of $T = $ Clock in a guard is to assign T the current value of Clock. That is, equality tests on unbound variables in the guards act as assignment statements. So T' is also set to the clock reading when the second Alert is observed.

When the trigger matches, the rule reacts by executing its body. The placeholders N, N1, S, S', T, T' are replaced in the body by their bindings. The body tests to see if the two nodes N and N1 are allocated to a common

network path. If so, the event Notify(...) is created by the **generate** statement and output by the parent.

Example 2: *Rule to mail requests for quotations*

```
// actions
in action ReceiveOrder(Customer Id, Item I, Quantity Q, Dollars Bid,
                                              Date ShipBy);
out action SendRFQ(Supplier S; Item I, Quantity Q, Dollars Limit,
                                        Date Deadline);
// functions
Boolean Valid(Customer Id, Item I, Quantity Q, Dollars Bid, Date ShipBy);
Dollars Margin(Dollars BidPrice);
// rule
(Customer Id, Supplier S, Item I, Quantity Q, Dollars Bid,
              Dollars Limit, Date ShipBy, Date Deadline, Time_Type T1)
ReceiveOrder(Id, I, Q, Bid, ShipBy) at T1
                    where Valid(Id, I, Q, Bid, ShipBy)
⇒
Deadline = ShipBy − 5 days;
Limit    = Margin(Bid);
while Supplier_List.HasMoreElements and Clock < T1 + 24 hrs {
  S = Supplier_List.NextElement;
if OnTimeRecord(S) > 90
    then
      generate SendRFQ(S, I, Q, Limit, Deadline);
}
```

This rule is triggered by receiving an order that passes a Valid test. We
assume this test includes not only the customer's credit rating and a price
check for the item, but also a check that the ShipBy date allows sufficient
time to fill the order.

A match of the ReceiveOrder pattern will bind all its variables to data
values and also T1 to the matching event's timestamp (see Section 8.8.3).
The body of the rule computes a value for the Deadline for replies to an
RFQ and an upper limit for a supplier's price of the item. It then iterates
through a list of suppliers as long as 24 hours has not elapsed since the order
was received. If a supplier's on-time record passes a test, a SendRFQ event
is created with appropriate data, including a dealine for a reply, and sent to
the supplier.

This rule would execute asynchronously with other rules for analyzing
the quotations that are received in response (see Section 2.4).

Our description of rule bodies is taken from RAPIDE but omits a lot of details. A language for CEP could be designed as an extension to Java, in which case the statements in rule bodies would be a subset of Java statements. Timing expressions are values of some local clock that is visible in the parent agent. There is a richer set of timing operators in RAPIDE whose purpose is to model the timing of events in causal event simulations of distributed systems.

9.3   Event Processing Agents

A class of EPAs is specified by an *interface* (see Figure 9.1). An EPA interface declares sets of input and output actions, and a *behavior* consisting of local types, variables, functions, and rules. There are three common types of EPAs: *filter, map,* and *constraint.* Each of these types restricts the kinds of rules its interface can contain.

9.3.1   Definition of EPAs

An EPA class interface is declared using the following syntax:

```
class  EPA_Class_Name  in  input_execution_type  out  output_execution_type {
                list of declarations
                list of event pattern rules
                list of event pattern constraints
                }
```

Execution types are sets of action declarations, discussed in Section 8.3.4. The input and output execution types can be declared as names of execution types or explicitly as lists of **in** and **out** actions. The list of declarations in the EPA interface can contain types, functions, and variables. Event pattern rules in the list of rules can only use actions, types, functions, and variables declared locally in the agent class interface (see Section 9.2.3).

Example 1: *Class interfaces of EPAs*

```
class Button
    in   action Press();
    out  action Move(), Release();
    {Press =>  generate Move();
                generate Release() after 0.1 sec;
    };
```

```
class Sensor
   in   action Activate(), DeActivate();
   out action Light(enum {On, Off} X;);
   {Activate  =>    generate Light(On);
    DeActivate =>  generate Light(Off);
    };
```

Button and Sensor are two classes of EPAs. Their **in** and **out** actions specify the types of events they can react to and create. The behavior rule of a Button says that a Press event triggers creation of a Move event, followed after 0.1 seconds by a Release event. The sensor's rules react to an Activate event by creating a Light(On) and to a DeActivate by creating a Light(Off).

9.3.2   Semantics of EPAs

Agent classes are types. Agents are objects of these class types. Agents can be created using the **new** operation with the class name (see Section 10.3.2). Agents can be started and terminated using the predefined **in** actions Start and Terminate of the primitive agent class shown in Figure 9.2. All agent classes are subtypes of the primitive class type.

EPAs execute independently as separate threads of control. Causal relationships between the activities of different EPAs result from the events communicated between them (see Section 10.2). Causal relationships between the activities of a single EPA result either from the semantics of

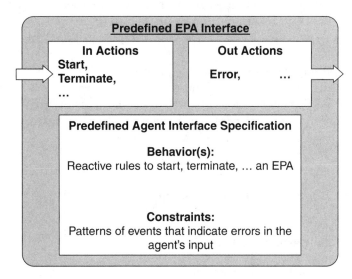

Figure 9.2: A predefined agent class is inherited by all agent classes

its rules or from the accessing of a state variable by two or more of its rules.

An EPA executes by processing the input events that it receives. Input events are processed one at a time to compute their contribution to matching the trigger of each rule. Whenever a match of a trigger is completed, the rule is executed, as described in Section 9.2.4. At any time, there may be a list of partial matches of triggers. Attempts to complete matches are performed one at a time.

A consequence of one-at-a-time event processing is that within a single EPA, rules do not access local state variables concurrently.

Matching of rule triggers and execution of rule bodies may include access to state variables of the parent agent. State variables are *protected*. This means that accesses such as reading or writing the value of a variable are causally ordered sequentially. Consequently, if a rule performs an activity, A, before it writes (or changes) the value of a variable, and a rule later reads the value and afterward performs an activity, B, then A will be a cause of B as long as the value of that variable has not been overwritten in between.

The semantics of EPAs described here is taken from RAPIDE. The RAPIDE model is very simple. Each EPA executes as a single thread of control. Multiple EPAs execute in parallel and communicate by means of events. They do not share global state. Coordination or synchronization of two EPAs is achieved through communication with a third EPA. Obviously, the predefined features can be extended to provide priorities, synchronization, and so on. The purpose of RAPIDE, however, was not to write complicated multithreaded programs, but to experiment with the use of causal event relationships in highly distributed, layered system models. This leads to the concepts of EPNs (see Chapter 10) and maps (see Section 9.5).

A second goal of RAPIDE was to structure EPNs into layered communication architectures of EPAs. The purpose here was to experiment with the abstraction principle and plug-and-play techniques of architecture modification. Consequently, an EPA can have a local EPN that is a lower-level architecture (see Chapter 10).

Example 1: *An airplane event processing agent*

```
class Aircraft
    in   action Enter(Aircraft NewId);
    in   action RadioReceive(Msg M);
    out  action RadioTransmit(Msg M);
    out  action RadarTransmit();
```

```
{   Aircraft Id = Null;
    Clock C;
    ...                          /* local functions, e.g., RequiredResponse.*/
/* behavior rules.*/
    (Aircraft ?NewId;) Enter(?NewId) =>Id = ?NewId;
                                      C.Start;
                                      generate RadioTransmit(Startmsg);
    (Msg ?M, ?Msg M', Time ?T;) RadioReceive(?M) at ?T  =>
    generate RadioTransmit(?M') where RequiredResponse(?M, ?M') within ?T+5;
    C.Tick => generate RadarTransmit();
};
```

The airplane example here has local state consisting of an Id, a clock object, and local functions. Clocks are objects that emit Tick events after they are started. An aircraft reacts to an input of an Enter event by initializing its Id, starting its clock, and creating a RadioTransmit event with the first message in some protocol. Whenever a RadioReceive event is input, it reacts by creating a RadioTransmit with another message in the protocol within five time units. The clock creates local events, which it outputs. These trigger a rule that creates RadarTransmit events, which the aircraft outputs.

In Section 10.5, we will show how aircraft can be part of a communication architecture, interacting with other EPAs.

9.4   Event Pattern Filters

Filtering is very important in processing large event sets. It lets us reduce the size of an event execution to relevant subsets of events. It is more practical to run analysis algorithms, which may be complicated or time-consuming, on those smaller subsets of the events.

An *event pattern filter* (abbreviated as *filter*) is an agent that uses event pattern rules to pick out a subset of the events in its input. If we pass an event execution to a filter, it picks out the posets that match the triggers of its rules and passes these posets on as its output. The output of a filter is a subposet of its input.

9.4.1   Definition of Filters

Filter classes are declared using the keyword **filter.**

```
filter F in T1 out T2 {
    declarations
    event pattern rules
    }
```

Here, T1 and T2 are execution types—that is, sets of actions (see Section 8.3.4). T1 is the type of the posets that can be input to the filter, called the *domain* type, and T2 is the type of posets it outputs, called the *range* type.

9.4.2 Semantics of Filters

The event types in the range T2 must be subtypes of the event types in the domain T1. A simple example is that the actions in T2 all belong to the set of actions in T1—see Figure 9.3.

A rule in a filter cannot have **generate** statements. It can be a **pass** rule or a state change rule. A filter outputs a subset of the actual events in its input. It never creates new events, not even copies of input events. This is analogous to the old programming concept of "pass by reference." The reason for this is *efficiency*. Filters exist to cut down the number of events to be processed. Making copies would be counterproductive.

Filters always preserve the timing relationship between input events that are passed to the output. Causal relationships can also be preserved, sometimes at computational cost. So filters are only guaranteed to preserve causality in postmortem filtering and may not do so in real-time filtering, depending upon the requirements of their application.[2]

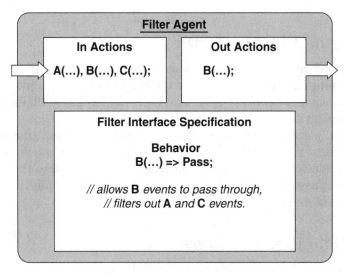

Figure 9.3: Example of a filter class

---

[2]Preservation of causality may depend upon whether the input event execution is persistent, the complexity of the filter pattern, and other factors beyond the scope of our discussion.

Figure 9.3 is an example of a very simple filter that can receive executions containing A, B, and C events and will pass on only B events. The **pass** rule could restrict the data parameters of the B events that are passed, but this detail is not shown.

Example 1: *Filter out small sequences of timeouts.*

```
filter OmitNormalTimeouts in S out T {
    Int Count = 0;

    // Rule 1: increment Counter, filter out normal TimeOuts.
    TimeOut where Count ≤ 5 => Count++;

    // Rule 2: pass TimeOuts after 5 have happened in one transmission.
    TimeOut where Count > 5 => pass;

    // Rule 3: reset when transmission terminates successfully.
    Acknowledge ⟶ Reset    => Count = 0;
}
```

This filter takes input events that are instances of actions named in S. They include TimeOut, Acknowledge, and Reset actions. The filter outputs events that are instances of actions named in T, which must be a subset of S. T includes the TimeOut action.

Typically, this filter would be applied to events in a communication network to filter out TimeOuts related to communication. For simplicity, we omit parameters for transaction Ids and so on.

The filter has three rules. The first rule triggers on the first five TimeOuts in an attempted communication. It increments a counter but does not pass on the TimeOuts. The second rule triggers on the subsequent TimeOuts after the fifth and passes them as ouput. The third rule triggers when an Acknowledge event causes a Reset event. Then it resets the counter to zero.

Notice that our use of the constant, 5, is unnecessarily restrictive. Instead, we could make a filter template with a Bound parameter. Also, this example filter is easily modified to deal with many different communication transactions concurrently. For example, if the TimeOut events include a communication Id, the rules can be modified to use that Id. The Count variable is changed to a structured object indexed by Ids.

The previous example is a very basic kind of filter that has many variations to deal with different domains of events. Its role is simply to count a number of input events before allowing events to pass though. For example, a similar type of filter is useful in differentiating between normal network activity and attempts to violate network security.

9.4.3   Action Name Filters

A very common use of filters is when we are only interested in events with some particular action names. So we want to keep only the events with these names and omit all the other events in some event execution. These are called *action name* filters.

Example 1: *Action name filters to pass on only ATM operations*

```
filter ATM_Operations_1 in S out T {
   Deposit or WithDraw or Transfer =>   pass;
}

filter ATM_Operations_2 in S out T {
   Deposit    =>   pass;
   WithDraw   =>   pass;
   Transfer   =>   pass;
}
```

Look first at the ATM_Operations_1 filter. The rule's trigger is a logical **or** of action names that we want to pass on. It will be matched by any event with one of these action names.

Imagine that the events generated by a bank's communication system are run through this filter. Its effect is to omit all those events that are not Deposits, WithDraws, and Transfers and to pass on *all* events with these three action names together with their timing.

If the filter maintains their causal relationship—remember, causality is transitive, so if we omit B from A $\longrightarrow$ B $\longrightarrow$ C we get A $\longrightarrow$ C—the output from this filter is the poset consisting of those events from the input execution that are instances of Deposit, WithDraw, and Transfer.

The ATM_Operations_2 filter does the same thing as ATM_Operations_1.

Action name filters are very simple and easy to understand, but they lack precision. Often, filtering needs to be based upon the content or context of the events.

9.4.4 Content Filters

Content filters use the contents of events to decide which ones to pass on to their output. This example uses the content-based matching example in Section 8.8.1.

Example 1: *Filtering stock quotations based upon their contents*

```
filter StockQuotes in StockMsgs out StockMsgs {

(StockTradeSymbol ?Sym, Dollars ?LatestPrice, Dollars ?LastQuote)
    StockQuote(?Sym, ?LatestPrice, ?LastQuote) where ?LatestPrice > ?LastQuote + $5;
=>   pass;
}
```

This filter checks the content of a stock quotation before passing it on. The quotation is passed on only if the latest price is $5 more than the last quote. The guard uses the content of the StockQuote event to make the test.

9.4.5 Context Filters

We need the full power of event pattern filters when the *context* of an event, such as its relationship to other events in the execution, is what makes it interesting. *Context filters* pass on subposets of their input that occur in a certain context. Contexts might involve, for example, the events that caused the events of interest, or the timewise preceding events, or the values of local variables in the state of the filter.

This example uses the network management types declared in Section 8.3.4.

Example 2: *A filter to omit transactions with normal completion times*

```
filter AbnormalTransactions in NetMngmt out NetMngmt {
    Time_Type Max is Const;
// rule to pass on abnormal transactions.
    (Time_Type ?T1,?T2; String ?I)
        (Send(Time is ?T1, Id is ?I) →
        Acknowledge(Id is ?I, Time is ?T2)) where T2 − T1 > Max
        =>
        Max = T2 − T1;
        pass;

};
```

The rule in this filter triggers on any poset containing the initial Send event of a message transaction and the final causally related Acknowledge event whenever those two events are more than Max time units appart. Max is set to the time difference between the triggering events. Then the events are passed on to the output. So the filter passes on causally related Send and Acknowledge pairs of events that have an increasingly long time difference. This could indicate a possibly deteriorating situation in a network. Other EPAs would be given this output to analyze.

9.5   Event Pattern Maps

An *event pattern map* (abbreviated as *map*) is a second type of EPA. It creates new events based upon the recognition of patterns of events in its input.

Maps let us *aggregate* events. Typically, maps are composed into EPNs that allow us to construct hierarchical views of event executions, as described in Section 7.4. We can search an event execution for a pattern of events that are related so that together they signify a higher-level activity in a system. When the pattern matches, the map outputs a higher-level *complex* event.

Figure 9.4 shows a class of map agents that aggregate causal sequences of events in their input and create Seq events summarizing the data in each sequence.

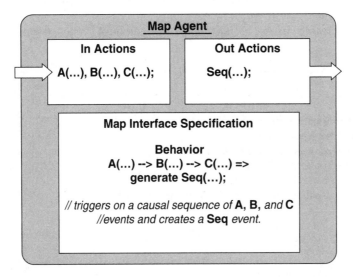

Figure 9.4: A map class to aggregate causal sequences in its input

Another use of maps is to *correlate* events. A map can be used to detect patterns of events that may be regarded as unrelated. Each match of the pattern results in creation of a "correlation" event summarizing the data in the match. Aggregation and correlation are similar operations. Correlation usually involves events that may be widely separated by time or origin and are not normally thought of as being related.

Maps can be applied to complex events that have been created by other maps. So we have a capability to define layers of complex events on top of the event executions generated by a target system. This capability is very flexible because it can be changed dynamically at runtime to meet changing monitoring and detection requirements.

In the most general use of maps, a response to detecting a match of a pattern in the input can be to output a poset of new events—not just one complex event.

9.5.1 Definition of Maps

A map class is declared using the keyword **map**.

map F **in** T1 **out** T2 {
    declarations
    event pattern rules
    }

Here, T1 and T2 are execution types. T1 is the type of the posets that can be input to the map, called the *domain* type, and T2 is the type of posets it outputs, called the *range* type.

9.5.2 Semantics of Maps

A rule in a map can change the state of the map or create output events using **generate** statements. A map cannot contain **pass** statements.

The new events created and output by a map may be causally related. The map constructs the causal relationship at the same time as it generates the new events. That is, the genetic parameters in output events expressing the causal relationship are computed by the rule bodies.

This causal relationship can result from the event pattern in a **generate** statement. Remember, the argument of a **generate** is a pattern. Whenever a rule triggers and executes a **generate**, the causal relationship between the new events is already defined in the pattern. A causal relationship may also exist between events created by different executions of **generate** statements. In this case, the latest events to be generated are causally related to previously generated events. The rule bodies must temporarily store the identifiers of events they create, to construct genetic parameters.

Example 1: *A map to aggregate trading transactions*

```
map GetTrades in MarketTransactionsType out TradesType {

    (TradeID ?ID; Customer ?C; Broker ?B; StockSym ?S;
            TradeKind ?K; Amount ?A; TimeType ?t1, ?t2)
    Order(?ID, ?S, ?A, ?K, ?B, performer is ?C) at ?t1 ⟶
    (Execute(?ID, ?S, ?A, ?K, ?C, performer is ?B) ~
    Confirm(?ID, ?S, ?A, ?K, ?C, performer is ?B) at ?t2 )
    ⇒
        generate Trade(?C, ?B, ?S, ?K, ?A, ?t1, ?t2);
}
```

This EPA is a map with a single rule. The rule aggregates posets consisting of three MarketTransactionType events into a single TradesType event.

The market transaction type, which is the input type of the map, consists of action declarations such as the following:

```
action Order(TradeID ?ID;  StockSym ?S; Amount ?A;
            TradeKind ?K; Broker ?B; Customer ?C);
action Execute(TradeID ?ID; StockSym ?S; Amount ?A;
            TradeKind ?K; Broker ?B; Customer ?C);
action Confirm(TradeID ?ID; StockSym ?S; Amount ?A;
            TradeKind ?K; Broker ?B; Customer ?C);
action BuyStock(TradeID ?ID;  StockSym ?S; Amount ?A;
            Broker ?B; Customer ?C);
...  // other action declarations.
```

The rule's trigger matches a pattern consisting of an Order that causes two subsequent events, an Execute and a Confirm. The Order is performed by a customer for some amount of a stock and sent to a broker. This event should cause an Execute performed by the broker that received the order, with the same data parameters for the stock and customer. The Confirm is also performed by the broker and sent to the customer. The order can be either a buy or sell order (trade kind). The Execute and Confirm events may or may not be causally related.

When this pattern matches, the map will generate a new event, a Trade. It contains data from the parameters of the triggering events, such as the broker, customer, and stock. It also contains the times of the start and end of the transaction—that is, the time the order was placed by the customer (?t1) and the time the broker confirmed the trade (?t2).

The output type of the map is TradesType, which contains the action declaration for the Trade event:

```
action Trade(Customer C; Broker B; Stock S; Kind K;
             Amount A; TimeType order, completion);
 ...    //  other action declarations.
```

The purpose of this map is to recognize posets of events that signify completed stock trades in an input execution. Each time the events constituting a trade are recognized, a new Trade event with summary data is generated. In this example, there is no causal relationship between any of the new Trade events in the map's output.

9.6 Event Pattern Constraints

An *event pattern constraint* (abbreviated as *constraint*) is an EPA that monitors its input execution for either the presence or the absence of a pattern and generates events to indicate the results. Event pattern constraints can be regarded as a special kind of map. However, the purpose of a constraint is not filtering or aggregation, but *detection*. This is a rather subtle distinction, but it is an important one.

Event pattern constraints have important applications in detecting violations of business or security policies in enterprise systems.

9.6.1 Definition of Constraints

A *constraint* is an agent class declared using the keyword **constraint** in place of **class**. The range type usually consists of one or two event types. Common examples of range types are {Satisfied(...), Violated(...)}, or simply {True, False}. The purpose of output events is to pass on information about whether or not instances of its pattern have been detected.

9.6.2 Semantics of Constraints

As we have said, the distinction between a constraint and a map is that a constraint is intended for detecting patterns. Three common kinds of constraints tend to be used over and over again.

1. **never** constraints. As described in Section 6.5, a **never** constraint says that such and such a pattern must never happen in its input. For example, "A Send event should never cause an Abort event."
2. **always** constraints. An **always** constraint says that some pattern of events must always occur in some relationship to some other pattern of

events. If the constraint's pattern involves causal or time ordering between two patterns—say, P $\longrightarrow$ Q or P $<$ Q—P initiates every check of the constraint.

- **always** P $\longrightarrow$ Q means that if P matches, the events in that instance of P must cause a match of Q.

- **always** P $<$ Q means that if P matches, a match for Q must happen later.

- **always** P **and** Q **during**(10, 20) means that the part of the execution in the time interval from 10 to 20 must match P **and** Q.

- **always** P **and** Q means that the entire execution must match P **and** Q.

To make checking practical, **always** constraints usually have a time bound in which the complete pattern must be matched and involve an ordering between events. For example, "A Send event must always cause an Acknowledge event within 15 seconds" means that every Send must cause an Acknowledge in 15 seconds, but not every Acknowledge has to be caused by a Send.[3]

3. **state** constraints. A **state** constraint requires some part of a system's state to satisfy certain conditions whenever a pattern of events happens. Usually, there is some time bound between the matching of the pattern and when the state must conform to the condition. A common example is that when the pattern of events happens, a database must contain certain data.

Figure 9.5 shows a class of constraint agents that check two constraints on their inputs. The first is a **never** constraint requiring that a B event never cause an A event. The constraint could involve relationships between the parameters—for example, it is violated only if the A event contains different data values from B's parameters. The second constraint is an **always.** Its initial event is an A. Whenever an A happens, a B and a C must happen within five seconds. Whenever constraints are violated, an error message is output.[4]

We can easily build maps to check for these commmon kinds of constraints, and indeed there is more than one way to do it with our event pattern–triggered rules. Figure 9.6 shows a class of maps that check the

---

[3]Normally, timing operators refer to a single global clock. In the case of multiple clocks, a particular clock can be referenced as a parameter of any timing operator (see Sections 8.7.1 and 8.8.3).

[4]The format of constraint error messages depends on the details of the CEP implementation and analysis tools.

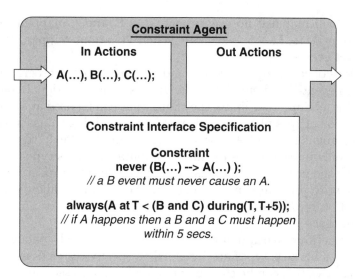

Figure 9.5: A class of constraint agents

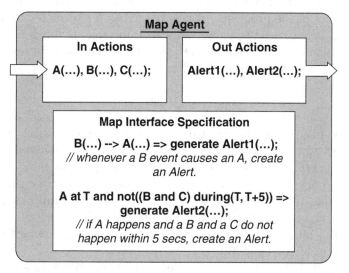

Figure 9.6: A class of maps to do constraint checking

constraints in Figure 9.5. The triggers are patterns whose matches imply violations of those constraints. The first rule triggers whenever a B causes an A, which violates the **never** rule. The trigger of the second rule can match whenever there is an A event at some time—T_0, say. This binds the variable T to T_0 so that the expressions in the **during** have values. Then the trigger will match if no events matching B **and** C happen during the interval from T_0 to $T_0 + 5$ (seconds). When violations happen, these maps create Alert events.

The idea of constraints can be found in many modern programming languages and event-based simulation languages. The traditional concept of a constraint is a bound that limits the values that can be used at some point in a computation. Types play the basic role in constraining values in typed programming languages like C++ or Java. For example, "Int I;" declares that I must take only integer values during a computation. This type restriction is enforced by the programming tools—language editor, compiler, or whatever we use to write programs in the language. We won't be allowed to include an instruction in our program that gives I a string value or anything other than an integer.

But sometimes types don't specify values accurately enough to avoid errors. That's because types are intended to specify restrictions that are so simple that a system can be checked at compile time to see if it satifies those restrictions. Constraints, on the other hand, are intended to specify more precise restrictions that usually can only be checked at runtime.

The integer I may need to conform to stronger restrictions at runtime at some points in the program—if it is passed as a parameter to a function, for example, it may need to lie within a certain range of integers. Languages like Eiffel [19], Anna [11], and VHDL [8] let us place further restrictions on I by using runtime assertions—for example:

$$\textbf{assert } f(x) \leq I \leq g(x);$$

An assertion like this one is a runtime constraint. It puts bounds on I, namely f(x) and g(x), that can only be computed at runtime when the assertion is executed. Generally, unless we are very careful programmers, we don't know when we compile the program whether or not it will satisfy the assertion. Standard kinds of programming tools don't help us with runtime constraints. So, when an assertion is executed, it tests to see if the constraint is satisfied. A violation of an assertion typically leads to a warning message or in some cases abortion of the program.

Now, we just take this idea of constraining the values in a computation at runtime and apply it to constraining the sets of events that are created in an enterprise system. The result is the concept of an *event pattern constraint*. An event pattern constraint specifies a pattern of events that must occur, or must never occur, in the events in its input. A constraint may even specify that the whole input execution must be an instance of a pattern. This gives us a very powerful kind of constraint that can express many business or security policies in enterprise systems.

9.6.3 Examples of Constraints

These examples show how to build maps that check for **never** and **always** constraints. We use the keyword **constraint** to indicate that the purpose of the map is constraint checking.

Never Constraints

Here's a generic way to program an EPA to check for **never** constraints like the one above. Suppose we want an EPA to check **never** P on some execution I, where P is a pattern of events that can happen in I. And we want the EPA to output Violation events with data about each violation when it happens. Also, we want the EPA to tell us if the constraint is satisfied by the execution I if and when I terminates. We would use two rules and a Boolean variable.

```
constraint NeverChecker in I out VS {
boolean Satisfied is true;
// rule 1 to detect violations.
P   ⇒   Satisfied = false;
        generate Violation(...);
// rule 2 to determine if the constraint is satisfied when the execution terminates.
Terminated(...) ⇒ if Satisfied   generate Satisfied(...);
}
```

The output execution type, VS, would contain the following actions:

```
action Violated (...);
action Satisfied (...);
```

As an instance of this template with a particular pattern for P, here's an agent that checks that a Send never causes an Abort.

Example 1: *A Send event should never cause an Abort event.*

```
constraint NeverChecker in I out VS {
boolean Satisfied is true;
// rule 1 to detect violations.
Send(...) ⟶ Abort(...) ⇒   Satisfied = false;
                           generate Violation(...);
// rule 2 to determine if the constraint is satisfied when the execution terminates.
Terminated(...) ⇒ if Satisfied   generate Satisfied(...);
}
```

Here's how this EPA works. If we feed it an execution as input, rule 1 will trigger if there is a Send(...) event that later on causes an Abort(...) event. The parameters, which we have omitted, can be used to ensure that the two events are related by common data—for example, they contain the same transaction Id. The rule 1 body then executes, setting the state variable to **false** and generating a Violation(...) event. Rule 2 triggers whenever a Terminated event happens, which indicates the end of the target system's execution. If the Boolean state variable is still **true**, rule 2 will generate a Satisfied event to report that the constraint was satisfied in the target's execution.

Our next example is a **never** constraint on events in an online trading system. The input execution type, MarketTransactionsType, includes event types signifying activities of brokers and their customers.

Example 2: *Constraint against brokers trading ahead of customers*

```
constraint DetectTradeAhead in   MarketTransactionsType out WarningType {
boolean Satisfied is true;
// rule 1 to detect trade–ahead violations.
 (String ?Symbol, ?Broker, ?Customer;
  Integer ?Amount1, ?Amount2;|Time|  ?t1, ?t2, ?t3)
  (Buy_Stock(?Symbol, ?Amount1, ?Broker, ?Broker) at ?t1) ⟶
  (Buy_Stock(?Symbol, ?Amount2, ?Broker, ?Customer) at ?t2) ⟶
  (Sell_Stock(?Symbol, ?Amount1, ?Broker, ?Broker) at ?t3) where ?t3 – ?t1 < 5 mins
  ⇒
  Satisfied = false;
  generate Buy_ahead(?Symbol, ?Amount1, ?Broker,  start is ?t1,  end is ?t2);

// rule 2 to determine if the constraint is satisfied when the execution terminates.
Terminated(...) ⇒ if Satisfied  generate Satisfied(...);
}
```

This constraint monitors executions of the MarketTransactionsType. Its purpose is to *detect* a particular pattern of events, in which a broker buys stock for its own account ahead of placing a customer's buy order for the same stock, and then quickly sells the stock from its own account. It reports violations in Buy_ahead events.

Obviously, many variations of the pattern can be considered as indicating possible suspicious activity. For example, the causal relation could be replaced by "∼" together with timing bounds requiring the events to happen close together. Also, the pattern could include more events, such as the customer's placing an order before the broker buys for itself.

Always Constraints

We can construct an EPA to check for an **always** constraint by using the following paradigm—it is more complicated than the **never** case.

Suppose we want **always** P to be satisfied in execution I. We will need an event store—say, a SetofEvents object. Let's call it Set. It must have common set methods—for example, we must be able to Put events into Set and Remove events from Set. In fact, we will need to Put and Remove events of any event type in the execution type I if they can contribute to matching the pattern P. Suppose A1, A2, ... An are the types of events that may contribute to matching P.

Example 3: *Template for checking **always** constraints*

```
constraint AlwaysChecker in I out VS {
// Object to store and remove events.
SetofEvents Set;
// rules to store each type of event that may match P.
A1(...) ⇒  Set.Store(A1(...));
A2(...) ⇒  Set.Store(A2(...));
     ...
An(...) ⇒  Set.Store(An(...));
// rule to detect  when instances of the constraint are satisfied.
P ⇒  Set.Remove(A1(...)); Set.Remove(A2(...)); ...  Set.Remove(An(...));
 // rule to determine if the constraint is  satisfied when the execution terminates.
Terminated(...) ⇒  if Set.Empty  generate Satisfied(...);
                else  generate Violated(Set);
}
```

This example assumes that Set.Remove(E) returns nicely (does not crash) even when the event E isn't a member of Set. So the parameters "..." must distinguish the events matching P uniquely from other events of the same type. For example, events that together form an instance of P may contain the same unique identifer signifying a transaction that they are part of. This would distinguish them from events in other instances of P.

Depending upon the actual pattern P, we can often improve upon this template to make the checker more efficient.

As an example, suppose the input execution consists of Send, Acknowledge, and Abort events, and we want to check that a Send always causes an Acknowledge.

Example 4: *A Send always causes an Acknowledge.*

```
constraint AlwaysChecker in I out VS {
// Object to store and remove events.
SetofEvents Set;
// rule to store incoming Send events.
Send(...) ⇒ Set.Store(Send(...));
// rule to detect when instances of the constraint are satisfied.
Send(...) ⟶ Acknowledge(...) ⇒ Set.Remove(Send(...));
// rule to determine if the constraint is satisfied when the execution terminates.
Terminated(...) ⇒ if Set.Empty   generate Satisfied(...);
                      else   generate Violated(Set);
}
```

This **always** checker works as follows. Whenever a Send event arrives, the first rule stores it together with its data in the Set object. The same Send event will also match the first part of the trigger of the second rule. When a matching Acknowledge arrives, rule 2 triggers and removes the Send event from the SetofEvents. Be aware that this implementation strategy depends upon *orderly observation* of events. Since the Send causes the Acknowledge, it must be received first by the EPA. So it is already stored in the Set. If and when the input execution terminates, the third rule checks to see if there are any remaining Send events. If not, the constraint is satisfied. But if there are, the constraint is violated, and rule 3 generates an event containing the set of unmatched Sends.

A couple of remarks about checking **always** constraints are worth making now. First, the pattern of our example constraint is very simple (Send ⟶ Acknowledge), so the EPA only has to store the Send events in its input. If the constraint has a more complicated pattern, we may have to store more types of events, especially when the events are not causally related so that their order of arrival is not guaranteed by orderly observation. This more general case is shown in the generic template for **always** constraints.

Second, if the input execution terminates and the constraint has been violated, the state of the EPA contains those events that were part of the violations. Our example passes these events in an event to notify that the constraint has been violated. They are very important, and in many cases we will want to submit them to other EPAs to analyze them and find out why the violations happened. But what if there are violations *and* the execution doesn't terminate? How do we know that an event is part of a violation then? Later on, we will discuss a small addition to EPAs to make it easy to pass on the events contributing to violations.

Third, efficiency considerations usually impose restrictions on the **always** checker. For example, the checking may terminate on a timer event rather than termination of the input execution.

State Constraints

The paradigm for checking **state** constraints is deceptively simple—the devil's in the details. Suppose that every time a pattern, P, happens we want to check that a database, D, satisfies a condition, DataTest.

```
constraint StateChecker in I out VS {
boolean Satisfied is true;
// rule 1 to check the data when the pattern occurs.
  P ⇒ if not D.DataTest(...) Satisfied = false;
                            generate Violation(...);
// rule 2 to check if the constraint is satisfied when the execution terminates.
Terminated(...) ⇒ if Satisfied   generate Satisfied(...);
}
```

Normally, there are references to clock readings in the pattern and in the DataTest to specify time bounds between the time the pattern P matches and when the database D must satisfy the test.

These kinds of constraints, where a pattern match triggers a test on state, can be viewed either as constraining the state *or* the triggering events.

- **state** constraint: Whenever P matches, D is tested.
- **never** constraint: P must never happen unless D satisfies the test.

Whichever view we take is a matter of intention. If we want to constrain the state, we make the test on the state in the body of the rule—after it has triggered. But if we intend to constrain the events, we use a **where** clause in the triggering pattern of the rule. For example,

```
// alternate rule 1 to constrain events.
    P where not D.DataTest(...) ⇒ Satisfied = false;
                                  generate Violation(...);
```

The next example is a **state** constraint to check that whenever a customer sends an order to a broker, the customer's account is active.

Example 5: *Constraining a broker's customers to have active accounts*

```
constraint DetectInactiveCustomers in MarketTransactionsType out PolicyType {
boolean Satisfied is true;
 (String ?TradeId, ?Symbol, ?Broker, ?Customer;
  Integer ?Amount; TradeKind ?Kind; Time ?T)
  Order(?TradeId, ?Symbol, ?Amount, ?Kind, ?Broker, ?Customer) at ?T
⇒
if not DataBase.Account(?Customer).Active
     Satisfied = false;
       generate Notify(Policy_Manager, "Account Alert", ?Customer, ?TradeId, ?T);
Terminated(...) ⇒ if Satisfied  generate Satisfied(...);
}
```

This is a **state** constraint on the database of customer accounts. Its intention is to check whenever a customer submits an Order to a broker that the customer has an active account in the broker's DataBase.

It works using one rule that triggers on Order events. Each time the rule triggers, its body checks the DataBase record of the customer's account—the customer's Id is a parameter of the Order event. If the account is not active, it generates a warning event with trade and time information.

9.7   Other Classes of EPAs

Event processing agents do not always fall into pure CEP categories, such as filters, maps, and constraints. There are agents that perform specialized tasks, such as merging event executions. Other kinds of agents, particularly those dealing with input to and output from CEP applications often need to be programmed as opposed to being specified by reactive behavior rules. Two of the most essential kinds of programmed EPAs are *adapters* and *indicators*.

One of the issues with programmed EPAs is the need to use them in EPNs. This is discussed in more detail in Chapter 10. Configuration tools utilize EPA class interfaces to aid in composing EPNs. So we need to be able to supply partial class interfaces for programmed EPAs that enable them to be connected to other EPAs in an EPN. A *partial* class interface has only some of the elements of an EPA class interface. For example, a partial interface may define the input or output actions only, or it may also define the constraints for the class of EPAs but omit the behavior rules.

Adapters are event proccessing agents whose task is adapting event executions to an event format needed by CEP applications, or conversely. Adapters are essential to configuring a CEP application to run on a given IT layer or event input. A class interface for an input adapter specifies the output event types. This enables configuraton tools to determine correct connection of the outputs of an adapter to inputs of other agents, such as filters. The interface for an output adapter that converts CEP event formats from EPAs to an external format specifies its input event types.

Indicators are event-driven agents that communicate the results of CEP applications to the external world. Indicators are output agents. They include several classes of event-driven agents. There are *visualizers* that present graphical views of their event inputs. Visualizers are essential in communicating the results of CEP applications to human users. Then there are various classes of warning agents called *monitors* whose job is to send alerts, warnings, or control events to the outside world. A class interface for an indicator specifies its types of input events. This enables configuraton tools to determine correct connection of the outputs of EPAs, such as maps, to the inputs of an indicator.

9.8 Summary

This chapter has outlined a language for specifying classes of event processing agents. CEP agent classes are specified by interfaces that declare

- **in** and **out** actions that define types of events
- Local state variables
- Behavior rules and constraints expressed in an event pattern language

An EPA is an object of a class. This is essentially an object-oriented language design. Thus CEP agents can be built in any language that allows, or can be extended to allow, these interface features. Obvious candidates are Java and C#.[5]

CEP agent classes can be constructed to perform many tasks in the event-driven world, from intrusion detection at the network level to controlling or viewing business processes at the strategic planning level.

Agents, and architectures of agents (see Chapter 10), can be run on event executions if we have an interpreter for the rules language. This provides a capability for simulation of EPAs and EPNs, as discussed in Chapter 4.

---

[5]Web search on "Java programming language" and "Microsoft .NET C#."

In fact, an interpreter may be sufficient for some real-time CEP applications. But generally, a compiler for an EPN language is needed together with underlying systems support for event processing. The RAPIDE event-based CEP system is an example of an early prototype system.[6] The technology to build support systems for CEP is rapidly emerging—for example, in the middleware, .NET, and Java worlds—and is discussed in Chapter 15.

---

[6]Web search on "Rapide simulation language."

Chapter $\boxed{10}$

Event Processing Networks

- *Common structures of event processing networks*
- *Rules for connecting agents*
- *Causal semantics of connections*
- *Rules for connecting dynamic EPNs*
- *Architecture classes*
- *Layered architectures—treating EPNs as agents*
- *Case study: viewing network-level activity*

This chapter presents simple language features for connecting EPAs to form *event processing networks* (EPNs). EPNs can be represented graphically as networks consisting of EPAs at the nodes and communication between the EPAs by means of events flowing on the network paths between the nodes. EPNs are examples of interface communication architectures, discussed in Chapter 4. Each EPA is an interface in a communication architecture. Each network path represents an event-triggered rule, called a *connection*, that transports events between EPAs.

The connection rules presented here are based on the RAPIDE architecture definition language. The presentation is informal and intended to illustrate the use of event pattern rules to define flexible, dynamic EPNs.

An EPN allows us to employ a network of communicating lightweight rules engines to build an application of CEP. The alternative to an EPN is a *rules engine*. A rules engine is a heavyweight EPA, containing all the rules for an application of CEP. Each alternative has some advantages over the other. The choice that will work best depends upon the target system and the particular application of CEP. EPNs give us a strategy for optimizing our use of rules and for breaking down complex event processing problems into simple steps. Rules engines, on the other hand, can optimize pattern matching on large sets of rules.

10.1   Common Structures of EPNs

To construct an EPN, we must link filters, maps, and constraints so that the output from one agent is the input to another agent. The agents communicate with one another by sending their output events along links to other agents. Figure 10.1 shows a typical EPN structure. Communication links must satisfy correctness rules. The process of correctly linking agents in a communication architecture is called *composition*.

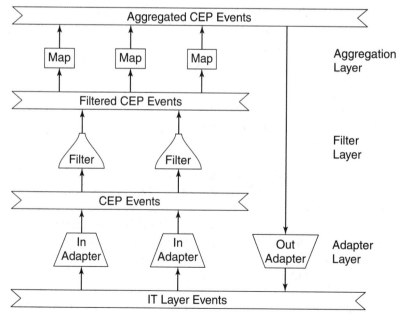

Figure 10.1: A conceptual view of deploying networks of EPAs

Some of the principal reasons to build EPNs are these.

- *Efficient event analysis.* The message traffic in a target system often contains large numbers of events that are irrelevant to the specific CEP application. For example, suppose we are monitoring a trading system to see if brokers are abiding by a set of business rules. All messages not concerned with trading are irrelevant and should be filtered out of the processing. This must be done as early as possible to prevent them from being used in attempts to match rule triggers, which wastes time.

  - Matching attempts, even failed ones, take time.
  - Events that are irrelevant to a CEP application can contribute to matching rules in that application. This can lead to lots of partial instances of triggers waiting for events to complete their match. The number of patterns to be matched grows to include partial matches that will never lead to a successful match.
  - Rules are simpler to write because they can assume the set of events has been filtered.

  Figure 10.1 shows how an EPN is structured to deal with events that are irrelevant to its purpose. At the adapter layer, events are being monitored from the IT layer and adapted to CEP format. The next layer of EPAs is filters that eliminate irrelevant events from any further processing. These are lightweight, fast EPAs—typically action name filters, as discussed in Section 9.4—designed to deal with large event throughput.

  The filtered events are passed on to a layer of maps and constraints that apply the rules involved in the CEP application—for example, monitoring event traffic for conformance to business policies.

  A rules engine would probably not organize its rules in this way—filters before maps and constraints. It puts the pattern triggers of rules in a tree structure. The pattern triggers are organized in tree structures according to similarities between the patterns so that if an event fails to match one pattern, further attempts to match patterns lower down that branch can be terminated. Ordering algorithms are designed to treat all patterns equally, their goal begin to reduce the number of matching attempts that cannot succeed. So filtering cannot be applied.

- *Global monitoring of distributed systems.* A CEP application may have to deal with events that are widely distributed across a large system. In this case, there are many monitoring points on the IT layer. The EPN must be structured to *merge* executions from various sources to present a coherent global view of system activity.

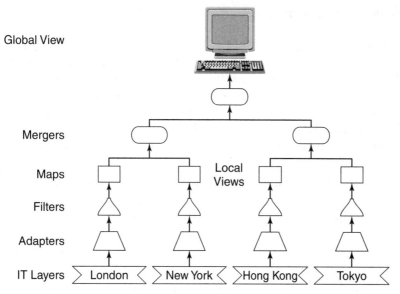

Figure 10.2: Structure of an EPN for a global view from
multiple locations

Figure 10.2 shows an example. The CEP applicaton must deliver a
view of system activity across the entire system. Examples of views
might be

- A view of distributed intrusions attempts that are in progress
- A statistical view of categories of IT traffic (e-mail, Web access,
  Telnet, and so on) in a large enterprise with multiple gateways to
  the Internet
- A global view of the progress of a logistics trip plan, incorporating
  events from each stage of the plan

In Figure 10.2 there are four monitoring sites where events are input
and adapted. Each site has a local CEP filtering and mapping network
that builds the local view. Different copies of the same type of view
from the local sites are merged. The oval-shaped EPAs represent
merger agents. Merger agents are maps that accept the same type of
event executions on multiple inputs and merge them into a single
execution of the same type as the inputs.

- *Implementation of abstraction hierarchies.* Applications of CEP can be
  constructed to deliver personalized system viewing (see Section 7.4).

    Several different views of the same event execution are constructed
by an EPN. This is achieved by implementing an event abstraction
hierarchy that specifies the views. We might expect, for example, to

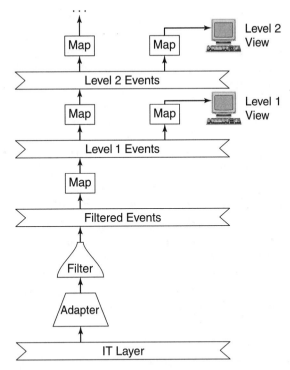

Figure 10.3: Structure of an EPN for multilevel viewing

deliver concurrently network management views, business-level views, and corporate-level strategic planning views.

A typical structure is shown in Figure 10.3. It consists of a sequence of filters and maps to construct the events corresponding to each abstraction layer, building more complex events from the simplest layer of IT events. Maps construct the views at each level. So in Figure 10.3, there is a map to aggregate filtered IT layer events to level 1 events. Level 2 events are aggregated from level 1 by one map, while another map is used to present a view of the level 1 events. A similar structure is shown at level 2.

10.1.1 Flexibility of Event Processing Networks

There are many other advantages to building EPNs.

- Agents can be reused easily. We may want to use generic EPAs from an event processing library, but there may not be a set of EPAs in the library that does exactly what we want. The easiest way to achieve our goals may be to build a network containing both library agents and some special agents for our purpose.

- EPNs can be composed dynamically. New agents can be linked into a network or existing agents cut out of a network on the fly, while the network is operating. The links between agents in a network can also be changed dynamically.

- CEP can be achieved in small steps. It is often more efficient to do complex event processing in small steps, using simple event patterns at each step, rather than to use complex patterns to do processing in big steps. To do small-step processing, we have to build an agent for each step and compose the agents to communicate the results of one step to the next. That leads to a network of agents.

- EPNs can be used for postmortem, or offline, CEP applications too. Offline EPAs can be heavyweight. Their patterns can be more complex, as would be needed in searching for complicated behavior. Offline we can afford the time to do complex pattern matching. So we expect that offline EPNs will be used to do postmortem analysis—say, looking for trends or patterns in large event executions.

10.2   Connecting Event Processing Agents

This section presents event pattern rules called *connections* for connecting EPAs to form an EPN. Connections are similar to reactive event pattern rules, described in Section 9.2. Connections use basic event patterns (see Section 8.5) and guards (see Section 8.8) to define communication of events between EPAs. Connections define causal relationships between the events that trigger them and the events they create.

10.2.1   Basic Connections

Basic connections connect **out** actions of EPAs to **in** actions of EPAs. They define causal relationships between output events and input events communicated between connected EPAs. A simple syntax is

> *sequential connection:*
> **connect**
> (*variable_declarations*)
> EPA1.out_Action(*parameters*) => EPA2.in_Action(*parameters*);
>
> *parallel connection:*
> **connect**
> (*variable_declarations*)
> EPA1.out_Action(*parameters*) ||> EPA2.in_Action(*parameters*);

EPA1 and EPA2 are names of agents, out_Action is the name of an **out** action of EPA1, and in_Action is the name of an **in** action of EPA2. A basic connection has a left side and a right side, both of which are basic patterns that match single events (see Section 8.5). EPA1 . out_Action (*parameters*) is the left side, and EPA2 . in_Action (*parameters*) is the right side.

The placeholders in both patterns must be declared in the variable declarations. All variables in the right-side pattern must also be in the left-side pattern so that any match of the left side results in an instance of the right side.

Semantics of Basic Connections

A basic *sequential* connection has similar semantics to a sequential event pattern rule (see Section 9.2.4). The events created by EPA1 are processed one at a time in their order of creation to see if they trigger the connection. If EPA1 creates an **out** event of type out_Action that matches the left side of the connection, the connection is triggered. The match results in placeholder bindings for all the placeholders in the right-side pattern. These bindings are substituted into the right-side pattern. The result is an event of type in_Action that is input to EPA2.

The triggering event from EPA1 *causes* the event input to EPA2. And all events input to EPA2 are causally ordered in a linear sequence. So the connection acts like a wire transporting signals. There is no overtaking. The triggering output events and resulting input events have a causal structure, shown earlier for reactive rules in Figure 6.3.

A basic *parallel* connection differs in that all the events it creates for input to EPA2 are causally independent of one another, as shown in Figure 6.4 (unless they cause events that trigger the connection).

Any two connection rules are independent. Therefore, events created by different rules are independent unless one of them caused an event that triggered the other rule.

These kinds of basic connections allows us to define *static* EPN architectures in which the numbers of EPAs are fixed so that they can be named.

Example 1: *A basic event pattern connection*

```
class Button
    in    action Press();
    out action Move(), Release();
    {Press => generate Move();
                generate Release() after 0.1 sec;
    };
```

```
class Sensor
    in   action Activate(), DeActivate();
    out action Light(enum {On, Off} X);
    {Activate  =>      generate Light(On);
    DeActivate =>      generate Light(Off);
    };

      Button   A_Button;
      Sensor   A_Sensor;
connect
      A_Button.Move    => A_Sensor.Activate;
      A_Button.Release => A_Sensor.DeActivate;
```

The example uses the EPA classes shown in Section 9.3 to declare two EPAs, A_Button and A_Sensor. There are two basic connections between the EPAs, as shown in Figure 10.4.

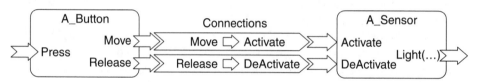

Figure 10.4: Basic connections between A_Button and A_Sensor

The first one is between the **out** action Move of A_Button and the **in** action Activate of A_Sensor. As a consequence, each Move event created by A_Button causes an Activate event to be input to A_Sensor. Because the connection is sequential, all the Activate events are causally related in a linear sequence. The second connection, also linear, connects the Release and DeActivate actions.

10.2.2   Guarded Connections

A content-based connection is a basic connection between two EPAs that depends upon the data in the **out** events. Each time an **out** event is created by one EPA that matches the left side of the connection, the data in the **out** event must satisfy a test before the connection inputs the matching **in** event to the other EPA. The test is called a *guard*.

```
connect
(variable_declarations)
  EPA1.out_Action(parameters) where C(parameters) =>
  EPA2.in_Action(parameters);
(variable_declarations)
  EPA1.out_Action(parameters) where C(parameters) ||>
  EPA2.in_Action(parameters);
```

The semantics of guarded basic connections is the same as for basic connections except that the connection triggers only when the guard, C, is true. C can test the parameters of an **out_Action** event. So whether or not the connection is made depends upon the contents of the triggering event.

Basic connections can also depend upon context. Here is a simple example.

Example 1: *Context-based basic connections*

```
Button[] Buttons = new Button[10];
Sensor   Up_Sensor;
Sensor   DownSensor;
connect
(Int ?Lvl)Buttons[?Lvl].Move where CurrentFloor > ?Lvl =>
                                   Down_Sensor.Activate;
(Int ?Lvl)Buttons[?Lvl].Move where CurrentFloor < ?Lvl =>
                                   Up_Sensor.Activate;
```

We have an array of ten buttons and two sensors, Up_Sensor and Down_Sensor. And we assume the buttons are part of an elevator. The function CurrentFloor returns the floor the elevator is currently at, which gives us a way to test the context of the elevator. Whenever a button creates a Move event, the context test determines whether the result is an Activate event input to the Up_Sensor or to the Down_Sensor.

10.2.3 Multiple Basic Connections

A multiple basic connection is simply a shorthand notation for several basic connections with the same trigger. As a convenience, we can write one rule with the basic event pattern trigger and a sequence of basic event patterns on the right side.

So, for example:

```
Button.Move ||> Sensor_1.Active;
Button.Move ||> Sensor_2.Active;
```

can be written as

$$\text{Button.Move} \;||> \text{Sensor\_1.Active,}$$
$$\text{Sensor\_2.Active;}$$

In general, the right side of a multiple connection can be a sequence of basic event patterns and also calls to functions and methods of objects local to the state of the architecture to which the connection belongs. An example is given in Section 10.5.

A second kind of multiple connection deals with connecting EPAs that output and input several actions. It is convenient to connect them with one rule rather than to connect each pair of **out** and **in** actions.

We can connect two agents, A and B, so that the output of A is the input to B by writing either

> **connect**   A.**out** => B.**in** ;

or

> **connect**   A.**out** ||> B.**in** ;

provided that the output execution type of A is the same as, or is a subtype of, the input execution type of B.

These kinds of multiple basic connections are equivalent to a set of basic connections that connect each **out** action of A to the **in** action of B with the same action name. The provision ensures that every event type in the input of B is output by A. So, B gets all the inputs it is designed to process.

10.3   Dynamic Event Processing Networks

An EPN is *dynamic* if the number of agents can vary at runtime and the connections between them can depend upon runtime tests. Building dynamic networks requires more flexible kinds of connection rules and rules that allow creation and termination of agents.

10.3.1   Class Connections

One kind of dynamic connection is basic connections that can have variables whose types are the EPA classes that are connected.

```
connect
Class1 ?EPA1, Class2 ?EPA2;
(variable_declarations)
 ?EPA1.out_Action(parameters) => ?EPA2.in_Action(parameters);
```

```
connect
Class1 ?EPA1, Class2 ?EPA2;
(variable_declarations)
   ?EPA1.out_Action(parameters) ||> ?EPA2.in_Action(parameters);
```

These are multiway connections from all agents of Class1 to all agents of Class2. If any EPA of Class1 creates an out_Action event that matches the left-side pattern, then, as before, the placeholder bindings of the action parameters are substituted for the action parameters of the right-side pattern, and the resulting event is input to *all* EPAs of Class2.

The events created by a sequential connection ($=>$) on any triggering are causally ordered in a sequence and are causally dependent upon the events created on previous triggerings. The events created by a parallel connection ($|| >$), on the other hand, are independent of one another unless they cause other events that trigger the connection.

Multiway connections, together with creation and termination rules, enable construction of dynamic EPN architectures that connect varying numbers of EPAs of type Class1 to varying numbers of EPAs of type Class2. The numbers of EPAs can vary during the operation of the EPN.

The semantics of dynamic connections is nondeterministic. One case of nondeterminism is when the EPAs they connect can be created or terminated on the fly. Therefore, the concept of *inputting* an event is dependent upon the timing of two separate activities: the triggering of the connection that creates an event to be input, and the creation or abortion of an EPA whose type is the input class of the connection.

Another case of nondeterminism is a fan-in connection, from several outputs to one EPA's input. If output events are simultaneous, the order in which the resulting input events are input is nondeterministic.

The definition of this semantics can be deferred to the implementor of the EPN language as being "implementation dependent," or it can be given a precise definition. Details are beyond the scope of our discussion here. In RAPIDE the runtime execution is multithreaded, and the semantics of inputting events created by connections in the nondeterministic situations we have described is not specified but may vary at runtime.

10.3.2 Creation and Termination Rules

A new agent of a class may be created by a creation rule. Creation rules are event-triggered rules. Typically, an EPN invokes a creation rule when it needs to configure itself to deal with a runtime situation such as increased demand for its processing.

```
connect
(variable_declarations)
    <complex_event_pattern> => new Class(parameters);
```

```
connect
(variable_declarations)
    <complex_event_pattern> ||> new Class(parameters);
```

Semantics of Creation Rules

When a creation rule is triggered, a **new** statement on the right side of the rule is executed. A new agent belonging to the class on the right side of the rule is configured, and a Start event is created with that agent's Id as a data element. The Start event is caused by the events that triggered the rule. A sequential creation rule implies that all the start events are causally related in a sequence, whereas a parallel creation rule implies that they are all causally independent. **new** statements have semantics similar to creation methods in languages like Java.

Similar rules can terminate an agent by using the keyword **terminate** followed by the name of, or reference to, the EPA.

10.3.3   Connection Generators

Class connections are one kind of connection rule that effectively connect many EPAs. However, in CEP applications with large numbers of EPAs, connections may need to be more structured than multiway. For example, CEP allows declaration of structures whose components are EPAs—say, an array of EPAs. It may be necessary to connect the corresponding components of two arrays—first EPA to first EPA, second EPA to second EPA, and so on.

Iterative programming statements such as **while** and **for** loops, can be used to generate sets of **connect** rules to create multiple connections. To do this, we need connection rule templates that are parameterized by the loop variable. The body of a loop statement is a **generate** statement whose body is a set of connection rule templates. On each iteration of the loop, the connection rules are created that are instances of the templates with the current value of the loop variable.

Rather than give a complete syntax for iterative creation of connections, we give some examples.

Example 1: *Generating a set of basic connections*

```
Int Count = 50;
Button[ ] Buttons = new Button[Count];
Sensor[ ] Sensors = new Sensor[Count];
```

```
connect
    for (Int I = 0; I < Count; I++)
        generate {
            Buttons[I].Move    => Sensors[I].Activate;
            Buttons[I].Release => Sensors[I].DeActivate;
        }
```

This example uses the EPA classes Button and Sensor, shown in Sections 9.3 and 10.2.1. Buttons is an array of 50 EPAs of class Button, and Sensors is a similar array of 50 Sensor EPAs.

The connection generator is a **for** loop containing a **generate** statement. Each iteration of the **for** loop executes a **generate** statement. The body of the **generate** in this example is a set of two connection rule templates with the loop variable, I, used to select an EPA component of the arrays. To execute the **generate**, first the current value of I is substituted in the templates. This results in two connection rules, which are then created.

Each instance of the first template is a connection rule that connects the **out** action Move of the Ith Button to the **in** action Activate of the Ith Sensor. Similarly, the Release **out** action of the Ith Button is connected to the DeActivate **in** action of the Ith Sensor.

The connections between each pair of Button and Sensor EPAs are independent of the connections between any other pair, as shown in Figure 10.5. So the result of the connection gnerator is an EPN with a parallel communication structure consisting of pairs of connected Buttons and Sensors.

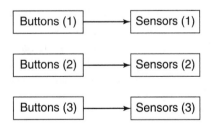

Figure 10.5: **One-to-one connection architecture**

Example 2: *Fan-in: a many-to-one connection*

```
connect
        (Button ?X)?X.Move ||> Sensors[1].Activate;
```

This is an example of a single many-to-one connection with a class variable. Because ?X can match any Button, any Move event created by a

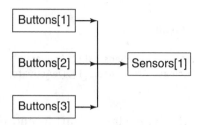

Figure 10.6: Fan-in connection architecture

Button EPA triggers the connection and results in an Activate event being input to Sensors[1]. This architecture is depicted in Figure 10.6.

An Activate event is caused by the Move event that triggered the connection. Simultaneous Move events result in each one triggering the connection, one at a time, in an unspecified order. Because the connection is parallel ($\| >$), all the Activate events it creates are independent of each other.

Example 3: *Fan-out: a one-to-many connection*

```
connect
        Buttons[ 1 ].Move  ||>
            for(Int I =  0;  I < Count;  I++)
                generate  Sensors[ I ].Activate;
```

In this example, the iterative connection results in 50 basic connection rules. This architecture is shown in Figure 10.7. A single Move action is connected by these basic connections to 50 Activate actions. Each Move event created by Buttons[1] triggers all the 50 basic connections, causing 50 Activate events. Each connection rule executes independently of any other.

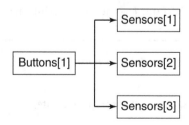

Figure 10.7: Fan-out connection architecture

Therefore, all the Activate events caused by a Move are independent of each other. Further, because the connections are parallel ($\| >$), Activates caused by different Move events are also independent.

Building large-scale architectures of EPAs requires practical ways of organizing both large numbers of EPAs and large numbers of connections. The class concept found in all object-oriented languages, going back to Simula67 [20], helps with organizing EPAs. Classes give us a way to classify EPAs into separate types and to relate them by subtypes.

Attempts are made in hardware simulation languages such as VHDL [8] to provide constructs for defining large numbers of connections in static architectures by means of iterative connection declarations. Connections in dynamic architectures were first tackled in RAPIDE, which has both the event pattern–triggered and iterative connections presented here.[1]

However, the number of connections between a single pair of EPAs can also be large. For example, suppose the EPAs are communicating by a protocol that has several stages, with different events being sent back and forth at each stage. An **out** action (say, A) in one EPA would allow an event to be sent. The same action would be an **in** action A in the other EPA to enable it to receive that type of event. Conversely, the next stage of the protocol would require an event of type B to go back the other way, leading to two more paired **in**, **out** actions, B. To deal with connections like this, the class interfaces can be structured into *dual* sets of actions, where each **out** action in one set is an **in** action in the dual set, and conversely. Connections between dual sets of actions in two EPAs can be made by a single *action set connection*. RAPIDE contains a concept of action set connection for this purpose.

10.4 Architectures and Event Processing Networks

An *architecture class* is a class of EPAs that encapsulate an EPN. The idea is to be able to treat a network of EPAs as just another EPA. This gives us a way to construct layered architectures such as described in Section 4.6. The visibility and connection rules of architecture classes enforce the abstraction principle for layered architectures.

---

[1] Web site: http://pavg.stanford.edu/rapide/

10.4.1   Architecture Classes

A class interface using the keyword **architecture** contains an EPN in place
of the behavior rules of a class of EPAs. The syntax is

architecture   *EPA_Class_Name* **in**   *input_execution_type* **out**   *output_execution_type*
       {
           list of declarations
           list of event pattern constraints
         connect
           list of connection rules
       }

Execution types are sets of action declarations, discussed in Section 8.3.4.
As in the declaration of EPA classes, the input and output execution types
can be names of execution types lists of **in** and **out** actions. The list of declarations in the architecture class interface can contain types, functions, classes
of EPA's, individual EPA's, and other types of objects. Instead of the behavior rules, an architecture class interface has connection rules. Connections in
the list of connection rules can only connect actions of EPAs declared locally
or actions declared in the architecture class interface. Guards in connections
are restricted to the types, functions, objects, and variables declared locally
(see Section 9.2.3).

Connections can either connect **out** actions of EPAs to **in** actions of
EPAs or connect **in** actions of the architecture class interface to **in** actions
of EPAs and **out** actions of EPAs to **out** actions of the class interface.
Figure 10.8 shows an EPN encapsulated as an architecture class. The connections are from the **in** actions of the class interface to **in** actions of EPAs
in the EPN, between EPAs in the EPN, and from **out** actions of EPAs to
out actions of the interface.

10.4.2   Semantics of Architecture Classes

An architecture class encapsulates an EPN. It specifies a class of EPAs.
The behavior of EPAs of the class is defined by the behavior of the EPN.
The EPN plays the same role as reactive behavior rules in class interfaces.
When an EPA of the architecture class (A, say) is declared, its declaration
implies the creation of a new set of all the EPAs in the EPN and their
connection rules. Creation of A implies creation a copy of the EPN that
executes locally to A and takes its inputs from the inputs to A and creates
its outputs as outputs of A. A itself can be connected by its **in** and **out**
actions to a higher-level EPN.

Events input to A trigger connections that input events to some EPAs
in the local EPN. Some local EPAs of the EPN are connected to **out** actions

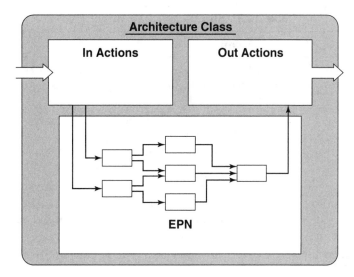

Figure 10.8: An architecture class encapsulating an EPN

of A. When those EPAs output events, connections to **out** actions of A are triggered and A consequently creates **out** events. The behavior of A must satisfy any event pattern constraints declared in A's architecture class interface.

When A terminates, all the local EPAs also terminate.

As shown in Figure 10.9, the visibility rules enforce that EPAs local to A can be connected only to each other or to A's **in** and **out** actions. This restriction on connections satisfies the abstraction principle of layered architectures in Section 4.6. The EPAs local to A communicate only through A's interface with an EPA in the architecture that A belongs to.

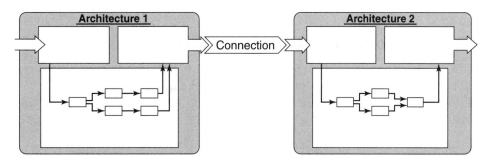

Figure 10.9: A layered architecture showing encapsulation
of lower-level EPNs

Table 10.1: Summary of Terminology

Terminology	Meaning
EPA	An event processing agent. An EPA is specified by an interface containing **in** and **out** actions, event pattern–triggered rules, and constraints.
Connection	An event pattern–triggered rule that communicates events between EPAs. A connection triggers on patterns of **out** events from EPAs and creates **in** events at other EPAs.
EPN	A network of EPAs that communicate over connections.
Architecture	An EPA that encapsulates an EPN. An architecture is specified by an interface containing **in** and **out** actions, constraints, and an EPN.
Layered architecture	An EPN containing EPAs that are architectures.

Layering and Plug-and-Play

Architecture classes provide a facility to build layered interface communication architectures (see Chapter 4) in which the interfaces are EPAs.

The semantics of connections between an architecture class interface and the EPN that is encapsulated by the class implies that plug-and-play techniques can be applied. For example, suppose we have two architecture classes, C1 and C2, encapsulating different EPNs N1 and N2. Suppose the interfaces of C1 and C2 are equivalent in the sense that they have the same sets of **in** actions and **out** actions and the same event pattern constraints. Suppose that an EPA of class C1 (A1, say) is connected as a component of a higher level EPN, N. Then A1 can be replaced by an EPA of class C2 (A2, say) without altering the behavior of N.

Table 10.1 summarizes the terminology of EPN's we have introduced so far.

10.5   Examples of EPNs and Architectures

This section contains some simple examples of EPNs and of architectures encapsulating EPNs. Other examples are in Section 10.6.

Example 1: *An EPN for checking timely message delivery*

```
// Execution type of Send and Acknowledge
typedef    execution {
```

```
            action  Send(Subject S; String Msg, String Id; Time T);
            action  Acknowledge(String Id; Time T)
    } SendAck;

// A Boolean message type
typedef  execution {
            action  Satisfy(String Id, Time T, Time T1);
            action  Violated(String Id, Time T, Time T1);
    } BooleanMsgType;

// a class of action name filters on network management executions
filter MessageAttempts in NetMngmt out SendAck {
        Send           =>  pass;
        Acknowledge    =>  pass;
}

// a class of constraints on message attempts
constraint MsgAttemptsCheck in SendAck out BooleanMsgType {
        Time ElapseLimit;
// rule 1.
    (Subject ?S; String ?M, String ?Id; Time ?T, Time ?T1)
        Send (?S, ?M, ?Id, ?T) ⟶ Acknowledge (?Id, ?T1)
        =>
            if ?T1 − ?T ≤ ElapseLimit then
                    generate Satisfy(?Id, ?T, ?T1);
            else    generate Violated(?Id, ?T, ?T1);

// rule 2
    (Event ?E, Subject ?S; String ?M, String ?Id; Time ?T, Time ?T1)
        Send (?S, ?M, ?Id, ?T) ~ ?E(Id is ?Id,  timestamp is ?T1)
        where  (?T1−?T) ≥ ElapseLimit =>
        generate Violated(?Id, ?T, ?T1);
}

// an EPN to monitor timeliness of message delivery
// agents
MessageAttempts NetFilter;
MsgAttemptsCheck Checker;

// A multiple connection between two agents
connect   NetFilter.out ||> Checker.in;
```

This example is a simple EPN consisting of two EPAs: a filter, NetFilter, that is connected to a constraint, Checker; see Figure 10.10.

NetFilter takes as input events of types Send, Acknowledge, Alert, Warning, and ConnectTime, which are the actions listed in the execution type, NetMngmt, shown in Section 8.3.4. NetFilter is an action name

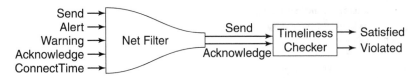

Figure 10.10: EPN for checking the timeliness of message delivery

filter. It filters out all the events except those with action names, Send and Acknowledge, which it passes to its output. These are the actions in SendAck.

The Checker EPA has SendAck as its input type. The connection between NetFilter and Checker is a multiple basic connection, as described in Section 10.2.3.

Checker has two rules. Rule 1 triggers on pairs of causally related events, Send$(\ldots) \longrightarrow$ Acknowledge$(\ldots)$, with the same Id data parameters indicating that they are events in a successful message tranmission. When it triggers, the rule first checks the time difference between the triggering Send and Acknowledge events. If they are within a bound, ElapseLimit, it generates a Satisfy event for the transmission Id. If not, it generates a Violated event to warn that the transmission took too long.

Rule 2 deals with attempted transmissions that may never complete. It triggers on a Send event and any other event with the same Id, either another Send or an Acknowledge whose timestamp differs from the Send event by more than the ElapseLimit bound. So whenever time goes beyond the time bound in which the transmission should have completed, rule 2 triggers and generates a Violated event for the transmission that the Send attempted.

Both rules may trigger on the same transmission attempts that do complete, but only if they exceed the time bound. In addition, rule 2 catches those attempts that exceed the time bound before an Acknowledge, including those that consist of many Sends and never terminate.

Example 2: *An architecture encapsulating the previous timeliness-checking EPN*

```
architecture SLAChecker in NetMngmt out BooleanMsgType {
    // SLAChecker encapsulates an EPN to monitor timeliness of message attempts.
    // agents
            MessageAttempts NetFilter;
            MsgAttemptsCheck Checker;
    // multiple connections between class interface actions and the two agents
        connect
            SLAChecker.in => NetFilter.in;
```

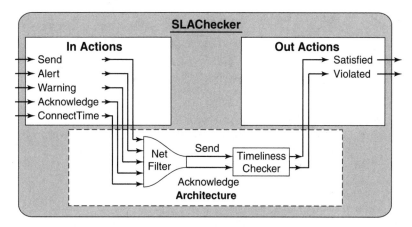

Figure 10.11: Architecture class encapsulating the EPN timeliness checker

```
NetFilter.out ||> Checker.in;
Checker.out    => SLAChecker.out;
}
```

SLAChecker (service-level agreement checker), shown in Figure 10.11, is an architecture class that encapsulates the EPN in the previous example. It defines a class of agents for checking the timeliness of message delivery. The input actions are Send, Alert, Warning, Acknowledge, and ConnectTime. Its output actions are Satisfied and Violated. The architecture uses a multiple connection to connect all the input actions from the class interface to the input actions with the same name of the filter agent. So, the first multiple connection in the example is equivalent to

```
connect
    SLAChecker.Send  => NetFilter.Send;
    SLAChecker.Alert  => NetFilter.Alert;
    SLAChecker.Warning  => NetFilter.Warning;
    SLAChecker.Acknowledge  => NetFilter.Acknowledge;
    SLAChecker.ConnectTime  => NetFilter.ConnectTime;
```

Similarly, the output actions of the Checker agent are connected to the output actions of the class interface. The third multiple connection in the example is equivalent to:

```
Checker.Satisfied   =>   SLAChecker.Satisfied;
Checker.Violated    =>   SLAChecker.Violated;
```

Example 3: *Simple air traffic control architecture*

```
class Aircraft
    in   action Enter(Aircraft NewId);
    in   action RadioReceive (Msg M);
```

```
      out action RadioTransmit (Msg M);
      out action RadarTransmit ();
 { Aircraft Id = Null;
   Clock C;
   (Aircraft ?NewId;) Enter(?NewId) =>Id = ?NewId;
                                      C.Start;
                                      generate RadioTransmit(Startmsg);
   (Msg ?M, ?Msg M', Time ?T;) RadioReceive(?M) at ?T   =>
    generate RadioTransmit(?M') where RequiredResponse(?M, ?M') within ?T+5;
   C.Tick => generate RadarTransmit();
 };


class ControlCenter
      in   action RadioReceive (Msg M, Aircraft A);
      in   action RadarReceive(Aircraft A);
      out action RadioTransmit(Msg M, Aircraft A);
      out action GoodBye(Msg M, Aircraft A);
{DataBase ...
  (Msg ?M, ?Msg M', Aircraft ?Id) RadioReceive(?M, ?Id) =>
   generate RadioTransmit(?M', ?Id) where NextStep(DataBase, ?M, ?M');
  (Aircraft ?Id;)RadarReceive(?Id) => DataBase.Update(?Id);
  (Aircraft ?Id;) RadarReceive(?Id) where DataBase.FinalStep(?Id) ||>
                                generate Goodbye(OutMsg, ?Id);

};


architecture EnRouteSector
   in   action HandOn(Aircraft A);
   out action HandOff(Aircraft A);
{SetOf(Aircraft) Airspace;
   ControlCenter Center;
connect
  (Aircraft ?A;) HandOn(?A) ||> Airspace.Insert(?A);
                                ?A.Enter(?A);
  (Aircraft ?A, Msg ?M;) Center.Goodbye(?M, ?A)
     where Airspace.IsMember(?A) ||>
                                ?A.RadioReceive(?M);
                                HandOff(?A);
                                Airspace.Remove(?A);
  (Aircraft ?A, Msg ?M;) ?A.RadioTransmit(?M)
     where Airspace.IsMember(?A) ||>
                                Center.RadioReceive(?M, ?A);
  (Aircraft ?A, Msg ?M;) Center.RadioTransmit(?M, ?A)
     where Airspace.IsMember(?A) ||>
                                ?A.RadioReceive(?M);
  (Aircraft ?A, Msg ?M;) ?A.RadarTransmit()
     where Airspace.IsMember(?A) ||>
                                Center.RadarReceive(?A);

}
```

EnRouteSector is a dynamic architecture connecting two types of EPAs: a single ControlCenter, called Center, and arbitrary many Aircraft. The architecture uses multiple basic connections, described in Section 10.2.3, to shorten the number of rules.

This kind of architecture could be used in event-driven simulations of air traffic control protocols, in the early-stage of developing management process as described in Section 4.2. Aircraft and control centers are modeled here as simple agents that react to radio events and output both radio and radar events. Their internal states include clocks and databases, the details of which are omitted.

EnRouteSector communicates with other agents by an **in** action, HandOn, and an **out** action, HandOff. By means of these actions, it accepts references to aircraft or hands them off. As a result of HandOn and HandOff events, EnRouteSector may be handling varying numbers of aircraft at any time. The aircraft currently in the sector are stored in a set called Airspace. Figure 10.12 depicts the architecture encapsulated in an EnRoute-Sector class.

A HandOn event triggers a multiple connection that inserts the aircraft into Airspace and starts communication with that aircraft. An identity is sent to the aircraft by inputting an Enter event.

A HandOff event is created by a connection when the Center sends a Goodbye event to an aircraft. The aircraft is deleted from the Airspace.

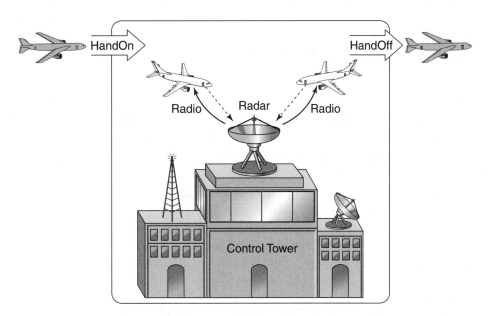

Figure 10.12: EnRouteSector architecture

Other connections trigger on radio and radar events and send radio events.

Remember that events are processed one at a time for triggering and executing connection rules, as described in Section 9.3.2. This applies both to events input to, or output from, an architecture EPA and to local events input to each EPA in the architecture. A consequence is that connection rules trigger and execute one at a time. So there is no concurrent access to local state such as Airspace. The order of execution is nondeterministic.

The EnRouteSector class imports the Aircraft and ControlCenter classes. Because these classes are not local to the EnRouteSector, and the connections use an Aircraft class variable, there is a possibility that its connection rules could trigger on an event from, or input an event to, an aircraft that is not in the local Airspace. This would violate the abstraction principle. In this situation, the connection rules should contain guards to ensure that the aircraft is a member of Airspace. As discussed in Section 9.2.3, this is to ensure that EnRouteSector conforms to the abstraction principle. For this reason, context guards that test membership in Airspace are included in the connection rule triggers.

10.6   Case Study: EPNs for Network Viewing

This section summarizes an actual experimental application of CEP to viewing a large university network (see Figure 10.13).[2] Simultaneous multiple viewing of network activity is a domain of applications where rapid composition of EPNs is a very powerful tool.

The network viewing domain has the following elements:

- Libraries of adapters for currently existing log file formats related to the myriads of commercial network products, including routers, intrusion detectors, and various network management tools.

- Libraries of filters and maps built in the course of developing viewing applications.

- Libraries of event-driven graphical meters for displaying abstract events in different formats and styles.

- A demand for a capability to rapidly reconfigure a running viewing application to provide a new view of network activity in response to a developing situation.

---

[2]The SUNet project, to apply CEP to the Stanford University Network

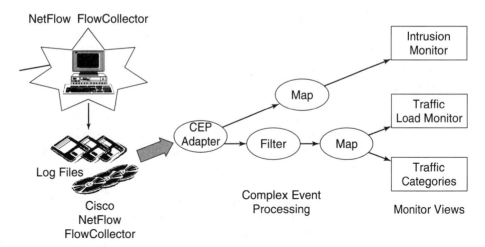

Figure 10.13: An EPN for viewing network traffic

A "developing situation" is when a viewing EPN detects an intrusion attempt in progress. A network manager would want to either reconfigure the EPN or set up a new EPN on the fly to track the activity of the target of the intrusion attempt and watch its activity closely. Another situation is a degredation in network performance. Again, a network manager would want to be able to configure an EPN to focus on just the subnet that is degrading, perhaps to correlate the storm of alerts arriving from various parts of the subnet.

The demand for rapid changes to EPNs leads to the need for tools that let us make and test changes quickly. These tools need to present EPAs and EPNs in graphical formats. Modifications to an EPN, such as, say, a change in connections or a change of EPAs, can be made graphically by drag-and-drop techniques. The type correctness of connections should be checked by the tool. In this study, a graphical EPN composition tool called RapNet was used.

Figure 10.13 depicts an EPN configured to monitor a network by taking input data from a commercial router. The router has an associated monitor of its own. The router's monitor produces log files that summarize the flows of packets through the router. Each log file covers a short time, usually one or two minutes. So the viewing EPN is running a minute or two behind the actual network activities.

Network managers were interested in several different views of the event traffic across the network. Interest depended upon each manager's job.

Security gurus, for example, want to monitor for various kinds of intrusion attempts. These included simple cases such as IP scans and port scans aimed at finding computers running versions of operating systems with known weaknesses. When a weak system is discovered, the next step in the intrusion is to exploit the weakness to gain access to that computer. There are commercial monitors that detect these kinds of scans. But they seldom detect slow scans designed to execute over several days or distributed scans designed to attack the network from different gateways.

Network managers are interested in detailed views of network traffic—for example, the top ten sources of Web traffic at a particular time of day, say, midnight; or the proportion of traffic that was local within the network as opposed to going out of the network, or coming from outside into local computers.

Figure 10.13 illustrates the CEP application. It was configured to provide simultaneously several different views of the same event execution. This was done by feeding the router log files to an EPN with branching paths consisting of filters, maps, and meters. A typical filter is shown in the following example.

The router's flow collectors could be configured to aggregate flows into log files in several formats. A CEP adapter breaks a router log file into several different types of CEP events—for example, Header, CallRecord, and DetailInterface—corresponding to the different log file formats. Each type of CEP event contains data such as the source and destination IP addresses, port numbers, and transport protocol related to a flow of packets. The set of these event types make up the execution type Sunet.[3] Examples of the forms of the log file events are discussed in Section 15.1, Example 2.

Example 1: *A typical filter*

```
filter StanfordSource in Sunet out Sunet {
  ( string ?sourceIP )
  CallRecord(srcaddr is ?sourceIP) where ((?sourceIP  =  "171.64.*")
          | (?sourceIP  =  "171.65.*") | (?sourceIP  =  "171. .66.*")
          | (?sourceIP  =  "171.67.*") | (?sourceIP  =  "36.*")
          | (?sourceIP  =  "172.16.*") | (?sourceIP  =  "172.17.*")) )
  => pass;
};
```

This is an example of one of many filters from the filter library. It is used to filter out flows of interest for a particular view. It simply processes the events from a CEP adapter and passes on the events from partic-

---

[3]Stanford University Network

ular subnets. The guard tests the source IP address. For example, any flow originating within the subnet 171.65.* is passed. Traffic from subnets not mentioned in the guard are filtered out.

Events from a filter are passed on to maps that are designed to supply a desired view. The following is an example of a simple map used to experiment with detecting IP address scans.

Example 2: *A map to detect suspicious IP address scans*

```
map multipleIP_noweb in Sunet out Forbidden {
// extensible arrays forming the local state.
    typedef array[string] of Int IPCountType;
    IPCountType IPCount = {default is 0};

    typedef array[string, string] of Int IPAccesstype;
      IPAccesstype IPAccess = {default is {default is 0} };
// behavior rule processing DetailInterface and CallRecord events.
    (String ?src; String ?dest; Int ?srcPort; Int ?destPort )
    DetailInterface( srcaddr is ?src, dstaddr is ?dest)
    or
    CallRecord(srcaddr is ?src, dstaddr is ?dest,
            srcPort is ?srcPort, destPort is ?destPort)
    => {
        if ( (?srcPort != 80) & (?destPort != 80) &
          ( IPAccess[?src, ?dest] ==  0 ))
          {
          IPAccess[?src, ?dest] = 1;
          IPCount[?src] = IPCount[?src] + 1;

          if (IPCount[?src] >= 10)
            {
            generate warning ( ?src, ?dest );
            }
          }
        }
      }
};
```

This map takes input events belonging to the types of Sunet and creates warning events of a type contained in the set of warning types called Forbidden. The forbidden event types could be displayed on a suitable graphical meter or sent to an EPA that outputs alerts.

The map uses a potentially large local state consisting of extensible arrays, IPCountType, and IPAccesstype to keep track of source IP addresses that are accessing different destination IP addresses. The time window is the one in which the EPN containing the map is operating.

CallRecord events signify a flow of packets between a source and a destination. If a flow is not related to port 80, which would indicate Web traffic, the source IP address is recorded as accessing the destination IP address. Once a source address has accessed more than ten different IP addresses in non-Web-related traffic, a warning event is created each time that source accesses a new IP address. The warning contains both the source and the destination.

Similar types of maps were constructed to track the volumes of different kinds of network traffic, such as e-mail, Web traffic, and Telnet. They also use extensible arrays in their local state. The lesson here is that detecting intrusions is not much different from viewing other aspects of the event traffic. Over time, libraries of EPAs were built to experiment with delivering the various views that were requested.

EPNs were constructed, as shown in Figure 10.13, that delivered both traffic information and intrusion attempt warnings from the same network router log files. Essentially, the EPNs were delivering simultaneously different views of network activity.

Another aspect of this application was the need to monitor activity on multiple routers. The target network contained multiple gateways to the Internet and between its various subnets. Global views across all routers were formed by merging the views of the activity on each router. EPNs were constructed to build a particular view for each gateway. These were instances of the same EPN architecture. Then a global view was developed using merger EPAs, as depicted in Figure 10.2.

This case study brought out several issues surrounding the construction of CEP applications. We discuss them briefly here in the context of this example.

10.6.1   Visual Tools for Constructing EPNs

One thing will have become apparent to the reader—the need for graphical support for constructing EPNs and architectures. It is very difficult with linear text, as shown in these examples, to quickly construct an EPN or an architecture or comprehend the flow of events in the communication structure of an architecture.

The EPNs in this study were constructed from the libraries of EPAs using a visual drag-and-drop tool. Different kinds of connections, such as described in Section 10.2, were represented by different kinds of visual links. A connection was made by drawing or placing the appropriate kind of link between the EPAs. For example, a link in the form of a single line from the output of one EPA to the input of another EPA had the semantics of a basic sequential connection (see Section 10.2.1). However, the visual tool implemented a link as a communication across a publish/subscribe middleware. Individual EPAs could operate either on the same machine or on separate machines. In either case, a communication link between EPAs entailed interposing an output adapter and an input adapter to convert CEP events to middleware messages on a unique subject, and conversely. This is depicted conceptually in Figure 10.1.

10.6.2 Security

To address security, communication across the middleware used the encryption capabilities provided by the middleware. However, the issue of how to protect an intrusion detection EPN from being attacked is a subject of ongoing research.

10.6.3 Scalability

Scalability is another ongoing research issue for network viewing. Another goal of the SUNet project was to determine if a prototype CEP implementation would scale to the task of event processing involved.

In this experimental application of CEP, the EPAs in the scan detection EPNs, running on a 400MHz processor, were processing events at rates of 1,000 events per second over time windows containing a million events. Remember, each CEP event from an adapter in these applications signifies a router flow that typically summarizes several hundred packets. It turns out that this rate of processing was sufficient to keep up in real time with the data generated in the router log files. In fact, it was found that the slowest EPAs in these applications were the event-driven graphical meters, which necessitated adding event caches to them.

Taking into account the prototype implementation of the pattern matching and event notification infrastructure, discussed in Chapter 15, these results were very encouraging.

10.7 Summary

This chapter presents techniques for constructing EPNs to implement CEP applications. An application is built as a network of communicating EPAs. Various kinds of connection rules allow us to compose sets of EPAs into communicating networks that perform the required tasks. EPNs can themselves be composed by first encapsulating them as architecture classes and then composing agents whose types are those architecture classes. In this way, we can build more complex applications from the EPNs that implement simpler applications. The architecture of a complex application is a layered interface communication architecture that we described in Chapter 4. An EPN is conceptually a single-level interface communication architecture, whereas the general concept of an architecture is multilevel.

We have outlined the language constructs for composing EPAs into communicating EPNs and for abstracting EPNs as EPA architecture classes. There are many options for providing the capabilities of these CEP constructs—for example, by implementing them on top of application servers, as discussed in Chapter 15, or as an extension of any modern computer language (Java, C#, and so on).

The connection and abstraction features presented in this chapter are simplified versions of architecture definition constructs in RAPIDE. In practical, scalable CEP applications, there is a need for connections between large sets of EPAs. A language of connections must provide succinct notation for large numbers of connections and for dynamic connections between varying numbers of EPAs. Further details can be found in the RAPIDE reference manuals.[4] Earlier examples of architecture connections for static hardware architectures are in hardware design languages such as VHDL [8].

Composition of EPNs must be supported by visual tools, especially because of the need for rapid configuration of EPNs to monitor new activities on a target network as they develop. There has been considerable development of various graphics-based composition tools—for example, for finite state machine systems, notably by David Harel et al., Statemate [6], and for business process systems, such as Microsoft BizTalk tools. Composition tools must enable real-time modification of a running EPN and the use of plug-and-play techniques. We ended this chapter with a short report on an actual research application of CEP to network viewing that was supported by a visual EPN composition tool called RapNet.[5]

Network management has traditionally been viewed as a rather low-level problem domain. It is commonly viewed as an entirely separate problem domain from, say, B2B process management. However, the truth is that network viewing and mangement has many aspects in common with strategic-level management domains in enterprise systems. For example, we expect that as the area of electronic B2B process collaboration develops, the B2B

---

[4]Web site: http://pavg.stanford.edu/rapide/
[5]Web site: http://pavg.stanford.edu/cep/

arena will share many of the problems and needs that are currently seen in network management. The domain of events will be abstract, higher-level events, but the detection and viewing problems will be similar. Therefore, a technology that can deal with the present and future problems of managing B2B-level processes should be powerful enough to be applicable to network-level management problems too.

Chapter 11

Causal Models and Causal Maps

- *Understanding systems*
- *What causal models are*
- *How to define causal models*
- *Building causal maps to make causality explicit*
- *Causal modeling as a process of continual improvement*

This chapter continues the discussion about causality that we began in Chapter 5. Perhaps we should start by rereading Section 5.7, particularly Example 3, *"Causality in inter-enterprise commerce."* Figure 5.5 depicts two causal models at the boundaries of two enterprises. The models are being used to add causal information to the transaction events that flow between the two enterprises.

This chapter introduces two concepts that are aimed at helping us use causal relationships between events. The first is the *causal model,* which is a set of rules that enable us to decide if events are causally related. The second is *causal map,* which is an EPA that adds genetic parameters to events. These genetic parameters implement the *causality* attribute of an event, a set of references to the events that caused that event. Causal maps *make causality explicit.* Causal models define causality and help us construct causal maps.

In this chapter, we discuss the kinds of rules that can be used in the causal models and how to construct a causal model for a system. We begin with a discussion of causality between events. Some of this repeats the discussion in Chapter 5 but goes further to discuss how the causal relationship between events is often dependent upon runtime conditions. The implication is that the rules for defining causality need to take runtime factors into account. Examples are given of both causal models and causal maps.

We phrase the discussion in terms of understanding a *system*. This is a general term that can mean any or all levels in an enterprise system, from the network up to a system of electronic business processes collaborating over the Internet.

11.1   Causality between Events, Revisited

Whenever we try to understand what is happening in a system we often find ourselves asking the question "What activities in this system led to the activity we are watching now?"

Examples of "interesting" activities and states that often get our attention are deadlock or thrashing among supply chain processes, response-time degredation in various applications, network-level message storms, repeated timeouts, and just plain "the system is dead." It is true to say that the ability to *find the cause* whenever an interesting activity or system state arises is the ultimate test of our understanding of a system.

In an event-based world, events signify activities that take place in a system. We can observe those events at some level of activities in the system, usually the IT layer—that is our basic assumption. And we want to use the events to answer the question "What is going on in the system?"—that is our basic problem.

Events can come from other places than the IT layer. For example, many systems have built-in instrumentation and monitoring tools that give us additional events carrying information such as CPU and disk space consumption from various components. That's nice information when you can get it. But we can't assume that we can always get this extra information, because various parts of a system and the applications running in it may not be instrumented to supply such information—and worse, may not be instrumentable.

Therefore, if we want to answer our question, we must be prepared to make the greatest use of the events we can observe. We want to know a lot about the events; for example:

- What activity an event signifies
- The time an event happened according to whatever clocks are available
- For any event, what other prior events led to that event

Notice one subtle problem implicit in our question. We want to know what *led to* a particular activity. This implies that whatever it was (and it might have been more than one thing) happened *earlier* than the activity we are interested in. What is the meaning of "earlier"? "Earlier" cannot always mean "earlier in time," because in distributed systems there is not always a global clock that timestamps all the events. Moreover, events that happen earlier in time than another event do not necessarily lead to that event—they can signify independent activities.

Instead of using the phrase "led to," we could have asked, "What caused this activity?" But "cause" is loaded with all kinds of everyday implications and assumptions. So we must be careful to say exactly what we mean by "caused." Here is what we mean.

A *caused* B: In the circumstances in which activities A and B happen, if A *had to happen* in order for B to happen, we say, "A caused B" in those circumstances.

One property of the *causality* relation, "A *caused* B," between activities A and B needs to be clearly emphasized: *Causality is dynamic.* "Dynamic" means that "A caused B" depends upon the circumstances in which the activities happened.

Sometimes you can say, "A always has to happen for B to happen"—but that depends on the nature of activities A and B. For example, if A is "eats cyanide poison" and B is "dies of cyanide," we have a pair of activities in which A always causes B. In this case, the causal relationship between A and B is *static*.

But the more common case is that the causal relationship is dynamic. For example, what caused the French knights on horseback to bog down on the battlefield of Agincourt—and thus become sitting ducks for Henry V's British archers? On that particular day in history, it was the previous days of incessant rain. But if history were replayed and it again rained incessantly, the French may not bog down, perhaps because they take off their heavy armor or because they ride on higher ground. Or they may bog down again, not because it rained, but because of carefully constructed hidden earthworks, ditches, and so on. So in this example, where A is "incessant rain" and B is "French knights bog down," we can have different circumstances where A causes B, where A happens but B doesn't, and where A and B both happen but there is no causal relationship between them.

We can take another example from our computer world. Sometimes one of our programs has a "memory leak." In certain situations, it allocates more and more memory and does not deallocate it. Let event A signify the leaking memory activity. Usually the first manifestation of A is that other programs running on the user's computer slow down. Let event B signify slowing down. Whenever A and B both happen, it may be that A is the cause of B. Or it may be that something else is the cause of B, and A is insignificant—A and B happen independently. Also, we can have B but not A, and vice versa.

So when activities A and B both happen within a system, one cannot always tell from the data contained in the events signifying A and B whether one caused the other. We have to look further to the circumstances. Causality is dependent upon runtime conditions. The dynamic nature of causal relationships between events implies that whatever techniques we use to track causality must be able to take account of runtime conditions.

11.2   Why We Need Causal Models

Imagine we are observing events generated by a target system. They come flying out of our adapters at great speed (see Figure 5.1) and with no apparent relationship to one another. An event may arrive at an adapter before the events that caused it, especially in a distributed system, where there may be no global clock but only lots of unsynchronized local clocks. Timestamps may not help us very much to understand what the causes of events are.

Generally, any activity can have a multitude of different causes. To figure out what is going on inside the system, we must know how the activities are related. This information would tell us what activities happened and what led to what during the execution we are watching. This is exactly the purpose of causal models, to define the causal relationship between events signifying activities so that we know what activities had to happen before something else happened.

We use a causal model to help us construct a *causal map*. A causal map makes the causal relationship between events in an execution *explicit*. The phrase "making causality explicit" means that a set of genetic data parameters that constitute a causal vector, which we described in Section 5.4.2, are added to each event. A causal vector parameter in an event implements the *causality attribute* of an event (see Section 8.4). It references those events that were the immediate causes of the event. A causal model tells us which events should be referenced in the causal vector of an event. A causal map constructs a causal vector of an event. In the coming Section 11.5, Figure 11.1 shows what we mean.

If we can make causality between events explicit, we can then make lots of questions about "what happened" and "what is happening" much easier to answer. That's because most of these questions involve searching for the causes of an event. An explicit causal relationship lets us do several important things in understanding a system and searching for answers.

- *Reduce the search space.* If we are looking for the cause of something, we can restrict our attention to the tree of events in the causal ancestry of that something (*looking backward*). Or if we are interested in what is happening as a result of something, we can look at the events that are caused by a given event (*looking foward*).

- *Prioritize the search.* Searching for causes can be prioritized. This means that we don't necessarily "believe" the causal model, but we have enough confidence in it to use it to make search priorities. For example, we can choose to first trace and search the causal ancestry of an interesting event before looking elsewhere for related events.

- *Drill down.* When we deal with aggregated events, say, in an event hierarchy as described in Chapter 7, we can use causality to drill down from a high-level event to the set of lower-level events that "caused it"—that is, that were aggregated to form that event.

- *Understand the system.* An explicit representation of causality between events in an event trace lets us "see" aspects of the system's behavior that are not otherwise evident. For example, we can more easily see the numbers of independent threads and processes executing concurrently at given times, how often they synchronize and what kinds of synchronization patterns are happening, synchronization bottlenecks, and so on.

Search prioritization, as we just described it, invokes a subtle point about our *confidence* in a causal model. We don't have to view a causal model as absolutely true in all cases for it to be useful, but it has to be correct most of the time. We'll come back to questions of confidence in Section 11.7. But first, we discuss ways of doing causal modeling.

11.3   What Causal Models Are

A causal model is a set of event pattern rules that enable us to tell which of the events we are observing from a system are causally related. Suppose we take two events that have just arrived from our input adapter in Figure 5.1. In fact, there may be several input adapters distributed around the target system. The rules tell us whether one of the events is a cause of the other or if they are causally unrelated.

That's quite a trick, when you think about it. Events generated on different executions of a system can signify the same activity and can look almost identical, but their circumstances and causes can differ from one execution to another. So the rules of a causal model must be able to determine the different causes of similar-looking events on two different executions. The rules must therefore be able to use other factors in addition to the events themselves, such as surrounding events and the states of system components in the two executions, to determine causal relationships. Consequently, the rules of a causal model must be written in a powerful language that allows this kind of genericity (more on this in the next section).

A causal relationship between events must satisfy certain general rules that we discussed in Section 5.3. It must be transitive and antisymmetric, and it must obey a very simple invariant with respect to the timing of the events that we called the *cause-time axiom*.

Here is a short recap of our discussion of these rules in Section 5.3.

Transitive means that if A *causes* B, and B *causes* C, then A *causes* C. This may seem a little counterintuitive with an everyday use of "cause." What transitivity says is that any event that caused something that caused C is also an event that caused C. Well, *it had to happen for C to happen,* didn't it?

When we use "cause" in everyday talk, we usually mean "immediate cause." But when we talk about a causal relationship between events in systems, we do not restrict the relationship to immediate cause. Remember the old nursery rhyme, "for want of a nail a Kingdom was lost"? That rhyme is about the transitivity of causality between events in a battlefield system. It teaches us, at a young age, to pay attention to details because a ridiculously small event can lead to successively larger events and finally to a catastrophic event—by transitivity. The ultimate lesson of the nursery rhyme is this: Any event that is in the causal history of C had to happen for C to happen and therefore is also a cause of C.

If we want to talk about A being an "immediate cause" of C, we have to use "immediate," meaning no other event happened between A and C—see Section 8.10, the example defining the *immediate cause* operator.

Asymmetric means A can't be a cause of itself. Not much counterintuitive about that! If A caused B and B could cause A (a symmetric situation), then by transitivity, A would be a cause of itself. So there cannot be any cycles in a causal relationship.

The *cause-time axiom* says if A caused B, then the timestamp of B cannot be less than the timestamp of A for the same clock. The cause-time axiom tells us that cause and time are related in a very simple way. An event can have a timestamp giving the reading of a clock when the event was generated. If we look at the timestamps giving the time according to a particular clock, an event can't have an earlier timestamp than some other event that caused it. This is a natural rule that corresponds to everyday experience. We call it an *invariant*—a relationship that is always true.

11.4   Defining a Causal Model and a Causal Map

Assume that we are given a target system and we want to construct a useful causal model for the events created by some set of applications running in the system. We might be interested, for example, in applications such as databases or process engines. Such a model is a precise set of rules that tell us what events caused what other events in an execution. Now, the first problem is how to get the information to construct the model.

First step: Read documentation for both the IT layer and the applications that we are interested in. The events created by these applications are the events of interest to us—not every event created in the system. Next step: Go talk to the people who own and use the applications and those who built them. Hopefully, they will understand how they create events and their causal dependencies. What you will probably find, however, is that people's knowledge of causality in complex applications is hazy and incomplete—and not precisely written down.

But all is not lost! There is usually a lot of useful information, based upon knowledge of the applications and the IT layer, that implies properties of the causal relation between events created by the applications of interest. This information is *implicit* in other information about the system that does not directly address causality. Our job is to turn the implicit information into *explicit* information about causality. So, we must expect to go through a process of discovery and refinement to get the information into a set of explicit rules. Typically, the process has these steps.

1. *Specify the set of events to be monitored.* First, we want to agree on which activities of the applications in the target system interest us. We must then specify the set of events that signify these activities. There may be several events needed to signify an activity. This step specifies the set of events for which the causal relationship should be made explicit. It assumes that a sufficiently rich set of events can be observed from the target system so that we can get these events.

2. *Describe how and when these events cause other events.* Having decided the events of interest, we want to describe how and when their activities immediately cause other activities in the system. This is where we have to dig into the implicit information, read documentation, talk to people who use or maintain the applications and the system, and so on, and come up with a description of the causal realtionships among the events of interest.

   The outcome of the first two steps should be an English description of the events, the activities they signify, and their causal relationships.

3. *Construct a formal causal model.* Here's where we must turn the informal knowledge into precise rules for constructing the causal relationship between events. We convert our English description into rules in some modeling language or notation, whatever seems easiest

as a first step. Examples of possible modeling languages that we might choose are finite state machines, Unified Modeling Language (UML) diagrams, sets of pairs of event patterns, or event pattern mappings. We'll illustrate the use of sets of pairs of patterns to model causality later on.

4. *Construct an EPA to add a causality attribute to events.* A causal map is an EPA that takes an event execution as input and outputs another event execution that is identical with the input except that each output event contains a causal attribute that specifies which events are the immediate causes of that event. Essentially, the role of a causal map is to add a causal vector that implements the causality attribute (see Section 5.4.2) to each event in the input.

Our final step is to use our causal model to construct a causal map. At this step, we write a map EPA to process events from the target system, and add causal attributes to them. We use the causal model rules to construct the triggers of the rules in the causal map, as shown in Section 11.6.

Step 2 recommends describing the immediate causes of an event in English because that seems to be the simplest way to focus on understanding causality in the target system separately from dealing with how to specify it in a formal notation. Issues of formalization are dealt with in step 3. At step 3, we are assuming that there is enough information in the events from a target system, and any observable state of the target system, to determine causality. We assume causality is implicit, and our job at steps 3 and 4 is to make it explicit. Step 4 suggests constructing a single map to implement the causality attribute of events. In fact, it may make sense in some cases to break this task into several EPAs in an EPN.

11.5 Using Pattern Pairs to Specify Causal Models

As we discussed in Section 11.3, a causal model for a system must specify the causal relationship between events in a generic way. It must apply to events in any execution of that system. Obviously, we also want the model to specify causality correctly—that is, if it defines two events as being causally related one did indeed have to happen for the other one to happen. These two requirements, genericity across all executions together with correctness, means that the rules of the model must be written in a very general and powerful language. The language must be precise (or formal) so that we can accurately predict the consequences of rules written in the language—for example, answer questions like "Do the rules imply that this event causes that event?"

In our presentation here, we propose that causal models be specified as sets of pairs of event patterns. Event patterns are written in RAPIDE-EPL, described in Chapter 8. So the rules that define causality between events are written using event patterns and guards that refer to state. We will argue later that this is a sufficiently powerful language to specify causal models for many different kinds of systems.

Each rule is written as a pair of patterns, a *left* pattern and a *right* pattern. Causality goes from left to right. So, we write a causal rule as follows:

$$A \longrightarrow B, \quad \text{where A and B are RAPIDE-EPL events patterns}$$

A is the left pattern and B is the right pattern. The rule means that for any set of events matching the right pattern, B, to happen, a set of events matching the left pattern, A, must have happened.

Usually, the right pattern, B, is a basic event pattern matching single events. The left pattern, A, matches the immediate predecessors of any event that matches B. In general, A can be a template for a poset. The data parameters in A and B should contain enough details to specify exactly the matches we want from our English description of events and their causes (steps 1 and 2) and no others.

According to this method, a causal model is a set of pairs of event patterns. We call the pattern pairs *causal rules*.

11.5.1   Using Causal Rules

Causal rules are used to determine causality between events by a *backward search* from right pattern to left pattern. In a typical use-case situation, events arrive from the target system and are put into an input event store, as shown in Figure 11.1 later in this section. Each arriving event, E, say, is tested to determine its immediate causes as follows.

- If E matches a right-side pattern of any rule in the causal model, the bindings of the match are applied to the left-side pattern of that rule. The result is either an instance of the left pattern or a partial instance that contains placeholders that were not bound to values by the match of the right pattern.

- In either case, a search is made in the input store for a poset matching that instance or partial instance. Such a poset is taken to be the set of events that are immediate causes of E according to the causal model.

Orderly observation of events from the target system, as we described in Section 5.8, has an impact on the simplicity and efficiency of the search for immediate causes of E. If orderly observation is possible, events arrive at the input execution in an order consistent with their causal order. So the immediate causes of an arriving event E will already be in the input execution. If, on the other hand, observation of events from the target system is not orderly, the search for a match of the instance of the left pattern may have to wait for the arrival of events that caused E.

11.5.2 Resolving Ambiguities

The rules in a causal model must have enough detail to be useful. The method of backward search can fail to produce an answer or can produce ambiguous answers.

1. Let's say we pick out an event E in the input store, and we ask, "What caused it?" If E doesn't match the right-side pattern of any rule, our causal model is telling us, "Nothing caused it." This could be a correct answer. Or the rules could be telling us, "Don't know." In this case, the set of causal rules is incomplete, and we need to add more rules.

2. If E does match a right-side pattern, we would like that there is only one set of events that matches the corresponding instance of left-side pattern of that rule. So there has to be a sufficient set of rules to deal with all the different cases in which events of type E can happen. We must ensure that the patterns in each rule have sufficient detail (for example, parameters of events and timestamps) that they give us an unambiguous match for the immediate causes of E.

   For example, the GetQuote event that caused a given PurchaseOrder event could be identified uniquely by data parameters in the PurchaseOrder event, such as a quotation number. Those parameters would need to be included in a pattern pair such as the following:

   GetQuote(Int ?Id, ...) → PurchaseOrder(Int ?Id, ...);

3. E may match more than one right-side pattern. This should mean simply that two or more events caused E, each rule specifying some of them.

   However, this situation could also lead to an ambiguous result because only one of the rules should apply. This case indicates the need to refine the existing rules by adding guards to the right-side patterns so that each rule applies exactly to the cases of events of type E that it should apply to. This may involve making copies of a rule and adding different guards to each copy.

Ambiguities can often be resolved by adding predicate guards to the right-side patterns of causal rules. In case 2, this may involve replacing a rule that leads to multiple matches of its left pattern by several versions of the rule with different predicate guards of the right pattern. In case 3, when the right patterns of multiple rules should not be matched by the same event, different predicate guards need to be added to those right patterns to make the rules more specific.

So a causal model is written as a set of pattern pairs with predicate guards:

$$(LeftPattern_1 \longrightarrow RightPattern_1) \; \textbf{where} \; Guard_1$$
$$\dots$$
$$(LeftPattern_n \longrightarrow RightPattern_n) \; \textbf{where} \; Guard_n$$

As a simple example, suppose we write the causal model for a single thread of control in our pattern pairs formalism. Thread T is our target system. A causal model should enable us to determine causality between events created by T, as depicted in Section 11.6, Figure 11.2.

Example 1: *A causal model for a single thread of control*

```
(Event ?E, Event ?F, Int ?C)
?E( thread is T, CounterValue is ?C) ⟶
                    ?F( thread is T, CounterValue is ?C+1);
```

In this example, **thread** is the predefined event attribute (see Section 8.4). Also, we are assuming that every event type created by a thread of control has a data parameter, CounterValue.

The model assumes that each time T creates an event, it inserts a counter value and it increments the counter value for insertion in the next event. So each event created by T has a unique CounterValue. Given an event, A, created by T, to find its *immediate cause,* we apply backward search by matching A to the right-side pattern. Suppose the binding for this match is the following pair of bindings:

$$< \; ?F \leftarrow A, \quad \textbf{thread} \leftarrow T, \; CounterValue \leftarrow V \; >$$

The immediate cause of A will be the event that matches

```
?E( thread is T, CounterValue is V−1)
```

According to our assumptions about T, there will be a unique event matching this instance of the left pattern. Notice that orderly observation is *not* assumed. The immediate cause event will be picked out whenever it arrives at the model. The result is a linear sequence of events, as shown shortly in Figure 11.2.

If our assumption about there being a thread counter is not correct, we must assume there is a clock that is fine enough that it can place a unique timestamp in each of the thread's events. The clock replaces an explicit thread counter. The thread is synchronized with the clock so that it generates events at time intervals of δ.

(Event ?E, Event ?F', Time ?Stamp)
  ?E(**thread is** T,   **timestamp is** ?Stamp) $\longrightarrow$
        ?F(**thread is** T,   **timestamp is** ?Stamp $+ \delta$).

These causal models for a single thread are simple. But they do not assume that the events on the left-hand side of Figure 11.1 arrive in an order consistent with their causal relationship—which is the order in which T created them.

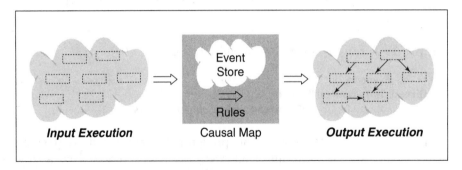

Figure 11.1: **Using maps to add causality**

Causal models are sets of rules for determining causal relationships between events. *Writing* a causal model is one step, and *implementing* it to make causality explicit is a next step, which may not be trivial.

11.6   Causal Maps

Given a causal model, step 4 in Section 11.4 is to construct a *causal map.* First, let's see what a causal map has to do.

Figure 11.1 shows what a causal map does. The map takes as input an execution containing events of interest that have been monitored on the target system and adapted to CEP format. The map creates another execution as output. The output is isomorphic to the input—but there's one big difference. Whereas the input execution does not show us how its events are causally related, the output execution does. Each of its events contains a causal vector whose elements refer to the events that are the immediate causes of that event. The causal vector is an implementation of the *causality attribute* of the event (see Section 8.4). So the map makes causality *explicit*, as described in Section 11.2. Now, whenever you look at an event, you can look at its causality attribute to see what its causal parents are.

How does a causal map work? See Figure 11.1 again. Input events are arriving dynamically from the adapter. They sit in the map's input event execution—an event pool or cache, if you will. The map processes events in four general steps, using the causal model at each step to make decisions.

1. *Processing input events.* The map's rules trigger on an event in the input execution only when all its causal parents (its immediate predecessors in the causal ordering) have already been processed by the map. The map's rules are constructed from knowledge of the causal model so that this is true. Guards in the pattern triggers of the map's rules refer to the local state. They prevent a rule from matching an event until its parents have been processed. Whenever the map triggers on an event, it puts a copy of that event object in its local store—the local store is shown as part of the state of the map in Figure 11.1.

2. *Adding causality to events.* The map operates on event objects that are in its local store. It adds a causal vector parameter to each event that contains the event Ids of causal parents of that event. Again, knowledge of the causal model is used to determine which event Ids are placed in the causal vector of each event. The Ids in the causal vector refer to events that have already been constructed and output. So the map must already have processed and output the parents of an event so that their event Ids are in its event store.

3. *Generating output events.* When the Ids of all causal parents of an event have been added to its causal vector parameter, the map generates an output event identical to that event object. The event Id of that output event is added to the event store. Note that this event Id refers to the output event, not to the input event that was used to construct the output event.

4. *Managing the event store.* The map has to keep in its local store any event that can be a cause of other events (that is, can be a causal parent) until all its causal children have been processed and output. Then, and only then, can the map delete the event from its local store—that is, manage its store. The causal model is used in deciding for each event in the local store when this condition has been met.

Implied by what we have just said is the fact that no matter what order input events arrive in, the map must process them in an order consistent with their causal order. So, the map uses the input execution as a "holding area" for events that arrive ahead of their causal parents. When the map wants to process an event, it must make a copy of it, by triggering a rule, and put the copy into its local store. Only then does it treat the event as an object and alter the local copy by adding the causal vector to the event's parameters, and finally generate a new event in the output execution.

11.6.1   A Small Example of a Causal Map

Perhaps a small example will help illustrate these ideas. Let's build a causal map for a single thread of control.

As we have seen, a single-thread system has a very simple causal model. Because its activities are executed in order, one by one, it has a thread counter. The thread counter is incremented every time the thread generates an event. We assume the counter value is a data parameter in each event. This assumption makes it possible to specify a causal model for a single-thread system. The model, in English, is as follows: Event E generated by thread T is the causal parent of event F also generated by T if the counter value of F is one more than the counter value of E.

Here's our previous causal model that formalizes this description:

```
(Event ?E, ?F; Int ?C)
?E( thread is T, CounterValue is ?C) ⟶
                 ?F( thread is T, CounterValue is ?C+1);
```

Now, we must assume that events from the thread may arrive at our adapter in an order that is not their causal order. A causal map should take these incoming events and output identical events in a linear causal chain, as shown in Figure 11.2. Their order is the order of their counter values inserted by the thread that generated them. Here's a causal map that does this.

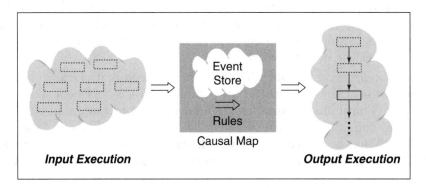

Figure 11.2: Causal map for a single thread

```
map M in ... out ... {
// local state
Int Counter = 1;
Event E = null;
Event LastEvent = null;
// behavior rules
// trigger when ?A matches the successor of the last event processed.
(Event ?A) ?A where ?A.Count = Counter  ⇒
    {  // save ?A as an object, E.
       E = ?A;
       // construct value of the causal vector attribute of E.
       E.Causality = Set(LastEvent);
       // create an event identical to the event E, and save its reference.
       LastEvent =  generate E;
       // update the thread counter value.
       Counter = Counter++;
    }
}
```

The map assumes that events in its input execution have come from the thread of control, so they all contain a thread Count parameter. In the trigger of the rule, the guard tests the Count parameter of an input event ?A to see if its value is Counter, which is the Count value expected for the "next event" from the thread. It triggers if ?A has this Count value. Incoming events stay in the input execution until they trigger the rule.

When the rule triggers, its body does the following processing. The input event is saved in the local store of the map as an object, E, (of type *event*). The causal vector attribute of E is constructed as a set of one element, the EventId of the last event that was generated by the map. That is the only change that is made to E. A new event is then generated that is identical to E, and its EventId is saved as the value of LastEvent. The generated event is placed in the output execution of the map. The Counter is updated.

Notice that the map's event store is just one event, E, the last event generated by the thread. Store management consists of overwriting the store with the latest event.

Why do we use EventIds instead of events themselves? Because we need to refer to an event that is already output when we construct the predecessor set of the next event. We can never generate the *same* event in the output execution twice, so we must use a reference to one we have already generated.

11.6.2   A Second Example of a Causal Map

As a second example, let us build a causal map for a distributed multi-threaded system—the one shown in Figure 11.3. The system contains

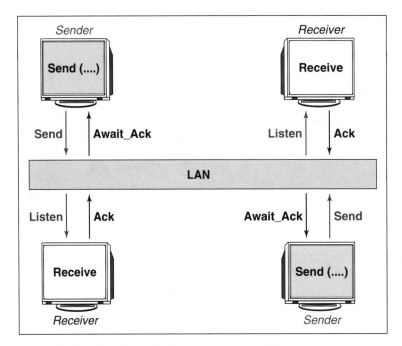

Figure 11.3: The Send/Ack system, a small messaging system

applications that communicate by broadcasting messages to one another on an IT layer. There are local clocks but no global clock.

Each application has an identifier that tells who it is: Id1, Id2, ... Some applications are senders of messages to others, and others are receivers that listen for and acknowledge messages. Application Ids are used in messages to indicate the sender and intended receiver. Each event also contains a message identifier, MsgId, which is an integer. A sender sends one message to an intended receiver and then it sends no further messages to that receiver until it gets an acknowledgment from that receiver. Receivers always acknowledge a message once, using the MsgId. A sender always increments the MsgId that was last acknowledged by a receiver when it sends a new message to that receiver. So, any transaction between a sender and a receiver is uniquely identified by the three Ids. The timing of these activities is not bounded. Also, senders can send to other receivers while waiting for an acknowledgment from one. If messages fail to be delivered or acknowledged often enough, the system eventually goes silent.

We'll call this the "Send/Ack" system. The activities of interest to us in Send/Ack are the sending and acknowledging of messages. These are the activities we want to monitor. They are signified by the messages we can observe in the system's IT layer. Our adapter can use each message to construct a very similar-looking CEP event that signifies that message—that is, the activity of sending or acknowledging a message.

Step 1: Specify the Events to Be Monitored

We construct our adapter to listen for the Send and Acknowledge messages, convert them to the CEP event format, and put all these events into an input execution buffer.

A typical set of events from the small Send/Ack system is shown in Figure 11.4. The events contain data such as the sender, receiver, and message Ids. The events are displayed according to the time they arrived at the adapter. The causal relationship between the events is not given. We have to infer it from the parameters and our knowledge of the Send/Ack system. The causal map we are going to construct will infer casuality and add it to the event parameters.

Step 2: Describe the Causal Relationship between the Events

Next we must describe how the events are causally related. We can try to do this in English as a first attempt. Here are some possible rules of causality.

1. Each application is a single thread, so all its events are causally ordered in a sequence according to their local thread counter values.

2. A Send event causes the Acknowledge event with the same Ids for sender, receiver, and message.

3. An Acknowledge containing a message identifier, MsgId, from a receiver to a sender causes the next Send event from the same sender to the same receiver and contains the message identifier MsgId + 1.

This description tells us that in this system, causality between Send and Acknowledge events can be figured out from the application Ids, the message Ids, and the counter values in the events. A causal model contains rules to decide whether any two events are causally related or causally independent.

Step 3: Define the Causal Model as a Set of Pattern Pairs

We convert the preceding English description to a set of three causal rules:

```
(ThreadId Id; AppId SourceId, DestId; Int MsgId, ThreadCounterValue; Event ?E, ?F))
1. ?E (Id, ThreadCounterValue)  ⟶  ?F (Id, ThreadCounterValue + 1),
2. Send(SourceId, DestId, MsgId)  ⟶  Ack(DestId, SourceId, MsgId),
3. Ack(SourceId, DestId, MsgId)  ⟶  Send(DestId, SourceId, MsgId + 1);
```

We can see from these rules that each **Send** and **Ack** event in the system (except the first events) will have two immediate causal predecessors,

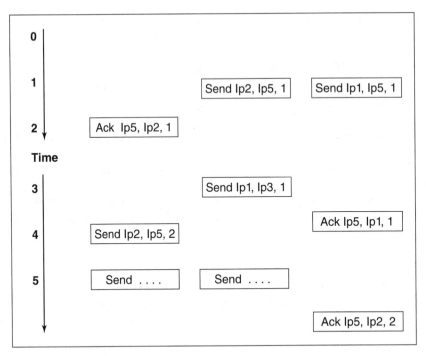

Figure 11.4: Events from the small Send/Ack system

one from the thread rule 1 and one from either the sending rule 2 or the acknowledging rule 3.

Step 4: Write a Causal Map
The execution type (see Section 8.3.4) of the causal map is

```
typedef   execution {
        Send(Appld Source, Dest; Int Msgld, Counter; String Message, ...);
        Ack(Appld Source,   Dest; Int Msgld, Counter; String Message, ...);
  } SendAckExecution;
```

The data parameters include Ids for the source and destination applications and for the message, and also a thread counter value. There is other data, such as a message and maybe a timestamp issued by a local clock at an application's node (workstation).

Next, we write a map to make explicit the causality specified by the model.

```
map SendAckCausalModel in SendAckExecution out SendAckExecution {
// Dynamic lists for storing application Ids, thread counts, and msg Ids.
```

```
Map<AppId, AppId, Event>  LastSend, LastAck;
Map<AppId, AppId, Int> MsgIdStore;
Map<AppId, Int> CounterStore;
Map<AppId, Event>  LastEvent;
Event E;          // event being processed

// behavior rules
// Rule 1: compute causal attribute for a Send event.
   (AppId ?S, ?R; Int ?MsgId, ?Count)
   Send(?S, ?R, ?MsgId, ?Count) where ?Count = CounterStore(?S)++ and
                                       ?MsgId = MsgIdStore(?S, ?R)++

   ⇒
   { E = Send(?S, ?R, ?MsgId, ?Count);
     E. causality = {LastEvent(?S), LastAck(?R, ?S)};
     LastSend(?S, ?R) =  generate E;
     LastEvent(?S) = LastSend(?S, ?R);
     CounterStore(?S)++;
     MsgIdStore(?S, ?R)++;
     }

// Rule 2: compute causal attribute for an Ack event.
   (AppId ?S, ?R; Int ?MsgId, ?Count)
   Ack(?R, ?S, ?MsgId, ?Count) where ?Count = CounterStore(R)++ and
                                      MsgId = MsgIdStore(S, R)

   ⇒
   { E = Ack(?R, ?S, ?MsgId, ?Count);
     E. causality = {LastEvent(?R), LastSend(?S, ?R)};
     LastAck(?R, ?S) =  generate E;
     LastEvent(?R) = LastAck(?R, ?S);
     CounterStore(?R) = CounterStore(?R)++;
     }

// Similar rules for the first Send or Ack event from each thread are omitted.
}
```

This causal map works in a similar way to the single-thread map except that each incoming event has two causal parents—unless it is one of the first events when the system starts up. The causal model tells us that each Send(S, R) event is caused by the last event created by S and by the last Ack(R, S) event. So we need to define data structures to "remember" these causing events for each pair of Sender and Receiver applications. We can use the data in the input Send or Ack events to guard the rule triggers so that a rule triggers only when the causing events have already been processed.

The event store makes liberal use of extensible arrays, data structures similar to C++ templates, to set up structures that can be indexed by application Ids. These data structures are LastSend and LastAck. They are used to store and access the event Ids of the last Send and Ack generated between any pair of applications. Similarly, CounterStore stores the next counter value for each application (which is a single thread), and MsgIdStore stores the next message Id to be used in the next transaction between any pair of applications.

LastEvent stores the last event generated by each application. If we want to find the last event generated by, say, an application with Id S, we look at the value of LastEvent(S). Finally, Event is the current event object being constructed and output.

We do not assume here that events from the Send/Ack system are arriving in an orderly manner at the adapter.

To see how the two rules work, imagine that the causal map has just finished matching and processing a pair of events, say, Send(S, R, 3, 10, ...) and Ack(R, S, 3, 25, ...). They are the tenth event from S and the twenty-fifth event from R, and they have transacted the third message between S and R. At this point, the MsgIdStore(S, R) contains the value 3. The next message in the Send/Ack system between S and R will have the integer MsgId 4. So, the first rule would match Send(S, R, 4, C, ...) (where C is 11 or greater). The second rule, however, would match Ack(R, S, 3, C, ...) (where C is 26 or greater) because the current value of MsgIdStore(S, R) is 3. But the Send/Ack system won't create another Ack(R, S, 3, ...) event. The next Ack event between R and S will be Ack(R, S, 4, ...).

So the second rule can't match until the first rule has matched a Send and incremented the MsgId value in MsgIdStore(S, R). Consequently, the rules can't match out-of-order Acks that arrive before the corresponding Sends.

Similarly, we can see that out-of-order Sends from the same thread will be matched in their proper order of generation because of the counter values in CounterStore.

This map takes as input a set of events such as those shown in Figure 11.4, with no explicit relationship between the events. The map adds causal vector attributes to copies of the input events. That is, the set of events generated by this map is isomorphic to the input set, containing all the input data, but in addition, it is a poset with an explicit causal relationship (see Figure 11.5).

11.7   Developing Accurate Causal Models

For us, a causal model is a set of rules for determining if events in a computer system are causally related. We are dealing with *computational causality*. If the system we are studying is complex, we will probably begin with an overly simple and incomplete model. An incomplete causal model may still

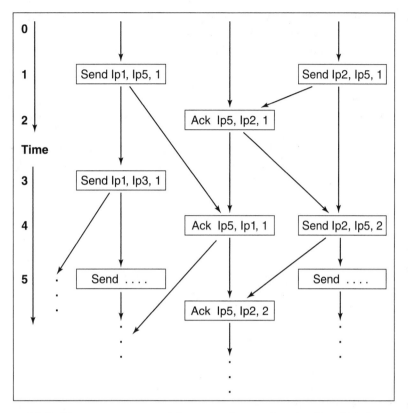

Figure 11.5: Poset constructed by causal map for the Send/Ack system

be useful in prioritizing searches for the causes of events and consequently making searches more efficient. A causal model of a complex system will be evolved and improved gradually, based upon the results of applying it to analyze the system's behavior.

Typical kinds of problems with causal models include the following.

- Inconsistencies. For example, the rules in the model may be inconsistent among themselves, or, more subtly, the causal relationship determined by the rules may contradict the timing relationship between events.

- Causal rules that are too strong. A model is *too strong* if it tells us that some pairs of events are causally related, when in reality they are not—too much causality.

- Causal rules that are too weak. A model is *too weak* if it tells us that some pairs of events are independent, when in reality they are causally related—too little causality.

Fixing these kinds of problems is part of developing an accurate causal model. Logical analysis of the causal rules can help eliminate inconsistencies. There are many techniques for making the rules in a causal model of a system more accurate. For example, properties of the target system that are depicted by a model of the causal relationships between its events, such as numbers of concurrent threads at a given time, should be compared with other knowledge about the system. Such comparisons can indicate where the model is incorrect and how the rules need to be changed. Rules that are too strong, or too weak, will be uncovered when the model is used to search executions for causally related events. More accurate rules will be suggested by the results of causal tracking searches.

11.8 Summary

Causality between events is an ongoing topic of scientific and philosophical discussion. There are multitudinous references on the topic, which are best discovered by searching the Web.

In this chapter, we have dealt with a limited concept of *cause* as it applies to events created in an electronic information system, perhaps best called *"computational causality."*

We have described some techniques for defining causal models and building causal maps. The purpose is to get our enterprise systems to output causal event executions rather than simple time-ordered event logs. This gives us many advantages when we need to understand the behavior of distributed systems. Early research in applying event causality to analyzing distributed and realtime systems is described in references [12], [13], [14], [15], and [23].

The techniques given in this chapter are by no means the only ones, nor may they be the best. Moreover, we didn't discuss the scalability of causal modeling. These questions ultimately reduce to similar questions about the fundamental operations, such as matching complex patterns of events. However, many applications of causal modeling are postmortem or offline applications related to analysis. For these applications, scalability may not be as important an issue as whether or not analysis techniques are improved by using causal models and yield better results more easily than before.

Case Study: Viewing Collaboration between Business Processes

- *A collaborative agreement between trading enterprises*
- *A causal model of events in the collaboration*
- *A causal map to add causal attributes to events*
- *Analysis of executions generated by collaborations*
- *Constraint checking as an integral part of collaboration*

In this chapter, we continue the discussion from Section 5.7 about applying causal modeling to collaboration between enterprise business processes. Example 3 in Section 5.7 discusses the advantages of adding causal tracking to events flowing across the Internet or a private commercial trading network. Those events signify steps in a collaboration between processes of the partnering enterprises. Example 4 in Section 5.7 shows an event execution resulting from a collaboration. We present this example in more detail here and illustrate how both constraint checking and causality are used to detect and analyze problems.

The objective of causal modeling of a collaboration is to create an event execution in which the causal relationships between events are explicitly represented by the causal attributes of the events (see the *causality* attribute, Section 8.4). These are the advantages of having casual attributes of events.

- Analysis of real-time event executions is more efficient, particularly tracking the progress of multiple, concurrent transactions.

- Diagnosing the causes of exceptional situations is easier. Tools that are designed to trace causal histories can be applied to the problems of how transactions failed to complete or deviated from the agreed protocol.

- Constraints expressing agreed policies are easier and simpler to express using a causal relationship.

- Violations of constraints can be detected more efficiently.

12.1 A Collaborative Business Agreement

Figure 12.1 diagrams the steps in an agreement between a merchant bank and a stock brokerage. The agreement presumably is written in English. It defines how each party agrees to interchange trading messages in a standard format, such as ISO 15022, with the other party. The agreed responses would be captured as event pattern pairs in a causal model of the collaboration.

The collaboration agreement would specify steps in a transaction to buy or sell bundles of financial instruments using messages of standard types specified in ISO 15022, perhaps as follows.

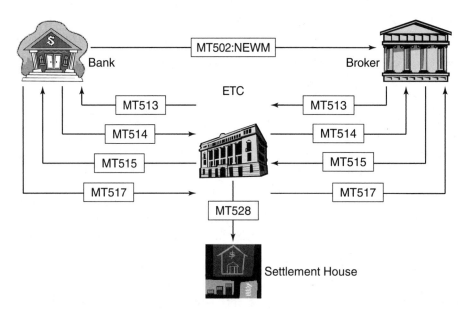

Figure 12.1: Enterprises collaborate across standard middleware

1. A message of type MT502 can be sent from the bank to the trading house to initiate a new order or to cancel a previous order, depending upon the values of its data fields.

2. A message of type MT513 must be sent from the trading house in response to an MT502 new order, via the ETC (an Electronic Trade Confirmation facility provided by the network), to the bank, confirming the execution of an order.

3. A message of type MT509 must be sent from the trading house to the bank in response to an MT502 cancel, either confirming or denying the cancellation.

4. One or more messages of type MT514 in response to an MT513 must be sent from the bank, via the ETC, to the trading house. Each message allocates all or part of a confirmed trade to its accounts. There may be several MT514 messages in response to one MT513. Together, these MT514 messages must allocate the total trade to the bank's various accounts.

5. A message of type MT515 in response to each MT514 message must be sent from the trading house, via the ETC, to the bank, confirming receipt of the MT514.

6. A message of type MT517 in response to a complete set of MT515 messages confirming all MT514 allocations must be sent from the bank, via the ETC, to the trading house, finalizing settlement of an order.

Details of the data contents of the messages would be spelled out as part of the agreement.

The agreement might also contain rules constraining the activity. Constraints play an important role in crafting agreements. The service provided by the ETC monitors for standard constraints—for example, that all the MT514 messages in a transaction allocate all of the trade. Additional constraints may be needed to finalize an agreement. These are some possible examples of constraints.

- *Global timing constraint:* All transactions shall be completed in three working days.
- *Consistent bank behavior:* The bank cannot issue an MT502 canceling an order after it has received an MT513 confirming the order.

  There may be variations of this constraint, allowing the bank to cancel if, for example, an MT514 allocation of an order is issued by the bank but no MT515 response is received within one working day.

- *Broker requirements:*   The broker will respond to an MT514 message only if it allocates a portion of a trade that is above a minimum value.

12.2   An Interface Communication Architecture

A top-level view of the communication architecture for this collaboration is shown in Figure 12.2. Events are communicated in the directions of the

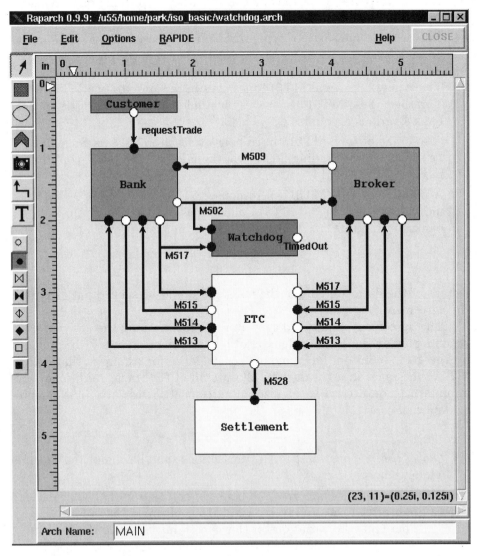

Figure 12.2: Top-level interface communication architecture

arrows, from an **out** action (white circle) to an **in** action (black circle). The figure also shows a *watchdog* EPA configured to monitor collaborations for conformance to the global timing constraint. Other constraints would be monitored by constraint EPAs positioned appropriately. For example, the bank's consistent behavior constraint might be monitored at the bank's interface with the financial trading network, and the broker's minimum allocation requirement might be monitored at the broker's interface with the network.

12.3 Causal Model

A causal model for the events created by these transactions is easily defined if there is some identifying data field of each event that indicates which order it is related to. This could be a unique order number agreed to by the partners. The causal model would consist of pairs of event patterns corresponding to the agreed rules of response in the collaboration agreement. For example, the following is a pattern pair rule for MT513 events:

```
(OrderId ?D, TradeRecord ?R) MT502(BANK_to_BROKER, ?D, ?R)
    ⟶    MT513(BROKER_to_ETC, ?D, ?R);
```

where ?D is a unique order number. It captures a broker's agreement to react to an MT502 new order with an MT513 confirmation. A similar rule expresses the causal relationship between MT515 events and the MT514 events that cause them. In each case where these rules match events, there will be a unique pair of events matching the left- and right-side patterns.

However, an MT513 can cause several MT514 events. So the right side of a rule for MT514 events may match several events, and each time the same MT513 event will match the left side. Since an MT517 event can be caused by several MT515 events, the left-side pattern for the MT517 rule may match several MT515 events. These cases make the reactive rules in a causal map more complicated, for example, by using guards.

12.4 Causal Map

A *causal map* transforms the events created during a transaction by adding a causal attribute to each event. This puts explicit references in each event to the events that caused it. A causal map creates a poset with the following properties.

- The events contain references to their immediate causal ancestors.
- The poset can be processed by analysis tools that track causality.

- The poset can be used in either of two ways:
    1. As a separate copy of the execution of the collaborative processes for analysis.
    2. Online to drive the collaboration.

In the first use-case, the causal map is used as a benign observer to record the activity. In the second use-case, it is positioned in the communication architecture so that it intercepts events, adds causal attributes to events on the fly as they are created by each enterprise, and sends those events to their intended destination.

We can choose to use causal maps in two ways. First, a causal map can be used to create an offline copy of a collaboration execution for analysis. The analysis can be done with a small time delay, after the activities of the processes have taken place. We call this "offline" use. Or the analysis can be postmortem, in response to questions about situations that arose. In either case, this is an after-the-fact use of causal maps.

The second choice is to use a causal map to perform an inline transformation of events as they happen in the execution. The transformed events are used to drive the steps in the collaboration between processes. The inline choice has the advantage of making causality available to the decision making components of the collaborating processes. The risk of slowing down the collaboration is minimal because transactions of the kind discussed here take place at speeds of events per minute. Experience with CEP experiments shows that slow down would happen at speeds of events per millisecond.

If the causal attributes were not added, assuming a unique OrderId in each event, the causal ancestors of an event could be found by searching the collaborative event execution for events of the appropriate type with the same OrderId. That is, to find the cause of an M513, search for an M502 with the same unique OrderId. But such a search gets complicated when we are looking for the causes of an M517 confirmation of a complete transaction event. There can be a number of M515 confirmations of account allocation that cause it. The actual number varies from transaction to transaction. So, we would need to search for all M515 events with the same OrderId as the M517 and determine when we have found them all.

Also, these searches using OrderIds would be repeated each time the causal information was needed. A causal map adds causal attributes to each event *once* to make the search simple. Construction of tools that use causality between events can rely on standard search programs based on causal attributes.

Naturally, there are many ways to implement causality explicitly. In simple collaborative protocols such as this one, where the events always follow a predetermined sequence, we may prefer a different technique from causal attributes.

12.5   Examples of Causal Rules

Here are some examples of the rules in a causal map for collaboration over the ISO 15022 standard. Because many transactions can be going on concurrently, extensible data structures that can be indexed by OrderIds are used in the local state to store events that are parents of events that have not been processed yet. The tricky cases are the handling of MT514 and MT515 events related to the same transaction. As the agreement is stated, these events can be flowing in both directions concurrently.

This map assumes orderly observation—events are observed in their causal order. Also, remember that input events are processed one at a time by EPAs, as described in Section 9.3.2. So there is no concurrent contention for local state.

```
map CollabCausalModel in ISO15022 out CollabPoset {
// Dynamic lists for storing sets of ISO events.
    Map<OrderNo, SetOf(Event)>  LastEvents, Temp514, Temp515;
    Map<OrderNo, Int>  Allocation;
    Event E, Parent;          // current event being processed

// behavior rules
// Rule 502: output copies of MT502 events with causal attribute, and store them
// for reference as the cause of later events.
(OrderId ?D, TradeRecord ?R) MT502(BANK_to_BROKER, ?D, ?R)
        ⇒  {
        E = generate MT502(BANK_to_BROKER, ?D, ?R); // no causal ancestors.
        LastEvents(?D) = {E};   // M502 is now the last event in the transaction.
        }

// Rule 513: output copies of MT513 events with causal attribute, and store them
// for reference as the cause of later events.
(OrderId ?D, TradeRecord ?R) MT513(BROKER_to_ETC, ?D, ?R);
        ⇒ {
        E =   MT513(BROKER_to_ETC, ?D, ?R);
        E. causality = {LastEvents(?D)}; // add reference to preceding M502.
        E  = generate E;
        LastEvent(?D) = {E};   // M513 is now the last event in transaction.
        }

// Rule 514: output copies of MT514 events with causal attribute, and store them
// until all MT514s have been processed. Then update LastEvents.
(OrderId ?D, TradeRecord ?R, Alloc ?A) MT514(BANK_to_ETC, ?D, ?R, ?A)
```

```
    ⇒    {
        Allocation(?D) = Allocation(?D) + ?A;
        E = MT514(BANK_to_ETC, ?D, ?R, ?A);
        E. causality = {LastEvents(?D)}; // add reference to preceding MT513.
        E = generate E;
        Temp514(?D).Add(E);
        if Allocation(?D) == ?R.Total
            {LastEvents(?D) = Temp514(?D);// All MT514s are the set of last events.
            Temp514(?D) = null;
            Allocation(?D) = null;
            }
    }

// Rule 515: output copies of MT515 events with MT514   causal attribute
// when all MT514s have been processed. Select correct MT514 ancestor.
(OrderId ?D, TradeRecord ?R, Alloc ?A)MT515(BROKER_to_ETC, ?D, ?R, ?A)
                            where Temp514(?D) = null
    ⇒    {
        Allocation(?D) = Allocation(?D) + ?A;
        E = MT515(BROKER_to_ETC, ?D, ?R, ?A);
        Parent = Select(LastEvents(?D).Member | LastEvents(?D).Member.Alloc = ?A);
        E. causality = {Parent}; // add reference to preceding MT514.
        E = generate E;
        Temp515(?D).Add(E);
        if Allocation(?D) == ?R.Total
            {LastEvents(?D) = Temp515(?D);// All MT515s are the set of last events.
            Temp515(?D) = null;
            }
    }
}    // end of map
```

Rules 502 and 513 are simple because those types of events are a unique ancestor of another event. Some of the other rules are more complex. Rule 514 has to collect all the MT514 events related to a single OrderId in a set of events, Temp514, until they have all been observed. The allocation test determines when all the MT514 events for an OrderId have been observed. Then the set of MT514 events in Temp514 is the set of LastEvents for that OrderId. The processing of MT514 events for that OrderId is complete, and Temp514 is set to **null**.

In the same transaction, MT515 events can be sent in response to MT514 events while other MT514 events are being created. Rule 515 holds up processing of MT515 events until all MT514 events have been processed. It selects as the cause of each MT515 the MT514 with the same allocation.

The causal map can be positioned anywhere in the collaborative architecture where all the events that signify collaboration can be observed. Typically, it would be a benign client on the trading middleware, just listening for collaboration events but otherwise not influencing the processes. It could also be designed as a distributed EPN with EPAs for managing the shared state, with some rules in EPAs at the boundary of each of the partners. Examples of the posets that CallabCausalModel produces are shown in Figures 5.6 and 12.3.

12.6 Examples of Constraints

The agreement may include constraints as we described earlier. For example:

```
// Global constraint on timing of all transactions.
  always (OrderId ?D, TradeRecord ?R, Time ?T)
      MT502(BANK_to_BROKER, ?D, ?R) at ?T  ⟶
          MT517(BANK_to_ETC, ?D, ?R) during (?T, ?T+72 hr);
```

```
// A broker requires a minimum amount for each MT514 allocation.
  never  (OrderId ?D, TradeRecord ?R, Time ?T)
      MT514(ETC_to_BROKER, ?D, ?R) where ( ?R.Alloc < MinimumValue);
```

```
// Bank must not cancel an order after receiving an MT513 confirming it.
never (OrderId ?D, TradeRecord ?R)
    MT513(ETC_to_BANK, ?D, ?R) < MT502(BANK_to_BROKER, "Cancel", ?D, ?R);
```

Each of these constraints can be used to build constraint EPAs, as described in Section 9.6. These constraints can be applied in two ways.

- *Real-time monitoring:* The constraints can be located appropriately to observe activity on the financial network in real time.
- *Offline monitoring:* The constraints can be applied to the output of the causal map, as part of the analysis that is offline and may be postmortem.

Figure 12.2 shows a watchdog EPA placed in the architecture to monitor in real time for the global timing constraint on transactions. Timeout events would be directed to a control console.

12.7 Analysis of Examples of Posets

Each of the following posets shows a small example of the output from a causal map of event executions signifying steps in transactions between the bank and the brokerage.[1]

Figure 12.3 shows the poset of a successful transaction in the communication architecture shown in Figure 12.2 implemented on the ISO 15022

---

[1]In these posets events, M502, M513, etc., signify ISO15022 messages, MT502, MT513, etc.

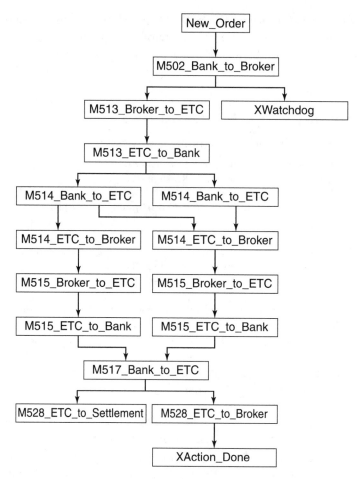

Figure 12.3: Causal history of a successful transaction

network. An order event from a customer to the bank causes an M502 event (signifying an MT502 message on ISO 15022) from the bank to the broker. This event causes a watchdog event, initializing a check for the global timing constraint, and subsequently also causes an M513 event from the broker to the ETC, and from the ETC to the bank. In turn, the M513 event causes two M514 events from the bank to the ETC and on to the broker. These M514 events, allocating portions of the trade to different accounts in the bank, happen at different times. The ETC tracks M514 events to check that a trade is completely and exactly allocated. This checking within the ETC invokes accounting applications that treat events in their time order of arrival. Thus, the two M514 events created by the ETC and sent to the broker not only depend upon the events from the bank, but also have a causal dependency. The second one depends upon the first. A causal rule to add these dependencies between M514 events depends upon knowledge of the ETC's internal processes. A less accurate causal map might omit them. The poset shows causal dependencies of subsequent M515 events and the M517 event from the bank that finalizes the transaction. The M517 is caused by both of the M515 events and causes settlement events between the ETC and settlement facilities to happen.

Figure 12.4 show a poset recording the events in a transaction that did not complete. The activity appears to have proceeded similarly to the first transaction except that

- The watchdog initialization event caused a TimeOut event, which in turn caused an Inconsistent event report.
- The broker appears to have failed to respond to an M514 event.

We might ask, "What caused the TimeOut event?" The computational cause is the M502 event that initialized the constraint check. The global timing constraint in Section 12.6 was violated because the M502 event did not cause an M517 event within the specified 72 hours. The M517 event is missing.

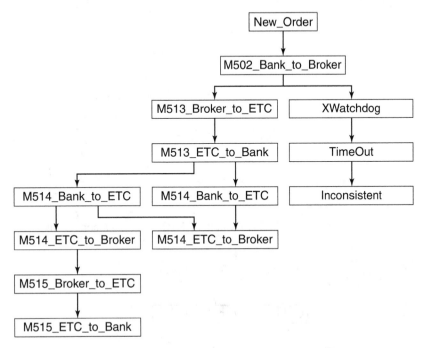

Figure 12.4: Causal history of a transaction violating the global timing constraint

Obviously, we want to know why the transaction failed. Such a failure is usually called an *exceptional situation*, even though in practice today it is very common. Exceptional situations are situations that the processes are not designed to handle—that is, to recover from and continue successfully. They usually simply terminate. Exceptions stall the process and lead to reduced transaction completion rates.

A solution must begin by solving the information problem: how to get accurate information needed to recognize the exceptional situation.

A more detailed picture of the transaction activity is given in Figure 12.5. Here the broker's requirements are also subject to online constraint checking. The second M514 event violated the broker's minimum requirement in Section 12.6 and caused another inconsistent event. Nothing further happened, and the transaction stalled, leading to the TimeOut.

Armed with this information, we might suggest several different approaches to fixing the problem. Some typical suggestions, and the reasons why they won't work, might be the following.

- *The agreement should be amended to cancel a trade when constraint violations happen.* This could lead to a high cancellation rate, which may be preferable to a high exception rate, but does not improve the collaboration success rate.

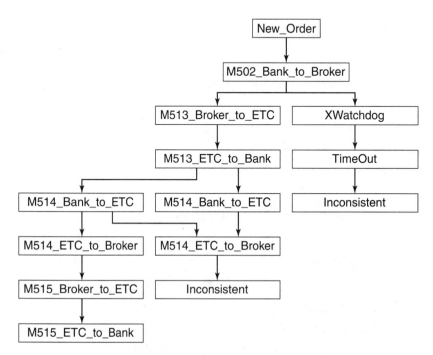

Figure 12.5: Causal history showing local and global constraint violations

- *The bank's allocation process should be upgraded to conform to the broker's requirement.* This may be impractical in a legacy system if, for example, the bank is doing business with many brokers, all having different requirements.
- *The broker should drop its minimum requirement.* Again, this may be unacceptable to the broker.
- *Violations of constraints should initiate a rollback in the transaction.* For example, violations of the broker's minimum requirement constraint should be reported to all three parties: the broker, the bank, and the ETC. The message protocol in the agreement should be extended with new message types to allow initiation of a rollback of all M514 events and M515 events they have caused.

    This solution may lead to a lot of thrashing and timeouts if violations continue to happen.

Solving these exceptional situation problems depends upon having the following two capabilities:

- *Constraint checking* to improve the diagnostic information generated during the execution of a transaction, and
- *Flexible processes that can be modified rapidly* to allow changes to processes to handle exceptions, and to reduce the constraint violations during execution of a transaction.

We can improve the diagnostics by using EPAs to check the transaction event executions online for constraint violations. The set of constraints must be as complete as possible, including not only constraints agreed to in the collaboration, but also requirements of each enterprise's business processes. The set of constraints may vary as each partner changes its business policies. The set of constraint EPAs that are monitoring the collaboration events can be changed to reflect changes in policy.

Reducing the constraint violations depends upon having the flexibility to change the processes as well as improving diagnostics. Essentially, processes need to be changed to conform to constraints and to handle exceptions. In the stalled transaction, for example:

- A constraint checker would notify of minimum requirement violations. This would improve diagnostics and give processes more information to work with.
- The broker's process could be changed to handle the M514 event that violates its requirements. For example, it might respond by sending the bank a repeat M513, allowing a rollback.

- The bank's process could be changed to not generate MT514 messages to the broker with allocations that are below the broker's minimum.

Improving diagnostics and rapidly modifying processes are the most promising approaches to improve the collaboration and increase the transaction completion rate.

12.8   Constraint Checking Becomes Part of the Collaboration

There may be problems with a collaborative aggreement that are easier to live with than to fix. For example, the constraint on the bank to behave consistently about canceling an order after a confirmation of it from the broker was intended to improve the trade completion rates. Even if the bank conforms to this constraint, the kind of situation shown in Figure 12.6 cannot be prevented. It shows a race condition between the bank's issuing an M502 cancellation of an order and the broker's issuing an M513 confirmation of the order. The second M502 Bank-to-Broker event is a cancellation of the order in the first M502 event. The M513 event was caused by the first M502 event. But the second M502 event happens independently of the M513 event created by the broker to confirm the order. The two events signify causally independent activities—there is no causal link between them in the poset shown in Figure 12.6. The confirmation must go to the ETC before it goes to the bank. While the M513 is en route, the bank cancels.

The timeline in Figure 12.7 shows the timing of the events according to a global system clock. The M513 confirmation is issued by the broker at

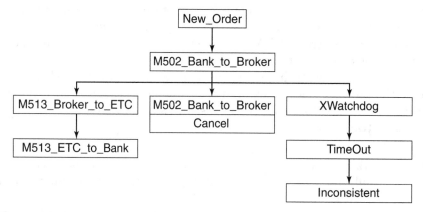

Figure 12.6: Causal history showing a race between M502 cancellation and M513 confirmation events

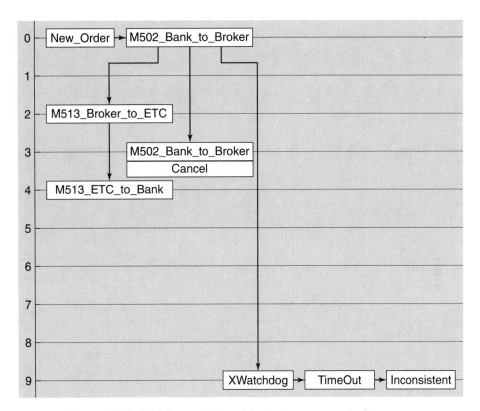

Figure 12.7: Timing relationship between events in a race

time 2, the M502 cancellation is issued by the bank at time 3, and the M513 is passed on from the ETC to the bank at time 4. Activity stalls, and the global time constraint violates with a TimeOut at time 9.

This is a race condition inherent in the agreement between the two parties because they are not constrained to synchronize every step they take with the other party. There are ways to prevent this race condition, but the solutions may be considered too cumbersome. In cases like this one, there is another option. It may be more practical to live with online monitoring of global constraints against the race condition happening in the system. These constraints warn when a race happens. The parties must agree upon how to handle the warnings. For example, a constraint against races could be expressed exactly as the **never** constraint on the bank in Section 12.6 with the timing operator, $<$, replaced by the parallel operator, $\|$. In this option, online constraint checking becomes part of the collaborative processing.

Chapter $\boxed{13}$

Implementing Event Abstraction Hierarchies

- *Specifying event hierarchies, revisited*
- *Using maps and EPNs to implement event hierarchies*
- *Induced causality*
- *The abstraction effect on constraints*
- *Bridging accessible information gaps*
- *Four steps to hierarchical viewing*
- *Example of viewing a fabrication line*

This chapter describes a strategy for applying CEP to view enterprise systems by means of event abstraction hierarchies. Here we lay the groundwork for applying the concepts explained in Chapters 10 and 11: *event processing networks* and *causal maps*. This chapter is a preparation for the case study in the next chapter. It goes into more detail about event hierarchies than Chapter 7 did.

    In the next chapter, we show how the strategy is applied. We describe an experimental case study to develop an EPN for hierarchical viewing and control of a stock-trading system. The hierarchy defines three levels of abstraction. The views are coordinated. The complex event patterns that are employed used causal relationships between events at various levels. Causality between events in the target system is defined by a causal model. To do all this, we must have a plan. This chapter is about the plan.

The challenges of keeping the human in control of the electronic enterprise were described in Chapter 3. The vision we proposed was to develop a CEP capability to build personalized, event-driven views of activity in a hierarchical system.

- The views should show activity at various levels of abstraction.
- Views should be constructed to meet individual users' personal requirements needed to perform their roles.
- Different views should be coordinated in the sense that they show views that are aggregated from the same set of monitored events at the same time—the views are "on the same page," so to speak.
- Views should be changeable on the fly to meet changing situations in the target system.

The problem to be surmounted in Chapter 3 to achieve this vision was the *information gap*—that is, the difference in information content between the events in the target system that could be monitored and processed by CEP, and the complex events that were needed to construct the desired views.

The key idea toward bridging the information gap was the *event abstraction hierarchy*. Chapter 7 gave an approach with simple examples of how to define and build abstraction hierarchies using event aggregation rules based upon STRAW_EPL.

Now that we are armed with RAPIDE-EPL, EPNs, and causal maps, we can revisit building event abstraction hierarchies and personalized viewing. First, the reader should briefly review Chapters 3 and 7. Now we are ready to proceed with a more detailed study of CEP applied to viewing the electronic enterprise and keeping the human in control.

13.1   The Accessible Information Gap

As we become more sophisticated in our demands for information, we want to monitor more complex activities in our systems and make more focused uses of the results. We described information gaps in detail in Chapter 3. In summary, the kinds of requests for complex monitoring and context-based operations that we hear frequently from managers of enterprise systems are things like these.

- *"We want to know in real time when a host outside our network makes an uninterrupted sequence of 50 or more connection attempts using IP addresses or a port number range."*—network managers trying to defend against security break-ins
- *"We want an online tool that lets us specify those aspects of the traffic on our network that we want to view at any given time."*—imaginative network managers
- *"We want to understand how performance degredation in our Web server or our partner's advertisement server affects our service-level agreements with our customers. We have all the log files, but we can't determine how they are related to the SLAs."*—ASP managers
- *"We want to route messages dynamically based upon their content and the context of other recent messages on related subjects."*—many Internet-based business applications
- *"We want to understand what patterns of repeated requests to our enterprise's secure databases from unauthorized entities happen, when they happen, and how they are related."*—privacy and security managers
- *"We wish we could understand the patterns of activities that lead up to the performance of one of our switches degrading in such and such manner—and detect them before performance degrades."*—providers of global communication services

To meet these kinds of requests, we need to monitor activities at different levels, and we need powerful pattern-based monitoring. Unfortunately, it often happens that the activities at the desired level—say, "degrading performance," or "attempted break-in," or "arbitrage opportunity"—cannot be monitored directly. Events signifying these kinds of activities just aren't generated in most systems or in most monitoring tools. We must construct such events from the information that is available—if that is possible!

If we are unable to monitor the activities we want but can only monitor lower-level information, like messages on the IT layer or summaries supplied by a network monitor, we have an *accessible information gap*. We want to view activities that interest us, and we describe those activities at a certain conceptual level, but there is no monitoring of our system at that level. Instead, we are given views of activities at a lower level, sometimes much lower.

The *accessible information gap* refers to the difference (or gap) between the level at which we can monitor activities in a system and the level of the activities we want to know about.

Event hierarchies let us specify how we can bridge an accessible information gap. They are a method we can use to specify what we want and how it can be extracted from, and aggregated from, the information we can get. But we have to be clever about how we do it. That's where event hierarchies help.

13.2 Event Abstraction Hierarchies, Revisited

The crucial aspect of our definition of an event abstraction hierarchy in Section 7.3 is to provide mappings between the events at different levels of abstraction. In the simple case described there, we used aggregation rules from STRAW_EPL. Now we can extend clause 2 of the definition to use EPNs that aggregate events between the levels. We can use connections between maps to build flexible viewing architectures.

The definition of a *concept abstraction hierarchy* must contain the following elements.

1. *A sequence of levels of activities.* Each level consists of a set of descriptions of system activities and, for each activity, a specification of the types of events that signify instances of that activity. Level 1 is the lowest level.

2. *A set of event pattern maps.* There is a map for each level (except level 1) that specifies the events of that level as aggregations of events at levels below. If there are multiple views at the same level, there may be more than one map to a level from lower levels. In the most general case, there may be an EPN, containing filters and maps, that maps events from lower levels to a level.

Figure 13.1 shows an outline of a hierarchy definition. Each level specifies a set of activities in the target system. We don't say how the activities are specified. They might be described in English or specified as functions, methods, system operations, and so on. What is important is that there is an action specification corresponding to each activity. The purpose of the action is to specify the types of events that signify an instance of the activity. The events should contain all the relevent data needed to determine which activity and which instance of it they signify.

For example, the figure shows that instances of level 1 activity O are signified by events that are instances of the action E_O. Similarly, other levels have actions and corresponding events to signify them. At the highest level, for example, activities A and B are signified by events of action types E_A and E_B, respectively.

The hierarchy definition must also contain event pattern maps, at least one for each level above level 1. The map or EPN for a level must specify the events at that level as an aggregation of events at the levels below it. In most examples, a map or EPN will aggregate only from events of the

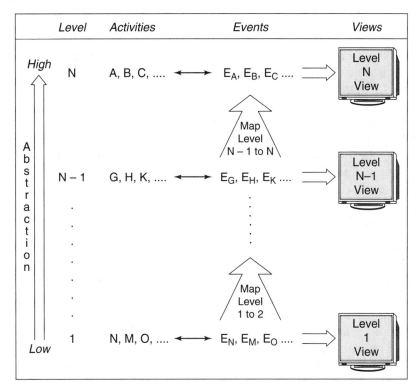

Figure 13.1: Concept abstraction hierarchies and how they are
implemented by maps

immediately lower level. However, in the general case, an event may be an
aggregation across several lower levels.

An event abstraction hierarchy definition in this format gives us a lot
of advantages.

- The abstraction hierarchy is specified precisely. We know
  mathematical relationships between the events at various levels.

- There is a unified EPN composed of all the maps or EPNs for the
  levels in the hierarchy definition. The unified EPN generates events
  signifying activities at each level, as they happen. This can be used to
  view the system at any abstraction level (see Section 13.3).

- The hierarchy definition is easily modified. We can add a new level
  by describing the new activities of that level and defining the corresponding events and aggregation maps from lower levels for those
  events. Similarly, we can change a level, or we can delete a level. This
  lets us specify abstraction hierarchies flexibly to account for variability

among people and for the variability of any person's view during the lifetime of the system.

- The levels in a hierarchy definition can be chosen arbitrarily. The only completeness criterion is that there must be a map specifying each level in terms of lower levels.

The maps specify mathematical relationships between events at different levels. Depending upon their actual details, we may be able to prove properties of events at some level—for example, the minimum time intervals that those events must take to happen or what causal relationships they must have.

13.2.1   Induced Causality

One aspect of event hierarchies is the causal relationships between events at higher levels. Suppose we have a causal model for the events at the levels that are being monitored. This model is inferred from properties of the target system. Events at higher levels are aggregated from sets of lower-level events. Are the higher-level events causally related?

A causal relationship between the higher-level events can be defined in a number of ways. These are called *induced causality* relationships, meaning that the causal relationships of the lower-level events imply a relationship between the higher-level events.

Strong induced causality. For example, the strongest form of induced causality is defined as follows:

1. If event A is an aggregation of lower-level events a_1, a_2, a_3, ..., and
2. B is an aggregation of lower-level events b_1, b_2, b_3, ..., and
3. for all i, j, $a_i \rightarrow b_j$, then
   A $\rightarrow$ B.

Essentially, strong induced causality means that if A is aggregated from a set of events, each of which is a cause of every event that B is aggregated from, then A is a cause of B.

Other definitions of induced causality use weaker conditions on the relationship between the sets of lower-level events. For example, if any a_i is a cause of all the b_j's, then $A \rightarrow B$.

Induced causality is often useful in drill-down searches for low-level causes of constraint violations expressed in terms of higher-level events.

13.2.2   Abstraction Effect on Constraints

Automated constraint checking is one of the tools we can employ to keep the human in control of the electronic enterprise (see Chapter 3). This technique allows us to automatically detect violations of business and security policies. It frequently turns out that a constraint, expressing some regulation or policy, can be formulated using events at more than one level in an event hierarchy. This is to be expected because events at different levels are related by aggregation maps.

The *abstraction effect* states that the higher-level version of a constraint is usually

- Simpler to express.
- More efficiently checked for violations.

The efficiency in checking for violations is gained not only because the higher-level form is simpler (for example, the constraint pattern contains fewer basic event patterns), but also because there are fewer higher-level events.

Because the aggregation to the higher level is already in place for viewing, it makes sense to take advantage of it for constraint checking too.

13.2.3 Modifiability

The point about easy modification should be emphasized. The idea here is that we can insert and remove levels at any time. To remove a level, say, level N, we need to define the map from level N−1 to level N+1. The new map will be the transitive composition of the map from level N−1 to N with the map from level N to N+1. The new map will aggregate level N+1 events from level N−1 events. To add a new level, say, level N, we must describe the activities and define the events of the level. Then for each new event, we must define a new map from level N−1 to the new level, N, that specifies how to aggregate the new event. We should also define a new map between the new level, N, and level N+1, but if we don't want to do that, the old map between levels N−1 and N+1 will do.

Omission of detail is also a powerful technique in constructing hierarchies. It lets us define the hierarchy of activities we want to discuss or view.

There is no need for a concept abstraction hierarchy to contain every possible detailed level of a target system. Indeed, one can argue that it is impossible for a hierarchy to be complete or absolute because new levels—however fantastic—can always be interpolated between existing ones. As a means of communication or as a monitoring device (see the next section), a hierarchy need specify only those levels of interest.

But there must be sufficient detail at each level for maps to the levels above to be correctly specified. This means that if the levels are widely separated in the complexity of their activities, the map to a higher level must make a bigger jump to aggregate from lower levels than it otherwise would if there were intermediate levels. Suppose there are three levels: L is lowest, M is in the middle, and N is highest. A map from L to N can always be constructed as a transitive composition of a map from L to M with one from M to N. Essentially, we trade off separation of levels and complexity of maps between levels.

Generally, there is no single way to define the hierarchical structure of a system. We refer to this as *variability* of hierarchical views, meaning variability among people and variability over time. Variability among people means simply that different people view the same components as being of different degrees of importance and as playing different roles in the system. People define differing hierarchical structures of the same system simply to show their own view of the system. For example, one man's application may be another's middleware. Variability over time happens because our views of a system can change. For example, we could draw a simple hierarchy, like Figure 1.4, as a first approximation of the system's hierarchy. Normally, we don't want to look at too many details at once. But at some point, we might decide that more detail was needed and that each level in this picture should be changed to show its components and their relationships. That would lead to a much more detailed picture of the system's hierarchical structure.

Since concept hierarchies are variable among people, and there is no single or standard way to define the hierarchy of a system, why are hierarchies useful?

First, some important hierarchies can be standardized. Second, variability in viewing a system is usually limited. This means there is some agreement among different people. If we look at a set of hierarchical views of the same system, generally if activities C and D are placed at different levels in one of them (say, C is at a lower level than D), none of the other views will place D at a lower level than C. In other views, C and D may be placed at the same level, or they may not appear at all. Of course, sometimes people do disagree dramatically in their views of a system.

But the important answer to the question of usefulness lies in the fact that we can't understand a complex system by looking at every activity at every level at once. We need a way to communicate with one another in discussions about a system. Hierarchies give us a way to focus attention on particular aspects and ignore, or "push down," other details. They let us communicate our system view to others. First and foremost, they are a communication device.

Going beyond simply communicating system views, abstraction hierarchies have been used to define industry standards. The OSI [9] seven-layer standard for communication protocols is a good example of this use. To do this, the ISO groups had to come up with a method of specifying the OSI hierarchy that went beyond the ordinary communication use. The OSI hierarchy had to be specified in a way that was precise and unambiguous.

The usefulness of abstraction hierarchies depends upon the kinds of techniques we employ to specify the hierarchy—how precise we can make the specification. Our goal is to show how to go beyond our informal use of hierarchies as communication. We can use them to automate the monitoring, viewing, and analysis of a target system at any level of abstraction.

13.3   Bridging the Information Gaps

Imagine that we are faced with an accessible information gap. We can monitor some level of activity in our system. But we want to view higher-level activities. One approach is to define a hierarchy that bridges the gap between the levels we can monitor and the levels we want to view.

We will try to define an abstraction hierarchy in which level 1 is the level of activities and events that can be monitored. Usually, this is the IT layer or some component of it, such as a set of log files or the system's information bus. The higher levels will define the activities we want to view. We have to describe these activities and specify the events that signify them.

Now comes the hard step—bridging the gap. We must specify how to aggregate the top-level events from the level 1 events that can be monitored. We do this by specifying maps that do the aggregation. But the job may be easier if we break it into steps. So we may want to specify intermediate levels of activities and events—that is, levels that lie above level 1 and below the top level.

We may run into problems at this step. Here are some we might expect.

First, it might not be easy to do—which is a good argument for building libraries of hierarchies and, indeed, standard hierarchies for each domain of system operations. Each system domain should have its own specialized standard abstraction hierarchies. There should be standard hierarchies for communication protocol systems, network management systems, finance and banking systems, microelectronic manufacturing systems, automated factory and warehousing systems, and so on. Domain-specific abstraction hierarchies are often related, particularly when one system is a subsystem of another. For example, one hierarchy may have a level that has the same kinds of activities and events as, say, the top level in another hierarchy. Whenever two levels in two hierarchies match in this way, hierarchies can be composed to form new hierarchies with broader coverage. Indeed, there are a lot of things we can do to make building hierarchies easier, but we'll delay talking about composition until later.

Another situation might be that the level 1 events do not supply enough information for an aggregation to the events we want. The system lacks instrumentation for the kinds of activities we want. Faced with this problem, we must go back to the system managers and implementers and try to find a way to insert extra instrumentation or extract it from subsystems that have heretofore been viewed and treated as closed systems. This is usually a difficult problem, often with political overtones within the enterprise. Its resolution requires justifying the work needed to do the additional instrumentation This reduces to an analysis of the effort versus the gain, for example, the ROI.

In practice, there is more than enough information at monitorable levels in distributed enterprise systems to bridge many gaps, indeed gaps that people have not yet begun to think about. This is one of the main reasons that many enterprises use firewalls—to prevent snooping the wealth of accessible information.

So, let's assume that we are successful in defining an abstraction hierarchy to bridge the gap in our system between the monitorable levels and the levels we want to view.

The final step is to apply the hierarchy to the system. What do we mean by "apply?"

We want to view the activities described in our gap-bridging hierarchy. So we must be able to either monitor or generate the corresponding events at each level whenever those activities, both low and high, happen in the system. The events drive viewers that let us "see the activities" in various graphical ways, as shown in Figure 13.1. Here's how we do it.

13.4 Steps to Apply a Hierarchy to a Target System

The following steps are applied iteratively, using EPA libraries and graphical composition tools.

1. *Add adapters to the target system to monitor level 1 events.* We assume that level 1 of the hierarchy specifies events generated by the system at components such as middleware and application log files that can be observed by adapters. We must place suitable adapters to monitor events at this level and convert them to the format used by our EPAs.

2. *Construct maps or EPNs as specified in the hierarchy.* This step uses the techniques described in Chapters 9 and 10.

3. *Construct suitable event-driven viewers.* Each view will be supplied by one or more event-driven viewers. Events from maps at various levels will drive viewer agents that let us view the activities we want to see. This is shown in Figure 13.1.

4. *Connect the maps, EPNs, and viewers to form an EPN implementing the hierarchy.* The filters, maps, and viewers are connected into an EPN, starting with the adapters and ending with the event-driven viewers. The output of the adapters drives the level 1 maps, whose output goes to the input of the level 2 maps, and so on.

If we apply the hierarchy, and our assumptions about level 1's events being monitorable are correct, we can view the activities of the system at any of the levels we choose. The way this works is very simple. When the target system generates events at level 1—the IT layer or at whatever layer is being logged—the adapters and each successive map in the EPN feeds its output to the next map in the hierarchy. Consequently, each map is triggered to generate events signifying activities at each of the levels in the hierarchy as shown in Figure 13.1. We can design whatever event-driven viewer agents we want and add them to the EPN. The events drive viewers that let us see the activities at each level in graphical ways we have designed ourselves.

This gives us *hierarchical viewing* of the target system—both real-time and postmortem. The flexibility to add and delete levels and expand the activities and events at any level, coupled with our ability to make corresponding reconfigurations of the EPN—like adding or deleting agents—lets us change a hierarchical view while it is in operation, in real time.

13.5   A Hierarchy for a Fabrication Process

To illustrate hierarchical viewing, we use a simplified model of a control system for a silicon chip fabrication line.

These kinds of systems consist of several hundred computers communicating across a middleware layer. Figure 13.2 shows a small subset of a typical fabline configuration with 11 computers. It contains most of the interesting *types* of computers as described in [1]—for example, work in progress (WIP), material handling system (MHS), statistical process control (SPC), and equipment control. In a full-scale system, there are a lot more pieces of equipment and their control computers.

The control computers communicate over a middleware layer using publish/subscribe messaging technology. Communication is by broadcasting and subscribing to (or listening for) messages on particular subjects on the middleware. Typical events at this level are Send(*subject, data*) and Listen(*subject, data*). Several of these events in a correct sequence make up a meaningful communication between a pair of controllers. When we view the event traffic on the middleware, we get a jumble of Send and Listen events corresponding to different transactions between different controllers. Figure 13.2 depicts the architecture of the fabline corresponding

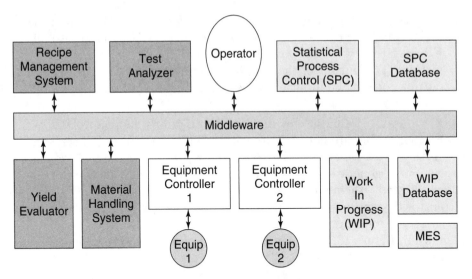

Figure 13.2: A fabline control system

to the lowest abstraction level, the middleware communication level in Table 13.1.

Any particular computer listens for messages of interest to it and is deaf to all other messages broadcast on the middleware.[1] So it is quite natural to define the next higher level of abstraction in an event hierarchy as a level that abstracts the middleware-level message sequences into *point-to-point* direct communication between pairs of computers. A point-to-point communication happens when two computers broadcast and listen for each other's messages according to some protocol. At this level, the middleware is hidden—point-to-point could take place on any middleware.

13.5.1   Personal Views

Different levels of events in this hierarchy will be of interest to different people. The lower two levels, the middleware level and the point-to-point level, would be of interest to a fabline control systems engineer. Such a person would typically view the fabline activity at the point-to-point level because it contains fewer events and gives a precise picture of the attempted communications between the control computers. When something goes wrong— maybe a communication times out because of a lost message or a too slow response—the engineer would use the point-to-point view to separate out

---

[1]This is implemented by a subject addressing scheme in middleware—one listens for subjects of interest.

Table 13.1: A Four-Level Event Hierarchy for a Fabline

Level	Activity	Event Types	No. Events
4. Product disposition	Disposition of lots	create_lot, fab_step_complete_lot, process_completed_lot	17
3. Fabline workflow	Machine status changes, movement and processing of lots	setup_machine, repair_machine, maintain_machine, position_lot, load_lot, process_lot, unload_lot	49
2. Point-to-point communication	communication between pairs of controllers	move_lot, move_lot_ack, setup_machine, setup_machine_ack, load_lot, begin_load, loading, end_load, begin_process, processing, end_process, lot_processed, unload_lot, begin_unload, unloading, end_unload, begin_repair, repairing, end_repair, begin_pm, maintaining, end_pm, idling	354
1. Middleware communication	Broadcasting messages on subjects, Subscribing to messages on subjects	Send($subject$, $data$), Listen($subject$)	1306

the middleware-level events that are relevent to that error. This requires using not only the abstract point-to-point events and the actual middleware events, but also the mappings between them.

The workflow level will be of interest to a production engineer who is interested in material processing and throughput, and equipment maintenance and utilization. Events at this level have abstracted away all the communication between control computers. They denote activities dealing with introduction, processing and movement of lots (cassettes of wafers), and various statuses of equipment. However, as we shall see, the systems engineer may also sometimes want to view at the workflow level.

The product disposition level deals with the manufacturing status of lots. All workflow activities have been abstracted away. This level would be of interest to upper management in the production organization.

13.5.2   Implementation

This hierarchy was implemented using event pattern mappings, as described in Section 13.4. The EPN used was a very simple linear composition of an adapter to the middleware and three aggregation maps between the levels. Different event-driven viewers were used at each of the four levels, as illustrated in Figure 13.1.

13.5.3   Diagnostics

Table 13.1 shows the exponential reduction in the number of events at each level during monitoring of events over a small time window.

Networked systems like fabrication lines often experience low-level faults that bring the system to a grinding halt. These faults can be very costly. Typically, the middleware can lose events, or the communication between the control computers is not robust under timing delays. The middleware, the protocols, or the software in the control computers could all be at fault.

Today, when such communication faults between controllers happen, a maintenance engineer is faced with a large level 1 event log. Typical diagnostic efforts to locate the causes of such faults have been reported to take up to two weeks. The engineer's first problem is to try to understand the level 1 log file in terms of level 3 activities that were going on when the fault happened.

Low-level errors tend to be first recognized at level 3, where expected events do not happen. For example, a cassette (or lot) that should have been processed by a given machine failed to be processed. In other words, an UnLoadLot event is missing at level 3 in the scenario of processing events.

When we implement an event hierarchy such as is shown in Table 13.1, we can use the records provided by the aggregation maps to drill down from level 3 to level 1. Here's how the drill down works.

- Suppose the last level 3 event to happen before the expected event was ProcessLot(6, 4). It signifies the processing of a lot, say, number 6, on equipment, machine number 4. Then we expected UnLoadLot(6, 4), but it never happened.

- We can trace down from the level 3 event, ProcessLot, to a set of level 2 events that it was aggregated from. We can do this using a poset browser that can access the recorded aggregation relationship from the maps implementing the hierarchy.

- From this level 2 set of events, we can drill down to a set of level 1 events. To see schematically what we are doing, look back at Figure 7.1 in Chapter 7. We trace down through the event shadows at successively lower levels as shown in this figure.

- This gives us, at level 1, a set of events that happened just before the set of events should have happened that would have been aggregated up to the missing level 3 event.

- We are now in the area of the level 1 log file that contains events in the causal history of events that should have occurred. We are close to where the error is located. Furthermore, we can view the level 1 log file as sets of shadows that correspond to level 3 events. And we have the causal relationships between the level 1 events and their time-stamps to guide us. All this information simplifies the search for the pattern that should have happened and why it did not happen—a missing level 1 event.[2]

In the next chapter, we give examples of the aggregation maps and drill-down techniques in a detailed case study.

---

[2]A report on this experimental application of CEP can be found on http://pavg.stanford.edu/cep/ [12].

Chapter 14

Case Study: Viewing a Financial Trading System

- *A distributed trading system using publish/subscribe middleware*
- *An information gap between the IT layer and desired views*
- *A concept hierarchy to bridge the gap*
- *Mapping between the levels in the hierarchy*
- *A causal model for communications in the trading system*
- *An EPN to implement hierarchical viewing of the trading system*
- *Viewing the trading system at each hierarchical level*
- *Using a hierarchy of views for drill-down diagnostics*
- *Constraints to help manage the system*

This chapter illustrates an application of hierarchical viewing to an event-driven model of a stock-trading system. The model is implemented on top of commercial middleware. We show how each of the steps described in Section 13.3 applies to this target system. Situations arising during the operation of the system are used to illustrate higher-level views and drill-down analysis to understand the activity in the system.

14.1   A Small Stock-Trading System

Figure 14.1 shows the top-level interface communication architecture of a model stock market trading system called the *small stock-trading system,* or STS. The system is hosted on a commercial publish/subscribe middleware called RV.[1] The components of the system are programmed in Java and use the RV API to communicate with one another. RV is the IT layer of the system. A similar system can be built on top of any middleware.

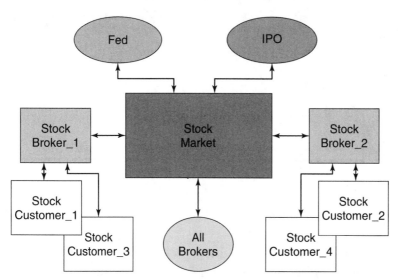

Figure 14.1: **A model architecture of stock market trading**

STS is a dynamic system in the sense that some of its components can be created and destroyed during operation. Figure 14.1 is a snapshot of its architecture when only two brokers and four customers are actively participating in the model. Communication in this picture is drawn as two-headed arrows between the system components so that the IT layer is abstracted out of the picture.

It helps to understand the system if we think of the components as falling into two groups.

- *Users.*   Components such as the Fed (Federal Reserve), Analysts, IPOs (investment banks that issue new stocks), Brokers, and

---

[1]TIBCO's Rendezvous information bus, usually called RV. "Information Bus" and "Rendezvous" are registered trademarks of TIBCO Inc.

StockCustomers. All these objects broadcast messages on RV to communicate with one another and with the market.

- *The market.* The market consists of a StockMarket component and arbitrarily many Stock objects, which are components of the StockMarket.

Here's what the STS components do.

IPO components create stocks and their initial prices. What happens is that an IPO broadcasts an RV stock creation message with a stock symbol and price as parameters, and the StockMarket subscribes to these messages. The StockMarket then creates a new Stock object and initializes it with its symbol and price. The Stock object then begins executing by generating a stream of RV messages containing its prices. A price can change randomly within certain bounds from the previous price and has a probability of being influenced by certain kinds of messages.

The **Fed** can generate RV messages that contain changes to the Fed's interest rate. They are broadcast on RV and subscribed to by the Stock-Market, which in turn passes them on to all Stock objects. An Analyst can generate RV messages containing favorable or unfavorable analyses of any stock. These messages are passed on similarly. Messages from the Fed or from Analysts may *cause* prices of some stocks to rise or fall—not always, but frequently.

The StockMarket has a two-level architecture because Stock objects are its components. The second level is not shown in Figure 14.1. Stocks are active components that continuously generate their current prices. The StockMarket broadcasts RV messages from the stocks to the outer world of all Brokers. It also handles messages from individual Brokers about trading stocks. Whenever a new stock is created, the updated list of stocks is broadcast to all Brokers.

A Broker communicates both with customers and the StockMarket by means of RV messages. A Broker can receive communication from the StockMarket in response to a request it sent, or it can get a message that is broadcast to all Brokers. A Broker keeps records of stock prices, stock lists, customer records, and the "stop loss" orders, called Alarm objects, that have been requested by its customers—until they are deleted by the customer.

StockCustomer components have the most complex interaction protocols. They communicate with Brokers. They can request any stock's price or the list of existing stocks, they can set an alarm condition on a stock's price (a stop loss order), and they can trade stocks. These requests are RV messages sent to a Broker, and the reply messages from the Broker are passed back on RV and subscribed to by the customer. A StockCustomer must always communicate with the same Broker—a simple constraint on this model.

A StockCustomer's requests for a stock price or the stock list goes to a Broker which then returns the Broker's latest price or list—which can be out of date. A StockCustomer can request a Broker to place a stop loss Alarm on a stock at some price. The request includes the name of the customer. The Broker then creates an Alarm object with the price bound and customer name. A StockCustomer can request the Broker to delete an Alarm that that customer has requested.

An Alarm defines a condition under which a customer should receive a notification. Whenever a Broker receives a price change, it checks all its Alarms; an Alarm is activated when the alarm condition is met. An activated Alarm sends a warning message to the StockCustomer.

A trade request is an RV message sent by a StockCustomer to its Broker. The trade event contains the stock's symbol and the number of shares to be bought or sold. The Broker checks the validity of the trade according to certain rules, which could be SEC rules and brokerage house rules. The Broker replies by sending a denial or confirmation message back to the customer. If a trade is valid, the Broker sends a message to the StockMarket requesting the trade, which may *cause* the stock's price to change. Confirmations of the trade's completion are returned from the StockMarket to the Broker and on to the customer.

The component All Brokers in Figure 14.1 is an adapter that allows us to easily add EPAs for constraint checking. Essentially, it is a monitoring facility. We describe how we use this facility in Section 14.5.

In this model, each component is treated as a single thread of control. Effectively, this orders the events each component publishes on the middleware in a linear sequence, ordered by a thread counter or a timestamp.

14.2   The Information Gap for STS

Now we have to decide what exactly we would like to monitor and view about STS and what we can actually log. This will tell us what our information gap is and what we have to do to bridge it.

Here's a short wishlist of views we might like to have.

- *Animation of the component-level communication:*   This is an animation of the message flow between the various components, as we have described it. We would like to see who is communicating with whom and the amount of concurrent activity. We want to get a visual feel for the activity in the system in terms of trades, price changes, and so on, not in terms of middleware messages.

- *Causality at the component level:* We want to view causality—for example, which messages are caused by a customer's request for a trade.

- *Statistics on activity at the component level:* We want to see a statistical bar graph of the percentage of different kinds of requests from customers—the percentage of requests that are price quotes, trades, stop loss orders (Alarms), and so on.

- *Performance of brokers:* How about the performance of the brokers? We want to monitor various aspects of their performance—how often they quote the latest available stock price, and how often the stop loss orders are executed when they should be. Each of these views requires that we look at several component-level events together with their causal order and timing. For example, a timely price quotation would need to aggregate a set of events consisting of the customer's request, the stock's price changes, and the broker's reply to the customer; some of these events are causally related, and their timing is critical.

- *Behavior of brokers:* We might like to know if the brokers conform to SEC regulations. Can we detect suspicious situations where brokers might not be adhering to regulations? Again, such views need to aggregate several events at the component level that obey specific timing constraints and may be related by causality.

All these views depend upon our being able to bridge the gap between them and the events we can monitor.

Now, what can we actually monitor? The answer is, messages on the RV middleware. These are messages that make up RV's communication protocols and are based on a subject addressing scheme for sending and subscribing to messages. The STS activities that interest us are described at the component level or above. They are completed requests for price quotes, trades, and so on. Each of these activities is an aggregation of several RV messages. So, there is a first gap between RV messages and the component activities we have described. Next, there's a question of causality. RV messages contain no explicit encoding about causality between messages. So causality is a second gap—we want to be able to track what caused what to happen. Finally, the performance and behavior activities consist of several related component-level activites—the third gap.

Conceptually, Figure 14.2 depicts the gap between information accessible from the IT layer and the views that we want to monitor. This is the gap between the messages on the information bus that can be accessed through the RV API (or an even lower level RV interface for packet-level information) and the level of events that signify aggregations of

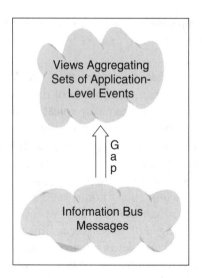

Figure 14.2: An accessible information gap in the trading system

component activities, such as statistics, performance measures, and illegal activity.

14.3   An Event Abstraction Hierarchy for STS

Our next step is to specify an event hierarchy to bridge this gap. We first need to describe a set of STS activities organized by levels. Table 14.1 shows a possible concept hierarchy for our STS system.

   This kind of table is not a standard for viewing financial trading systems. It is simply our view of a reasonable levelwise set of activities. What is fixed is the lowest-level IT middlware messages—that's what is accessible. The rest is open to change and revision. These are the important properties.

1. Level 1 describes the accessible activities.
2. Any activity at a higher level can be specified as an aggregation (a map or an EPN) of activities at the levels below it.
3. Each desired view can be constructed as a map from a subset of the activities.

   Each activity should have a corresponding action declaration that specifies the type of events that signify instances of that activity. Each level 2 activity is an activity of a component in the STS. For example, customers make requests to their brokers, and brokers respond to the customers and

Table 14.1: STS Activities Organized into Three Levels

Level	Activity Class	Activities	Event Types
3	Customer-broker transactions	Buy or sell transactions, setting stop orders, price enquiries	*Price query* *Buy action* *Sell action* *Alarm creation*
	Broker performance	Inaccurate price quote, late stop order execution, illegal trading	*Late price* *Late alarm* *Buy ahead* *Sell ahead*
2	Customer actions	Requests for prices, buying, selling	*Get price* *Buy* *Sell* *Create alarm*
	Broker actions	Replies to customers, requests to stock market	*Broker reply* *Buy stock* *Sell stock*
	IPO actions	Creating stocks	*Create stock* *Spead rumor*
	Stock market actions	Stock price changes, buy or sell transaction results	*Stock create* *Set price* *Price change* *Buy result* *Sell result*
1	Middleware messages	Publish messages, receive messages	*TIB_Message*

make requests for trades to the market. The level 3 activities consist of posets of level 2 activities. Some of them represent a completed transaction between components of the trading system—for example, a Buy transaction, which involves a customer, a broker, and the stock market carrying out related level 2 activities. Other level 3 activities represent performance measures on brokers; they consist of related sets of activities of a broker.

14.4 Building the Event Abstraction Hierarchy

Our next task is to construct aggregation maps for the event types of levels 2 and 3 in Table 14.1. Figure 14.3 shows our strategy. We will build a map to causally order component communication events at level 2. Then we will

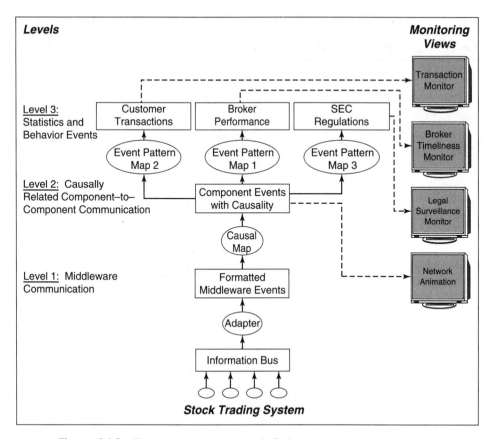

Figure 14.3: Event pattern maps defining an event abstraction hierarchy for STS

build three maps to deliver level 3 views of the lower-level activity. These are the views in our wishlist in Section 14.2. We configure these maps, together with event-driven viewers, into an EPN that implements the hierarchy. The kinds of visual tools discussed in Section 10.6.1 are used in the configuration.

The next sections show how we tackle building the event hierarchy from the bottom up.

14.4.1   Level 1

The level 1 events are the events that are output by an event adapter (see Sections 5.2 and 10.1) applied to the middleware. This adapter listens to the StockMarket message traffic on the RV middleware—the messages can be monitored through the RV API. Essentially, these level 1 events signify messages broadcast on the information bus. They are instances of an action declaration that specifies the messages:

```
action TIB_Message (String   Subject,
                     ThreadId Sender,
                     String   Message,
                     String   Symbol,
                     Float    Price,
                     Int      Shares);
```

An event at level 1 signifies the activity of broadcasting a message on RV containing the data in that event. The data tell us the subject of the message, which component initiated the message, and its contents. We can also find out who is subscribing to the subject of the message by using some specialized interfaces of RV. In Figure 14.3 these level 1 events are shown as the formatted output of the adapter.

14.4.2   Level 2

At level 2 we have two goals. Our first goal is to specify the types of events that signify communication activities between components. These activities are classified in level 2 of Table 14.1. We want to define the actions that signify communication between pairs of components (the Java objects in the StockMarket model). The level 2 events will be instances of these actions.

The second goal is to specify the causality between these events.

Event types signifying the component-to-component communication activities described in Section 14.1 are specified by the following actions. We give some examples.

```
// activities of IPOs
action CreateStock (String Symbol, Float Price );
action SpreadRumor (String Symbol );
    . . .


// activities of StockMarket
action StockCreate (String Symbol, Float Price );
action SetPrice (String Symbol, Float Price );
action PriceChange (String Symbol, Float Price );
action BuyResult (OrderId Order, String Symbol, Float Price, Int Shares, String Message,
                  ThreadId Customer, ThreadId Broker );
action SellResult (OrderId Order, String Symbol, Float Price, Int Shares, String Message,
                   ThreadId Customer, ThreadId Broker );

    . . .


// activities of Customers
action GetPrice (String Symbol, ThreadId Customer, ThreadId Broker);
action Buy (OrderId Order, String Symbol, Int Shares, ThreadId Customer,
       ThreadId Broker );
```

action Sell (OrderId Order, String Symbol, Int Shares, ThreadId Customer,
 ThreadId Broker);

action CreateAlarm (OrderId Order, String Symbol, Float Price, ThreadId Customer,
 ThreadId Broker);
 . . .

// *activities of Brokers*
action BrokerReply (OrderId Order, String Symbol, Float Price, Int Shares,
 String Message, ThreadId Customer, ThreadId Broker);
action BuyStock (OrderId Order, String Symbol, Int Shares, String Message,
 ThreadId Customer, ThreadId Broker);
action SellStock(OrderId Order, String Symbol, Int Shares, String Message,
 ThreadId Customer, ThreadId Broker);
 . . .

Types such as OrderId and ThreadId are predefined enumeration types that can be used to index structured types.

To keep these examples simple, we've omitted the predefined parameters of events, such as timestamps and thread counter values that are defined in Section 8.4.

A Causal Model

Our second goal is to specify the causal relationships between these events by a causal model. The model will act as a guide to programming a causal map. Following step 3 in Section 11.4, we write down the immediate causal relationships between events in a convenient, precise modeling language.

As discussed in Section 11.4, we could choose any modeling language, such as state machines, UML, or something else. In this study we will use our event pattern language to specify a model of causality. To do this, we write down a set of pattern pairs based upon our intuitive understanding of the STS. The right-hand pattern is a level 2 event and the corresponding left-hand patterns (there may be more than one rule with the same right-side event) are its immediate causal predecessors—the level 2 events that caused it to happen. The use of pairs of event patterns to model causality follows our discussion in Section 11.5.

Here are some of the pattern pairs in a model specifying the immediate causes of STS level 2 events. We describe how to determine causality and the assumptions under which the model yields reliable results.

Example 1: *A causal model for STS using pattern pairs*

// **rules of threads of control:**
0A. (Event ?E, ?F; ThreadId ?TId; ThreadCounterValue ?TCV)
 ?E(?TId, ?TCV) $\longrightarrow$?F(?TId, ?TCV + 1);

0B. (Event ?E, ?F; ThreadId ?TId; ThreadTimeStamp ?TTS)
$$?E(?TId, ?TTS) \longrightarrow ?F(?TId, ?TTS + \delta);$$

// **rules of STS transactions between components:**
1A. An IPO setting a stock price and a customer requesting a price quote together cause a broker's reply with a price quote:
(OrderId ?OI, Symbol ?S, Price ?P, Int ?Shares, Customer ?C, Broker ?B)
    SetPrice (?S, ?P) **and** GetPrice (?S, ?C, ?B) $\longrightarrow$
        BrokerReply (?S, ?P, Message **is** "quotation", ?C, ?B);

1B. A stock price change from the stock market and a customer's price request together cause a broker's reply with a price quote:
(Symbol ?S, Price ?P, Int ?Shares, Customer ?C, Broker ?B)
    PriceChange (?S, ?P) **and** GetPrice (?S, ?C, ?B) $\longrightarrow$
        BrokerReply (?S, ?P, Message **is** "quotation", ?C, ?B);

2. A customer's Buy order causes a broker to initiate a BuyStock transaction:
(OrderId ?OI, Symbol ?S, Price ?P, Int ?Shares, String ?Msg, Customer ?C,
        Broker ?B)
    Buy (?OI, ?S, ?Shares, ?C, ?B) $\longrightarrow$ BuyStock (?OI, ?S, ?Shares, "buy", ?C, ?B);

3. A customer's Sell order causes a broker to initiate a SellStock transaction:
(OrderId ?OI, Symbol ?S, Price ?P, Int ?Shares, String ?Msg, Customer ?C,
        Broker ?B)
    Sell (?OI, ?S, ?Shares, ?C, ?B) $\longrightarrow$ SellStock (?OI, ?S, ?Shares, "sell", ?C, ?B);

4. A broker's transaction request to buy or sell causes a stock market response:
(OrderId ?OI, Symbol ?S, Price ?P, Int ?Shares, String ?Msg, Customer ?C,
        Broker ?B)
    BuyStock(?OI, ?S, ?Shares, "buy", ?C, ?B) $\longrightarrow$
        BuyResult(?OI, ?S, ?P, ?Shares, ?Msg, ?C, ?B);

(OrderId ?OI, Symbol ?S, Price ?P, Int ?Shares, String ?Msg, Customer ?C,
        Broker ?B)
    SellStock (?OI, ?S, ?Shares, "sell", ?C, ?B) $\longrightarrow$
        SellResult (?OI, ?S, ?P, ?Shares, ?Msg, ?C, ?B);

1C. A stock market response causes a broker to report the result of a transaction:
(OrderId ?OI, Symbol ?S, Price ?P, Int ?Shares, String ?Msg, Customer ?C,
        Broker ?B)
    BuyResult(?OI, ?S, ?P, ?Shares, "confirmed", ?C, ?B); $\longrightarrow$
        BrokerReply (?OI, ?S, ?P, ?Shares, "bought", ?C, ?B);
    BuyResult(?OI, ?S, ?P, ?Shares, "denied", ?C, ?B); $\longrightarrow$
        BrokerReply (?OI, ?S, ?P, ?Shares, "failed", ?C, ?B);
    SellResult(?OI, ?S, ?P, ?Shares, "confirmed", ?C, ?B); $\longrightarrow$
        BrokerReply (?OI, ?S, ?P, ?Shares, "sold", ?C, ?B);
    SellResult(?OI, ?S, ?P, ?Shares, "denied", ?C, ?B); $\longrightarrow$
        BrokerReply (?OI, ?S, ?P, ?Shares, "failed", ?C, ?B);

. . .

Types Customer and Broker are ThreadId types, and Symbol is a String type. We've left out some of the rules—for example, those dealing with stop loss orders (Alarms)—in order to shorten this example. And, as before, we've left out some parameters of events as well—for example, thread counter values and TimeStamps.

This model is a way of specifying for STS what events are the immediate predecessors of an event. A pattern pair means that for any event matching the right side to happen, a poset of events matching the left-side pattern must have happened.

By applying these rules successively to each event in a set of STS events, we can construct explicit causal relationships between all the events in a transaction. We start with an event and work backward, applying the rules from right side to left side.

For example, there are several ways a broker's BrokerReply event can be caused, as shown in rules labeled 1A, 1B, and 1C.

For example, this event

     BrokerReply(OI#N, IBM, 100, 500, "bought", McDuff, Merrill, ...)

signifies a report of a successful transaction with OrderId OI#N to buy 500 shares of IBM at $100 for the customer account McDuff. This event matches the right sides of two rules, 1C and 0A. So the immediate causes of this event, according to our model, are events that match the left-side instances of these two rules. The left side of rule 1C matches an event generated by the StockMarket:

     BuyResult(OI#N, IBM, 100, 500, "confirmed", McDuff, Merrill, ...)

The left-side instance of rule 0A matches the last event generated by the broker according to its thread counter.

In a transaction to buy stock, as shown in Figure 14.4, each arrow is labeled with the rule that specified its existence. Boxes labeled "activity" in

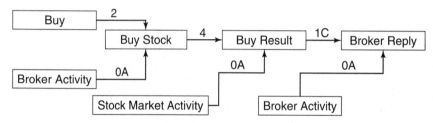

Figure 14.4: Causal relations between events in a Buy transaction

the figure stand for an immediately preceding event created by the broker thread or stock market thread, as the case may be.

However, the model, as we have stated it here, has certain ambiguous cases. For example, a PriceChange event may match the left side of many instances of rule 1B as a cause of a BrokerReply quoting the price of a particular stock. But clearly, the intention of the rule is to choose the timewise latest PriceChange that has been received by the broker. So the rule needs to be refined by adding guards that reference the timestamps of the events—for example, so that only a PriceChange generated within a time window of length δ before the BrokerReply will match. Even so, the model may yield incorrect results—see the discussion in Section 11.7.

As discussed in Section 11.5, we may need to separate the cases in which each rule applies by adding guards to the right sides. Or we may need to use timestamps in the rules to resolve ambiguous cases, such as repetitions of a transaction, that may lead to events with identical data except their timestamps. Or, finally, we may need to observe a richer set of events to allow more accurate rules than 1B.

By the way, we have given two forms of the rule of threads, one using a counter value attribute (see Section 8.4) and the other using a thread clock with a sufficiently fine granularity, δ.

Causal Map

Now comes our final step—to construct a map that not only generates these level 2 events from the level 1 events, but also adds the causality attributes to the level 2 events to make their causal relationships explicit. To simplify this step, we separate it into two maps.

The first map takes the level 1 formatted CEP events from the adapter and generates corresponding level 2 events. It generates a set of level 2 events that are instances of the preceding action declarations. This first map doesn't worry about the order of events. Each level 1 event that enters its input event pool matches its rule. It figures out the level 2 action name from the TIB_Message subject parameter in the level 1 event and uses the other level 1 parameters in the level 2 event. For example, a broadcast on the subject Stock.Customer.Buy is converted to an event with the action name Buy generated by a customer.

input event from level 1
  TIB_Message (Stock.Customer.Buy, OrderNo, "IBM", 500, "MacDuff", "Merrill")

corresponding level 2 output event.
  Buy (OrderNo, "IBM", 500, "MacDuff", "Merrill")

The output of the first map is fed to a second map that has to add the causality attributes. The composition of these two maps is called the "causal map" for STS in Figure 14.3. It is the map from level 1 to level 2 of the event hierarchy.

Corresponding to each pattern pair in the causal model is a rule in the map that creates a new copy of the right-side event that contains a causal attribute. As an example, let's take the case of BuyStock events created by Brokers and sent to the StockMarket. We use a rule with a trigger similar to the pattern pair in rule 2 of the model.

Example 2: *Plan for a rule to create BuyStock events with a causal attribute*

```
(OrderId ?OI, Symbol ?S, Price ?P, Int ?Shares, String ?Msg, Customer ?C,
            Broker ?B)
    BuyStock (?OI, ?S, ?Shares, "buy", ?C, ?B) where    condition 1 and
                                                        condition 2
⇒
{
    Step 1   construct references to the causal predecessors of the BuyStock
                event;
    Step 2   create a new BuyStock event with a new parameter containing
                references to its predecessors;
    Step 3   store references the new event for future use as a predecessor
                of other events;
}
```

Rule 2 in the causal model tells us the BuyStock event always has a causally preceding Buy event. So the idea is to trigger on BuyStock only *after* the preceding Buy has been processed. The **where** condition 1 is used as a guard in the trigger to achieve this by testing the state of the map to see if another rule in the causal map has triggered on the Buy event and processed it. In so doing, the other rule stores a reference in the state of the map to the new copy of the Buy event that it creates. Condition 1 in our rule's trigger tests the state to see if the other rule has stored a newly created Buy event with the same OrderId.

Similarly, condition 2 ensures that the BuyStock event is not processed until it is the next event in the broker thread (rule of threads). If the previous event in the broker thread has been processed, its counter value will be stored in the map state. So condition 2 tests whether the counter value parameter of the BuyStock event is the next counter value in the broker thread. When our rule triggers on the BuyStock event, it carries out the three steps. It constructs a set of references to the causal predecessors of BuyStock—they are already stored in the map state. It creates a copy of the BuyStock event with the set of references to predecessors as a new causality attribute parameter. And it stores references to this event for use as a predecessor of future events.

Here are some examples of mapping rules in the casual map.

Example 3: *Some of the rules for computing causal attributes of level 2 events*

map CausalMap **in** Level 2 **out** Level 2 {

```
/*****************************************************************
 *          TYPES  AND  STATE  VARIABLES                       *
 *   the following array structures are extensible to accommodate *
 *   new OrderIds and ThreadIds.                               *
 ***************************************************************** /
```

```
// array type indexable by OrderIds used to store the latest event
// in each current transaction.
typedef array [OrderId] of event   LastTransactionType;
LastTransactionType LastTransaction = { default is null };
```

```
// array indexable by ThreadIds, used to store last event of each thread.
array [ThreadId] of event LastSenderEvent = { default is null };
```

```
// array used to store last counter value of each thread.
array [ThreadId] of Int LastCounterValue = { default is 0 };
```

```
// set of events that are predecessors of the current event to be created.
Set[Event] Preds;
// current event
Event E;
```

```
/*****************************************************************
 *                    RULES                                    *
 *   trigger on any event whose predecessors have been processed, *
 *   and generate a level 2 event that includes a causal attribute *
 ***************************************************************** /
```

```
// Rule for Buy events. Buy events created by customers initiate new transactions.
(OrderId ?OI, Symbol ?S, Price ?P, Int ?Shares, String ?Msg, Customer ?C,
            Broker ?B)
Buy (?OI, ?S, ?Shares, ?C, ?B) where ?C.CounterValue = LastCounterValue[?C]++
    ⇒ {
```

```
// clear the previous event's set of predecessors
Preds . Clear ();
// if there is a LastEvent from this customer add it to predecessor set
if (LastSenderEvent[?C] != null)
        Preds . Insert(LastSenderEvent[?C]);
// construct a new Buy event with same data
E = Buy(?OI, ?S, ?Shares, "buy" ?C, ?B);
 E. causality = Preds;   // add causal attribute.
// create and output a level 2 customer Buy event with causal attribute,
// and save the new event as the latest event in the current transaction
LastTransaction[?OI] = generate E;
// ...and as the last event recorded in the state for this customer
LastSenderEvent[?C] = LastTransaction[?OI];
// ... and update the thread counter value recorded in the state for this
//   customer
LastCounterValue[?C]++;
}


// Rule for BuyStock events from brokers. BuyStock events are created by Brokers
// in response to customer's Buy events.
(OrderId ?OI, Symbol ?S, Price ?P, Int ?Shares, String ?Msg, Customer ?C,
            Broker ?B)
BuyStock(?OI, ?S, ?Shares, "buy", ?C, ?B)
    where LastTransaction[?OI].ActionName = "Buy" and
            ?B.CounterValue = LastCounterValue[?B]++
⇒ {
// clear the previous event's set of predecessors
Preds . Clear ();
// if there is a LastEvent from this broker add it to predecessor set
if (LastSenderEvent[?B] != null)
Preds . Insert(LastSenderEvent[?B]);
// add the Customer's Buy order for this transaction as a predecessor
    Preds . Insert(LastTransaction[?OI]);
// construct a new BuyStock event with same data
E = BuyStock(?OI, ?S, ?Shares, "buy", ?C, ?B);
 E. causality = Preds;   // add causal attribute.
// create and output a level 2 broker BuyStock event with causal attribute,
// and save the new event as the latest event in the current transaction
LastTransaction[?OI] = generate E;
// ...and as the last event recorded in the state for this broker
LastSenderEvent[?B] = LastTransaction[?OI];
// ... and update the thread counter value recorded in the state for this broker
LastCounterValue[?B]++;
}


// Rule for BuyResult events from StockMarket in response to brokers' BuyStock
// events
(OrderId ?OI, Symbol ?S, Price ?P, Int ?Shares, String ?Msg,
```

```
                        Customer ?C, Broker ?B)
        BuyResult (?OI, ?S, ?P, ?Shares, "confirmed", ?C, ?B)
            where LastTransaction[?OI].ActionName = "BuyStock" and
                  StockMarket.CounterValue = LastCounterValue[StockMarket]++
    ⇒ {
        // clear the previous event's set of predecessors
        Preds . Clear ();
        // if there is a LastEvent from the StockMarket add it to predecessor set
        if (LastSenderEvent[StockMarket] != null)
            Preds . Insert(LastSenderEvent[StockMarket]);
        // add the broker's BuyStock event for this transaction as a predecessor
        Preds . Insert(LastTransaction[?OI]);
        // construct a new BuyResult event with same data
        E = BuyResult (?OI, ?S, ?Shares, "confirmed" ?C, ?B);
        E . causality = Preds;    // add causal attribute.
        // create and output a level 2 BuyResult event with causal attribute,
        // and save the new event as the latest event in the current transaction
        LastTransaction[?OI] = generate E;
        // ...and as the last event recorded in the state for the StockMarket
        LastSenderEvent[StockMarket] = LastTransaction[?OI];
        // ...and update the thread counter value recorded in the state for the
        //   StockMarket
        LastCounterValue[StockMarket]++;
        }


    // One of the rules for BrokerReply events to customers in response
    // to StockMarket BuyResult events
    (OrderId ?OI, Symbol ?S, Price ?P, Int ?Shares, String ?Msg, Customer ?C,
                Broker ?B)
        BrokerReply (?OI, ?S, ?P, ?Shares, "bought", ?C, ?B)
            where LastTransaction[?OI].ActionName = "BuyResult" and
                  LastTransaction[?OI].Message = "confirmed" and
                  ?B.CounterValue = LastCounterValue[?B]++
    ⇒ {
        // clear the previous event's set of predecessors
        Preds . Clear ();
        // insert the LastEvent recorded for the broker into predecessor set
        Preds . Insert(LastSenderEvent[?B]);
        // add the StockMarket's BuyResult event for this transaction as a predecessor
            Preds . Insert(LastTransaction[?OI]);
        // construct a new BrokerReply event with same data
        E = BrokerReply (?OI, ?S, ?P, ?Shares, "bought" ?C, ?B);
        E . causality = Preds;    // add causal attribute.
        // create and output a level 2 BrokerReply event with causal attribute,
        // and save the new event as the latest event in the current transaction
        LastTransaction[?OI] = generate E;
        // ...and as the last event recorded in the state for the broker
        LastSenderEvent[?B] = LastTransaction[?OI];
```

```
// ...and update the thread counter value recorded in the state for the
//   broker
LastCounterValue[?B]++;
// end of this transaction; reclaim storage
LastTransaction[?OI].Erase;
}


// similar mapping rules corresponding to other pattern pairs in the causal
// model.
...
}
```

We make some simplifying assumptions in this example. First, we assume the input consists of level 2 component-to-component communciation events output from our first map. Secondly, we assume each component in STS is a single thread—customers, brokers, StockMarket, etc. This lets us omit the details for dealing with multiple threads in a component. It is simple to extend this example to deal with multi-threaded components. Thirdly, we assume each transaction has a unique OrderId. This simplifies both the state of the map and the triggers of the rules that deal with sequences of buy, sell, and stop loss transaction events. On the other hand, we have not assumed orderly observation.

The example works as follows. The state of the map stores a reference to each event that has been output by a rule until all the events it causes have been output. The latest event output in each transaction is stored and can be retrieved using the OrderId. Each event output by the map is also stored according to the thread that created the corresponding input event, and can be retrieved using that thread's ThreadId. The guards encode knowledge of the communication protocols in the STS.

When a rule triggers on an input event, it creates a copy of the event and adds the set of references to the output events that are immediate causal predecessors of this new event. This set of references is the causality attribute of the new event. Finally, the rule adds a reference to the new event to the appropriate data structures in the maps state for later use as a predecessor of a future event to be created.

Not all the rules are as simple as the rules for transactions with OrderIds. For example, a rule to output BrokerReply events that are price quotations and contain a causal attribute, must trigger on the input BrokerReply event and also itscausally preceding GetPrice and PriceChange events. This rule exemplifies the situation where OrderIds are absent. The state must store a set of recent GetPrice events from the Customer, and PriceChange events from the Stock, or StockMarket. Guards in the rule trigger must not only access ThreadCounterValues of the Customer and StockMarket to ensure that the GetPrice and PriceChange events have already been processed. They must also encode more knowledge about the timing of events in the STS to select the causally preceding events. This kind of rule may lead us back to the discussion of accuracy of causal models in Section 11.9.

In general, the state of a causal map can be an association of input event Ids with corresponding output event Ids. Triggers can be multi-event patterns whose guards access references to the corresponding output events to enable rule bodies to construct causality in the output event execution. These details are beyond the scope of our discussion here.

One of the purposes of this example is to show how a map can allow for disorderly arrival of input events—that is, an event may arrive in the input pool before that event's causal ancestors have arrived. The triggers are designed so that the rules process those events in an order consistent with their causal relationship.

The level 2 events created by the causal map are shown in Figure 14.3. They are used to drive an animation of the communication that happens in STS on a picture of its architecture, such as Figure 14.1. Each level 2 event is animated as a message traveling between the component that generated it and the intended receiver. In the hierarchical picture, Figure 14.3, we show the level 2 events being fed to an animation viewer. The viewer is just another event processing agent that accepts events from the causal map and puts out a graphical depiction. Causality plays an important role in sensible animation of communication. Because the causal map outputs events in an order consistent with causality, the events are fed to the animation in an orderly way so that no event is depicted before its causal predecessors.

14.4.3 Level 3

So far we have bridged part of our information gap, as depicted in Figure 14.2. We have defined the maps between level 1 and level 2 of Table 14.1. More importantly, we have been able to define a causal map for the events at level 2. Now we must look at the rest of our viewing wishlist in Section 14.1. We want to see

- A statistical breakdown of customer's trading activities
- The timeliness with which brokers perform their activities
- Any illegal trade-ahead activity

These views of our STS system are aggregations of activities at level 2 and, in most cases, activities that are causally related. In our hierarchy they are level 3. Our plan, shown in Figure 14.3, is to deliver these views by three separate aggregation maps.

Customer Trading Activities

Here are level 3 actions defining event types that signify multievent transactions at level 2 that are initiated by customers.

```
// Level 3 actions signifying trading activities initiated by customers
action PriceQuery(String Symbol, Float Price, ThreadId Customer, String Message,
            ThreadId Broker, Time StartTime, Time EndTime);
action BuyAction(OrderId OI, String Symbol, Int Shares, Float Price, ThreadId Customer,
            ThreadId Broker, Time StartTime, Time EndTime);
action SellAction(OrderId OI, String Symbol, Int Shares, Float Price, ThreadId Customer,
            ThreadId Broker, Time StartTime, Time EndTime);
action AlarmCreation(String Symbol, Float Price, ThreadId Customer, ThreadId Broker)
```

These level 3 trading activities take place over a time interval defined by the timing of the level 2 events they are aggregated from. They have a *start* and an *end* timestamp.

A PriceQuery, for example, takes place over a period of time starting whenever a customer requests a price quotation from a broker. It ends when the broker generates a BrokerReply to that customer that is causally related to the price query. It contains the same Stock Symbol, Customer, and Broker parameters. So, a PriceQuery is an aggregation of the two level 2 events, one generated by the customer and the other by the broker. It takes place in the time interval over which the two events happen.

An AlarmCreation is similar. It signifies the level 2 activity of setting up a stop loss order. The BuyAction and SellAction actions signify completed transactions consisting of four level 2 events that we have already described—for example, see Figure 14.4.

These level 3 events are generated by map 2 in Figure 14.3. They drive the transaction monitor, which shows graphically the numbers of each kind of event. The display of a graphical agent during an execution of STS is shown in Figure 14.6 later in this chapter. It is a continuously varying bar chart that shows the relative numbers of each kind of trading transaction and thereby gives us a view of the mix of customer activities in any execution.

Typical rules in map 2 are shown in the next example. One of the interesting aspects of this map is that because it takes its event stream from the causal map, it can assume orderly observation, and its triggers can be restricted to matching on causally related events. It doesn't have to remember any events in its state. It is simple and efficient.

Example 1: *Examples of rules in map 2 from level 2 to level 3*

```
// rule to detect completed price query transactions.
(Symbol ?S, Float ?P,   String ?Msg, Customer ?C, Broker ?B, Time ?t1,
Time ?t2)
GetPrice(?S, ?C, ?B) at ?t1  ⟶  BrokerReply(?S, ?P, "price", ?C, ?B) at ?t2
 ⇒
  generate PriceQuery(?S, ?P, "price", ?C, ?B, StartTime is ?t1, EndTime is ?t2);
```

```
// rule to detect successful buy transactions.
(OrderId ?OI, Symbol ?S, Float ?P, Int ?Shares, Customer ?C, Broker ?B,
            Time ?t1, Time ?t2)
Buy (?OI, ?S, ?Shares, ?C, ?B) at ?t1  ⟶
    BuyStock (?OI, ?S, ?Shares, "buy", ?C, ?B)  ⟶
        BuyResult (?OI, ?S, ?P, ?Shares, "confirmed", ?C, ?B)  ⟶
            BrokerReply (?OI, ?S, ?P, ?Shares, "bought", ?C, ?B) at ?t2
 ⇒
  generate BuyAction(?OI; ?S, ?Shares, ?P, "bought", ?C, ?B, StartTime is ?t1,
                                                  EndTime is ?t2);
```

The trigger in the PriceQuery rule will match a GetPrice event generated by a customer and the first causally following BrokerReply with the same Symbol, Customer, and Broker parameters. It will have additional parameters for Price and the message "price". When the rule triggers, it generates a level 3 event, PriceQuery, containing the data parameters from the match of the trigger. This rule uses the causal relationship ($\rightarrow$) between level 2 events to distinguish between similar transactions.

The rule to aggregate events in a Buy transaction triggers on instances of the causal chain of level 2 events shown in Figure 14.4. The messages "bought" and "confirmed" are important in distinguishing a successful Buy from one that was requested but failed. The rule generates a single level 3 event, BuyAction, that summarizes the data and timing of the whole transaction.

Broker Performance

Now we come to viewing the performance of brokers. We want to look at the timeliness with which they execute their services for customers and determine whether they keep to the trading rules. So we specify level 3 actions that signify aggregations of level 2 events that will give us these views. First, here are the level 3 actions.

```
// Level 3 actions signifying various aspects of broker performance:
// price quoted by Broker is not latest stock price.
action LatePrice(String Symbol, Float Price, ThreadId Customer,
          ThreadId Broker, Time StartTime, Time EndTime);
// stop loss order is not executed by a broker when it should be.
action LateAlarm(String Symbol, Int Shares, Float Price, ThreadId Customer,
          ThreadId Broker, Time StartTime, Time EndTime);
// suspicious activity signifying broker possibly trading ahead on customer's order.
action BuyAhead(String Symbol, Int Shares, Float Price, ThreadId Customer,
          ThreadId Broker, Time StartTime, Time EndTime);
action SellAhead(String Symbol, Int Shares, Float Price, ThreadId Customer,
          ThreadId Broker, Time StartTime, Time EndTime);
```

Each of these level 3 actions is an aggregation of level 2 events, as described in the following examples.

Example 2: *A rule in map 1, Figure 14.3, for detecting quotations of old prices*

```
(Symbol ?S, Float ?Price, Float ?Lastprice, Customer ?C, Broker ?B, Time ?t1,
Time ?t2, Time ?t3)
(GetPrice(?S, ?C, ?B) at ?t1 ⟶
    BrokerReply(?S, ?Price, "price", ?C, ?B) at ?t2) ~
    PriceChange (?S, ?LastPrice) at ?t3 where (?t2−δ < ?t3 <?t2) and
                                       (?Price ≠ ?LastPrice)
    ⇒
    generate LatePrice (?S, ?Price, ?LastPrice, ?C, ?B, StartTime is ?t1,
                                       EndTime is ?t2);
```

The timeliness of a broker's price quotation to a customer has to take into account when the customer requested a price quotation, what price the broker sent in response (causally related to the request), and what price the stock market had most recently set for that stock before the broker responded. The stockmarket's price change is not causally related to what goes on between the customer and the broker. So timeliness aggregates three level 2 events, two of which are causally related, and all three must bear a specific time relation to one another.

This rule uses some timing knowledge about the STS—that the stockmarket price changes for a given stock are issued exactly δ time units apart. So the rule's trigger compares the broker's price quote issued at time t2 with the price change for that stock issued within δ before t2. If the price quoted by the broker differs from the latest price in the system, a LatePrice event is generated with the data involved. These events are created by map 1 in Figure 14.3 and used to drive the broker reliability monitor "broker Response Time" shown in Figure 14.8 later in this chapter.

Example 3: *A rule in map 1, Figure 14.3, for detecting late stop loss executions*

```
(Symbol ?S, Float ?Price, Float ?Sellprice, Int ?Shares, Customer ?C,
 Broker ?B, Time ?t1, Time ?t2, Time ?t3)
(CreateAlarm (?S, ?Price, ?C, ?B) at ?t1  ⟶
 BrokerReply (?S, ?SellPrice, "StopLossExecution", ?C, ?B) at ?t2 ) ~
 PriceChange (?S, ?Price) at ?t3 ) where (?t1 < ?t3 < ?t2) and (?SellPrice < ?Price)
 ⇒
    generate LateAlarm (?S, ?Price, ?SellPrice, ?C, ?B, StartTime is ?t1,
                                                          EndTime is ?t2);
```

A LateAlarm event signifies that a broker has executed a stop loss order later than it should have been—it should have been executed when a stock's price reached a value specified in the order, but by the time it was executed the price had changed. The trigger in this rule checks for a pattern of three events. A customer makes a stop loss order (CreateAlarm) at t1, and the broker replies to this order (a causally related reply) at a later time, t2, with a lower price (SellPrice), than was requested. If during this time interval, say, at t3, the price of the stock did reach the price in the customer's order, the order should have been executed at t3. But the price went even lower before execution. This is somewhat simplified from real-life situations and doesn't check for all the ways a stop loss can be wrongly executed.

Example 4: *A rule in map 3, Figure 14.3, for detecting suspicious broker behavior*

```
(String ?S, Float ?BuyPrice, Float ?SellPrice, Int ?Shares1, Int ?Shares2,
 Customer ?C, broker ?B, Time ?t1, Time ?t2, Time ?t3)
(Buy (?S, ?Shares1, ?C, ?B) at ?t1  ⟶
 BrokerReply (?S, ?BuyPrice, ?Shares1 "Bought", ?C, ?B) at ?t2 ) ~
(BuyStock (?S, ?Shares2, ?B, ?B) at ?t3,  ⟶
 SellStock (?S, ?SellPrice, ?Shares2, ?B, ?B) at t4 )
 where (?t1 < ?t3 < ?t4 < ?t2 < ?t1 + TimeWindow)
 ⇒
    generate BuyAhead (?S, ?BuyPrice, ?SellPrice, ?C, ?B StartTime is ?t1,
                                                          EndTime is ?t2);
```

A level 3 BuyAhead event signifies that a broker, after receiving a buy order from a customer, has executed a buy order for its own account on the same stock before executing the customer's order. And then the broker executes a sell order for its own account after executing the customer's buy order. This is a suspicious situation, in which the broker may be taking advantage of knowledge of a customer's buy order to profit from the effect of that buy order. The rule generates a BuyAhead warning. Trading ahead of customers' orders is against SEC regulations.

However, note one subtle issue with the rule's trigger. There need not be an explicit causal relation between the customer-broker transaction and the broker-broker transaction. The ~ operator relates the two. It is unlikely that such an explicit "message trail" would exist in a real-life system's IT traffic to allow an inference of explicit causality. The trigger uses a proximity TimeWindow as a rough measure of suspiciousness. This is a parameter of the map that can be adjusted.

BuyAhead events drive one of the views delivered by the viewing agent whose display during an execution of STS is shown in Figure 14.8.

These maps—map 1, map 2, and map 3—are simple examples aggregating level 2 events into level 3 events signifying activities we are interested in viewing.

14.5 Implementing Hierarchical Viewing for STS

Our next step is to program EPAs for all the maps and viewers we have discussed so far in this chapter for STS. We also need a CEP adapter for the RV messaging middleware that is the STS IT layer. These EPAs are added to the library of a visual EPN composition tool described in Section 10.6.

Figure 14.3 is a design for an EPN that will generate and display the views of our three-level event hierarchy. Following this design, the CEP adapter is configured to run as a client of RV. The STS architecture in Figure 14.1 shows an interface called All Brokers for the CEP adapter. The adapter's output is connected to the input action of the causal map, TIB_Message (see Section 14.4.1, the first map). In turn, the causal map's outputs are connected to an animation EPA and to the three maps from level 2 to level 3. Connection rules described in Chapter 10 are used, following the communication structure in Figure 14.3. The output from each of Map 1, Map 2, and Map 3 is connected to a special graphical EPA that depicts those level 3 events in an appropriate form—for example, a bar graph for the customer trading statistics and time charts for brokers' behaviors.

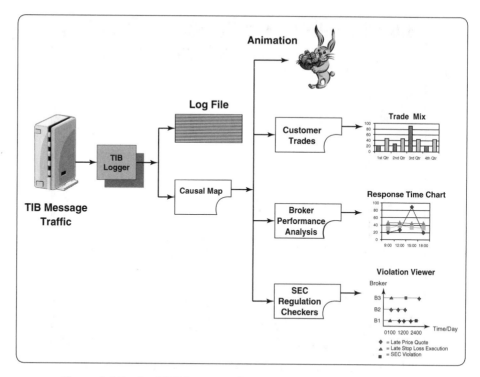

Figure 14.5: An EPN composing maps and viewers for STS

The EPN we have composed is depicted in Figure 14.5. This EPN bridges the information gap between STS messages on the middleware and the activities we were interested in viewing. It *implements* the three-level abstraction hierarchy defined in Section 14.3. Essentially, it is a communication network of EPAs fed by an adapter that monitors the middleware for STS message traffic. The EPN delivers the wishlist of views that we asked for in Section 14.2.

The following figures are snapshots of the event-driven viewers taken during an execution of STS. These viewers alter their graphical display each time they receive an event.

Customer Initiated Transactions (Figure 14.6) shows the total numbers of price quote requests, buy and sell trades, and stop loss orders in a bar graph format.

Broker Response Time (Figure 14.7) shows each of two brokers' response times to customer requests. Broker-2 clearly had some trouble responding quickly early on in the STS activity but later achieved a similar performance to Broker-1.

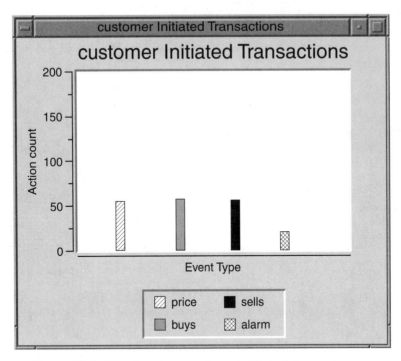

Figure 14.6: Viewing transactions initiated by customers

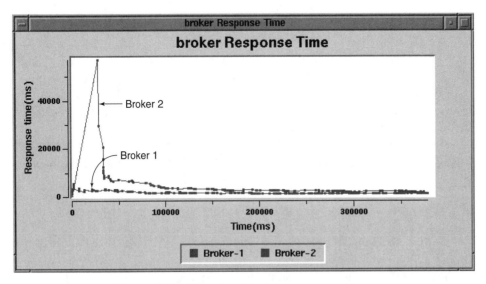

Figure 14.7: Viewing broker response time

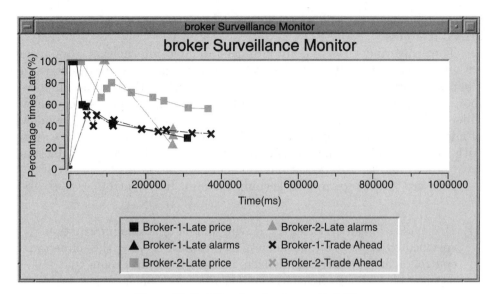

Figure 14.8: Viewing broker reliability

The *Broker Surveillance Monitor* (Figure 14.8) records all the events at level 3 that signify that a broker quotes a stock price that is not the latest one (squares) in the system, or fails to execute a stop loss order at the earliest possible time (triangles), or generates a sequence of stock trades that could indicate a violation of SEC trading regulations (crosses).

14.6 Three Steps toward Human Control

Now we return to the discussion in Chapter 3. How does our application of CEP to STS realize the ideas we discussed for keeping the human in control of the electronic enterprise?

We started out by defining an event hierarchy for STS so that the higher-level events signified activities we were interested in knowing about (see Section 14.3). We then developed a causal model of STS and maps to aggregate views of these higher-level events according to our event hierarchy (see Section 14.4). And finally, we constructed event-driven viewers to deliver the views in visual forms that we can easily understand (see Section 14.5).

Representing causality between events by causal attributes made the job of defining the higher-level maps easier. Producing an orderly poset of events at level 2 allowed us to take advantage of orderly observation to make the maps from level 2 to level 3 relatively simple. Another advantage is that the pattern matching of their rule triggers, which involve complex patterns with causality, is more efficient than it would be in the case of out-of-order arrival of events.

The maps and viewers deliver understandable information about the activity in the system. It is problem-relevant information, as we discussed in Chapter 3, directly related to the uses we are making of the system. Furthermore, at any time, all the views are "on the same page." That is, they show different higher-level events that are aggregated from the same time window of middleware events. This lets us correlate the behaviors shown in one view with those shown in another view. In fact, we can introduce additional EPAs into the viewing EPN to do various kinds of correlation for us.

Here are three steps toward keeping the human in control.

1. *Personalized high-level views:*   Having understandable information, specified by the human, is the first step toward keeping the human in control of the enterprise. It delivers problem-relevant events that tell us directly, without further reasoning, what we want to know.

2. *Diagnostics driven from high-level views:*   The second step toward keeping the human in control is having diagnostics that are driven from the higher-level views. Questions about how system performance is affecting our applications are formed from the views related to our particular uses and interests in the system.

   Drill-down techniques allow us to explore lower-level events that caused the situations at the higher-level that we are interested in analyzing. The higher-level event focuses the search of a large set of low-level events to the subset related to it by vertical causality.

3. *Constraints:*   The third step is to automate our diagnostics as we learn more about how our system behaves. Adding constraint EPAs to the viewing EPN to warn us when special situations arise is a powerful weapon in our struggle to stay in control.

14.6.1   Drill-Down Diagnostics

Viewing level 3 information often leads us to look for additional details. Usually, a problem in an enterprise system is first observed at a high level. As we view our own application-level activities, that is when we first notice things going wrong.

Often, we cannot assess the *cause* of particular activities at this level. High-level views may show us that something is wrong but not *why*. For example, a broker may quote an old price because it has not received the latest price that the stock market has generated. This could be a latency problem in the trading network. Or it could be that the broker has received the latest price but simply has not updated its internal database. The causes of the old price quote must be investigated further.

In these situations, we want to *reverse* the hierarchical event aggregation. We want to use vertical causality to start from the high-level activity that interests us and track downward through the lower-level events that it was aggregated from. Vertical causality is a powerful tool in focusing the search for "what happened."

This process is called *drill down*. It is transitive. We can apply it level by level, downward. Our CEP infrastructure lets us drill down easily because it stores the aggregation relationships between sets of low-level events and higher-level events. Whenever a map triggers, the infrastructure records the triggering set (see Section 8.4) and the high-level events that are then generated. So drill down can be supported by tools that use this store of vertical causality in the infrastructure.

Typically, we need to do drill down when we are doing postmortem diagnosis—but not always postmortem. Sometimes drill down can be applied during online diagnosis as well.

As an example, let's see how a postmortem drill down could be used when we are analyzing what happened in STS.

Figure 14.5 shows an EPN configured on middleware. In real time the maps in this network aggregate messages from the middleware communication of the trading system (level 1) up to level 3 abstract events that drive viewers of activities and performance of the applications running on the system.

Now suppose we want to investigate a level 3 event that appears in the Broker Surveillance Monitor shown in Figure 14.8. We turn on a CEP diagnostic tool, a multilevel graphical browser called POV (poset viewer) that can display posets at multiple levels. It uses the CEP infrastructure event storage to browse events and track both their horizontal and vertical causal ancestry. It lets us trace through successive levels to see what events, either at the same level (horizontal causality) or at lower levels (vertical causality), led to any events we choose.

In Figure 14.9 we're looking at a set of level 3 warning events indicating potential trade-ahead situations. They are the same events that are depicted as crosses in Figure 14.8, but now we are looking at them with POV. POV shows events as boxes labeled by their types (action names).

To get the details of the event we are interested in, we simply click on the event circled in POV. A pop-up window, also shown in Figure 14.9, displays the data parameters of the event. It indicates a possible buy-ahead by broker 1 trading 300 shares of IBM stock over the time period 166383 to 167333.

This event was aggregated by a CEP agent, SEC Regulation Checkers (see Figure 14.5), from a pattern of level 2 events used to define an

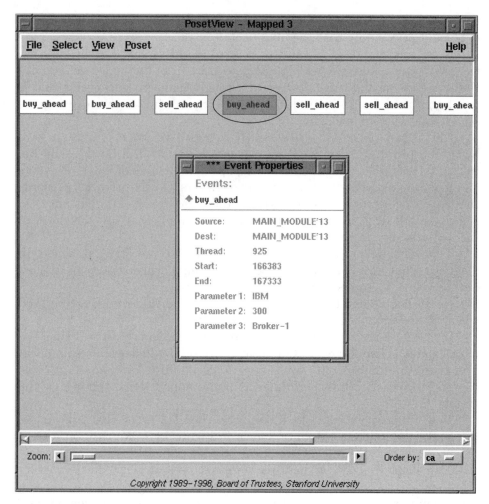

Figure 14.9: Abstract events at level 3 warning of possible illegal trading

aggregation rule in map 3 (see Section 14.4.3). When we click on this trade-ahead event at level 3 in POV, it shows us the four level 2 events that led to it, shaded in Figure 14.10. The browser uses the aggregation relationship stored by the CEP infrastructure to do this.

By highlighting the level 3 event in POV, we have drilled down to level 2. We have exactly the level 2 events that were aggregated to cause (vertical causality) our level 3 event.

POV depicts explicitly the horizontal causal relationship between events at level 2. Figure 14.10 shows events as boxes and their causal relationships as arrows. The causal relationships result from knowledge about the STS trading system that was encoded in the causal map described in Section 14.4.

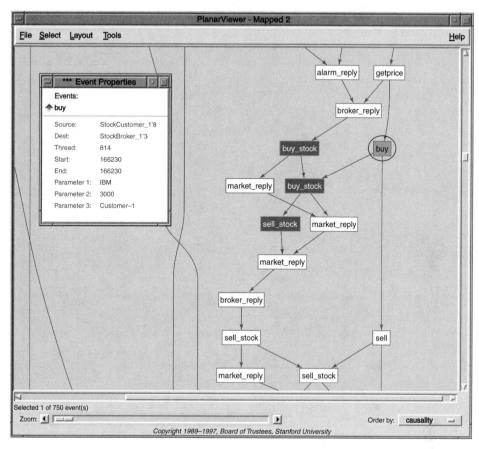

Figure 14.10: The shaded level 2 messages causing a trade-ahead warning

The pop-up window in Figure 14.10 shows details of the circled customer's buy order for 3,000 shares of IBM, placed with broker 1 at time 166230.

Figure 14.11 shows additional pop-up windows giving details of the three shaded broker's trading actions that triggered the warning event. The earliest broker event, at time 166383, shows the broker buying a small number of IBM shares, 300, for its own account. The next event, where the broker executes the customer's buy order, takes place at 166931. The processing elements in the system, threads and publish/subscribe actions, causally relate the customer's buy order *and* the broker's earlier buy for its own account, to this buy order on behalf of the customer. Finally, the third triggering event, in which the broker sells 300 shares of IBM for its own account, happened at 167333. All four events must happen within a specified time window for a warning event to be generated by the rules in map 3.

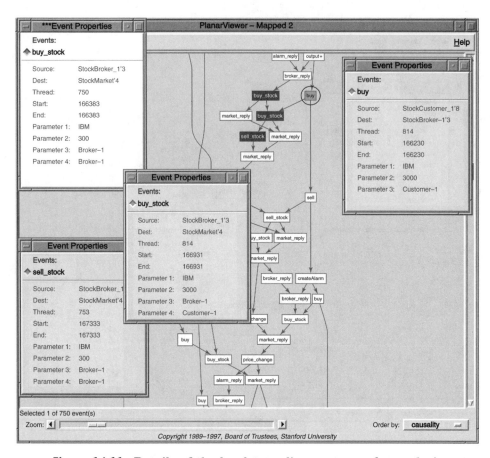

Figure 14.11: Details of the level 2 trading messages for analysis

Figure 14.11 shows no causal link between the customer's buy order and the broker's buy for its own account. But the timing of the events shows that the customer's order is earlier by a small time. This illustrates a fact of life with event logs from IT layers. Not all the information we would like to have is placed in messages on the IT layer where it can be monitored. But enough suspicious activity appears to warrant a warning that flags the situation as "suspicious."

14.6.2 Detecting Constraint Violations

As we learn more about a target system, we can construct new EPAs to deal with troublesome situations for us. New EPAs are added to the EPN that we set up to do the hierarchical viewing. Often, these situations are not predicted when the viewing EPN is first configured, but result from experience with the views. When something "interesting" happens, we want to do more than passively view the activity. We may want the viewing EPN to automatically take additional actions. A common action is to generate warnings to various sites within the target system or, more often, to managers of the target system. Warnings, of course, are passive because they do not, by themselves, affect the system. There are many ways to achieve a proactive capability. One way is to add EPAs to broadcast messages on the IT layer that control the lower-level resources or higher-level applications in the system.

Constraints that automate monitoring and detection are often added to the viewing EPN. The reason for using the viewing EPN is that these constraints are easier to express, and violations are more efficiently detected, using the higher-level events and event causality.

Policies and Regulations

Any enterprise system has to conform to policies and regulations, either its own internal policies or those of some regulating body. Almost as soon as we set up a viewing EPN, a layer of constraints to detect violations of policies or regulations will be configured on top of the EPN.

Here is an example in English of the kinds of constraints that we might want to add to the viewing EPN for the STS. They are easily expressed in RAPIDE-EPL.

As a result of the 1987 stock market crash, the Securities and Exchange Commission (SEC) regulations require small orders, generally not more than a thousand shares, to be executed in a timely manner. STS might be required to conform to these rules.

> <<*Regulation for small order execution*>>
> **never**: A trade for a small order in stock S is requested at time
> *T*, and the same broker receives a large order trade request in stock
> S at time *T1* where *T* ≤ *T1*, and the small order trade is completed
> *after* the large order trade.

We can set up EPAs to automatically check STS activity for conformance to this kind of policy. We can construct a constraint as outlined in Section 9.6. It can be designed to take level 2 event executions from the viewing EPN and check them for conformance to this constraint.

Here is one way this regulation could be expressed by constraint. The constraint is a pattern of two pairs of causally related events at level 2. The pairs may happen independently.

(OrderId ?OI1, OI2; Symbol ?S; Int ?Shares1, Shares2; Broker ?B; Time t1, t2, t3, t4)
never (Buy(?OI1, Symbol **is** ?S, ?Shares1, Broker **is** ?B) **at** t1 **where** ?Shares1 < 1000 →
    BuyResult(?OI1, Symbol **is** ?S, ?Shares1, "confirmed", Broker **is** ?B) **at** t2) ~

(Buy (?OI2, Symbol **is** ?S, ?Shares2, Broker **is** ?B) **at** t3 **where** ?Share2 > 1,000 $\longrightarrow$
     BuyResult (?OI2, Symbol **is** ?S, ?Shares2, "confirmed", Broker **is** ?B) **at** t4)
     where t1 < t3 **and** t4 < t2

Note that in this example we have omitted some of the unneeded parameters in the events Buy and BuyResult. We have used the named parameter format to indicate important parameters. There are other ways to express this constraint. However, all forms of the constraint must use *context,* either by multiple event patterns or by state references.

Trading systems today within brokerage houses ensure conformance to small order execution system (SOES) regulations by using programs that employ databases to track account activity. Until this kind of software was developed, SOES processing was tedious paperwork taking days to complete a transaction. Now it takes a matter of seconds. However, hard-coding conformance checking leads to systems that are not flexible and that quickly become "legacy."

The CEP constraint checking illustrated here could be put in place to detect violations within a brokerage house or across the stock market system globally. And it is very flexible. It does not depend upon any particular databases or accounting systems. It relies only upon the ability to observe events in the enterprise IT layers. High-level-language constraints are easily changed to reflect changes in regulations or to use alternative detection strategies.

14.6.3   The Abstraction Effect

Sometimes it is possible to express constraints at different levels of abstraction. Often, using a higher level of abstraction can have the effect of

- Simplifying the constraint
- Making checking the constraint more efficient

For example, here is a different way to express this SOES regulation that uses level 3 events instead of level 2. It uses the level 3 action defined in Section 14.4.3, which aggregates four level 2 events.

action BuyAction(OrderId OI, String Symbol, Int Shares, Float Price, String Message,
          ThreadId Customer, ThreadId Broker, Time StartTime, Time EndTime);

We can define a constraint with a pattern of two level 3 events instead of four level 2 events. It is more efficient to check this constraint for violations because only two events are involved in the pattern, and the level 3 execution will contain exponentially fewer events than the level 2 execution. Overall, there will be exponentially fewer attempted matches and a higher percentage of successful matches (that is, detected violations).

```
(OI2; Symbol ?S; Int ?Shares1, Shares2; Broker ?B; Time t1, t2, t3, t4)
  never(BuyAction(Message is "bought," Symbol is ?S, Shares is ?Shares1, Broker is ?B,
               StartTime is t1, EndTime is t2) where ?Shares1 < 1,000 ~
       BuyAction(Message is "bought," Symbol is ?S, Shares is ?Shares2, Broker is ?B,
               StartTime is t3, EndTime is t4) where ?Shares2 > 1,000 and
                                                    t1 < t3 and t4 < t2 );
```

In comparing this level 3 constraint with the previous level 2 constraint, there is a fine point about whether the intention of the regulation is to include the time taken for the communications between the customer and broker that start and end the BuyAction. If not, a quick drill down to the eight level 2 events that caused the level 3 violation will enable a check of the timing between the broker and the StockMarket.

Many other SEC regulations are amenable to systemwide automated monitoring for violations using CEP constraints.

14.7 Summary

We have given a step-by-step overview of a case study to apply CEP to help understand the real-time activities happening in a distributed messaging system.

A three-level event hierarchy was defined that corresponded to views chosen by humans to understand ongoing activities in the system. This hierarchy was implemented by an EPN that monitored messages on a commercial messaging IT layer at the lowest-level. Event causality and aggregation were employed to provide higher-level, event-driven views. Views included visual displays of

- Relative proportions of application-level activities
- Performance of components in terms of timing and correctness
- Violations of regulations by components of the system

The case study illustrated the use of the event hierarchy in drill-down diagnosis of the causes of high-level events, such as violations of regulations.

Finally, we discussed how constraints could be added to the viewing EPN to aid in automatically detecting context-sensitive situations involving multiple trades of a stock.

This case study embodies the main concepts of CEP. It illustrates how they are applied to enable personalized viewing and management of electronic enterprise systems by humans.

Chapter $\boxed{15}$

Infrastructure for Complex Event Processing

- *The role and structure of event adapters*
- *The functionality of CEP infrastructure*
- *Interfaces and components of infrastructure*
- *Off-the-shelf infrastructure—reality or dream*
- *Design of pattern matchers*
- *Rules management—a future battleground*
- *CEP analysis tools*

This chapter deals with the questions of what kinds of infrastructure facilities are needed to enable complex event processing, which of those facilities will be supplied as an integral part of commercial information technology, and which of them are unique to CEP.

We give a broad outline of an answer to the questions. The main theme of the discussion is that a certain core functionality for CEP has to be built outside of mainstream commercial development and that most everything else will be supplied by commerical products in the middleware and Computer Aided Software Engineering (CASE) tools industries.

We omit description of foundational algorithms for basic operations, such as pattern matching. And we do not discuss details of how infrastructure components can be implemented on top of the many modern commercial systems that support event-driven applications, such as Java 2 Platform Enterprise Edition (J2EE) servers or .NET. Such topics, in detail, would occupy an entirely different book.

In the previous chapters, we have presented the basic concepts of CEP and how to apply them. We have assumed that there is an infrastructure that enables event executions to be stored, EPAs to communicate events to one another, events to be fed to pattern matching engines, rules to be executed, and so on.

CEP *infrastructure* is a basic layer of event processing facilities needed to make the visions presented in Figures 1.1 and 1.2 in Chapter 1 a reality. These pictures show distributed event-driven systems in which event distribution is implemented by high-bandwidth communication layers. The communications in the financial trading system in Figure 1.1 are a combination of Internet, cell phones, private networks, and other kinds of communication systems. In Figure 1.2 the command-and-control system's event distribution IT layers share commercial networks and also contain communications systems specialized to miltiary requirements. Both IT layers include very high performance networks and various layers of technology. The role of a CEP infrastructure is to interface with the IT layers in these kinds of systems, and to provide a platform on which to implement complex event processing to view and manage the systems.

15.1   Examples of Forms of Observed Events

This section is about the kinds of observed events the CEP infrastructure has to deal with.

Observed events are carriers of information. And it's that information in a format suitable for event processing that CEP needs. Unfortunately, the forms of observed events vary greatly between systems and between levels in a system. This makes setting up CEP on a new target system with a new event format more tedious than we would hope because a new adapter from observed events to CEP events usually has to be written. However, the "proliferation of adapters" problem is not unique to CEP. Most commercial applications face this problem. Libraries of adapters will be needed.

In this section, we look at a few examples of forms of observed events from different systems and how the forms encode the activity signified by the event.

The first examples of observed events are taken from messaging middleware.

Example 1: *Events from a publish/subscribe middleware*

```
Event 0: RT_MESSAGE( 28158, "/data_sample", "numeric_data",
                     100, "val", 1.450100, ... )

Event 1: RT_MESSAGE( 53271, "/data_sample", "numeric_data",
                     100, "val", 2.328500, ... )

Event 2: RT_MESSAGE( 28158, "/data_sample", "numeric_data",
                     125, "val", 3.000000, ... )

Event 3: RT_MESSAGE( 28158, "/data_sample", "numeric_data",
                     100, "val", 4.007500, ...)

Event 4: RT_MESSAGE( 53271, "/data_sample", "numeric_data",
                     125, "val", 5.094700, ... )
```

These events were observed on a commercial publish/subscribe middleware layer. They are middleware messages that have a specified format, called a message type in that middleware. The format of these messages is

```
machine address      /* address of the machine that generated
                        the message */
subject              /* subject to which the message is
                        published */
message type         /* the type name of the message type */
int4                 /* number of data fields */
str                  /* a string field */
real8                /* real number */
...                  /* any number of <str, real8> pairs */
```

In this sample, there are two publishers of messages, machines 28158 and 53271. They published messages to a subject, "/data_sample". The type of the messages is numeric_data. The numeric data type can have any number of pairs of data fields, consisting of a string and a real number.

Any other machines that are interested in these messages can subscribe to that subject, "/data_sample". Then they will be sent these messages. If CEP can act as a client to the middleware, it can subscribe to all subjects, usually by subscribing to a subject such as "*", which tells the middleware, "I'm interested in everything." Then CEP will observe all the messages flowing between components of the system.

The messages, which are observed events signifying middleware activities (publishing messages), are fed to an adapter for that particular middleware. The adapter translates them into CEP events. The CEP events will contain the data of the messages and additional parameters for event Ids, timestamps, and causal relationships. Unique event Ids will be added. The observed messages may also contain a timestamp from the middleware; if not, the time of arrival at the adapter will be used as the event's time-stamp. Causality data will be added by the adapter based upon knowledge of the system. For example, if the activities of publishing messages by one ma-chine, say, 28158, are sequentially ordered, the signifying events are causally related (an earlier one had to happen before a later one). So the adapater will place the Id for event 0 in the causal data of event 2. And the Id of event 2 will be in the causal data of event 3. Publishing activities executed on different machines, however, will be unrelated. So, the Id of event 0 will not be in the causal data of event 1 or event 4.

Events observed on middleware are relatively high-level events compared with events observed from the network layers of a system. So, just to see what relatively low-level events look like, our next example is taken from the log files of a typical high-bandwith network router.

Example 2: *Events from a network router monitor*

```
SOURCE jenkins—gateway
|FORMAT A|AGGREGATION CallRecord|PERIOD 10|STARTTIME
911499298|ENDTIME 911499898|FLOWS 34940|MISSED 0|RECORDS 31956
171.64.71.157|171.64.200.202|47070|6000|6|5|2|920|1|911499438|911499438|0
171.64.7.99|171.64.204.155|53|2475|17|1|2|464|1|911499465|911499465|0
208.144.175.21|171.64.206.97|1353|27920|17|0|6|232|1|911499536|911499537|920
171.64.20.172|172.24.189.8|1083|161|17|95|2|140|1|911499659|911499659|0
172.24.189.4|171.64.20.172|161|1083|17|100|2|148|1|911499368|911499368|0
205.188.252.37|171.64.200.213|4000|1030|17|0|7|751|1|911499335|911499366|30928
171.64.158.135|172.24.195.107|202|202|17|10|15|1215|1|911499592|911499608|16452
171.64.200.213|205.188.252.37|1030|4000|17|0|2|112|1|911499817|911499817|0
199.181.172.249|171.64.193.55|80|1138|6|90|10|7241|1|911499410|911499411|1168
171.64.7.99|171.64.204.155|53|2478|17|0|2|468|1|911499467|911499467|0
....
```

Messages are broken down into sequences of bits, called packets, that routers understand and can send from a source machine to a destination machine. Some of the bits in a packet play a role in telling where the packets came from and where they are going—the so-called header of the packet. The rest of the bits are data. Routers set up a connection between a source and a destination and hold that connection open for a time to transport several packets at once. The sequence of packets flowing along one open connection is called a flow. A monitor is associated with the router and produces log files consisting of summaries of the packet headers of each flow. A log file is produced for every one-minute time window. Router monitors can generate several gigabytes of log files per hour.

The flow log files are sent to a CEP adapter, which processes them into CEP events signifying the network activities summarized in the flows.

The first two lines of this example router log file will be processed into a CEP event having the event type Header and containing data fields defined as follows:

```
action Header(string source, string format,
            string aggregation,
            int period, int starttime, int endtime,
            int flows, int missed, int records);
```

For example, *source* is the name of the network gateway, *format* is the type of format of the flow records, *aggregation* is the type of flow record (in this example, it's a "CallRecord"), and there are time interval parameters and so on. The CEP adapter would add event Ids and timestamps—it might use the start and end times as the event timestamps. Causal relationships would be omitted as unknown.

The other lines in this example are all CallRecords summarizing flows across the router between a source machine and a destination machine. They will be processed into CEP events having the event type CallRecord and containing data fields defined as follows:

```
action CallRecord(string srcaddr, string dstaddr,
                int srcPort, int destPort,
                int protocol, int ToS,
                int packetCount, int byteCount,
                int flowCount,
                int firstTimeStamp, int lastTimeStamp,
                int totalActiveTime);
```

The first two paramenters are the source and destination machine IP addresses; the third and fourth are the source and destination ports. These parameters give us information about the activity: who is sending a message to whom, and what kind of message it is (e-mail, Web traffic, FTP, and so on). The adapter would add an event Id, timestamps (which may reuse the system timestamps).

Our final example is taken from an experimental event format being developed as a possible standard for communication between intrusion detectors.

Example 3: *An intrusion warning event from a network monitoring system*

```
(HelpedCause
        (ByMeansOf
                (Login at A)
                (Telnet 0—>A)
                (Passwd "joe")
        )
        (CommonCause
                (Mail password A  —> info@belgrade.com)
                (Telnet A—>B)
                (Telnet A—>C)
                (HelpedCause
                        (Telnet A—>D)
                        (CommonCause
                                (Mail password D  —> info@belgrade.com)
                                (ByMeansOf
                                        (Login at A)
                                        (Telnet D—>A)
                                        (Passwd "joe")
                                )
                                (Telnet D—>B)
                                (Telnet D—>C)
                        )
                )
        )
)
```

This is a simplified outline of an event output from a network security application in a standard format called GIDO (general intrusion detection object).[1] Similar Internet standard formats for intrusion detection alerts output by commercial applications use XML. This example is simplified for readability—we use "A," "B," and so on in place of IP addresses.

This is an example of an observed event (called an *alert*) from an intrusion detection system. It signifies activity of intruding into a network. It contains a trace of an intrusion, which may be summarized as "This intrusion uses one password; comes in from outside; visits multiple hosts on subnets; mails back password files."

According to the alert, the intruder, which is probably an automated script called a worm, comes in by successfully logging in from machine O (outside the network) to machine A (inside), trying a password on account

---

[1] A proposed intrusion detection standard format developed under DARPA security research programs.

"joe". The technique the worm uses on this attempt is to try to log in via Telnet using a login/password combo. If successful, it mails the password back to info@belgrade.com.

From machine A, the worm attempts to Telnet to machines B, C, and D. It is only successful at logging in to machine D. From D it attempts to log in to A, B, and C. It succeeds only on A, but then detecting that A is already infected, it terminates immediately.

GIDOs are a form of observed events that would be transformed by a CEP adapter into CEP events. A possible goal would be to use CEP to correlate alerts from many different detectors all outputting alerts in the standard GIDO format. Event-based rules in CEP would be used to compare and correlate the alerts to increase the overall reliability of the detection system and to reduce the false alarm rate. The CEP correlator would need to be able to output its results in GIDO format, so an output adapter from CEP to GIDO would also be needed.

15.2 Interfacing CEP Infrastructure to Target Systems

A CEP system is interfaced to the target system to receive and process events as depicted in Figure 15.1. The CEP infrastructure is fed by event adapters that monitor a variety of event sources in the target system. If the target is a globally distributed system, several adapters will be dispersed across the target, as shown in Figure 15.1. Each adapter is interfaced to a subsystem in the target and gets the events that can be monitored locally. Each adapter is usually hosted in close proximity to the local subsystem that it is monitoring.

The role of adapters is to monitor for events, messages, or whatever forms of activity records come from the target system. Monitoring is done benignly, which means that the target system is not affected in any way. An adapter converts its input into events in formats used by CEP. Any implementation of CEP needs events in a particular format, and an adapter's job is to put the events it gets into this format.

The set of adapters may be heterogeneous, containing different classes of adapters. In complex applications, adapters are fed by event sources that are not only located in local subsystems, but may also deliver events from different layers of the target. As we discussed in the previous section, different types of events may be observed, varying from network-level packet dumps to application-level messages on information buses. Each type of event source requires its own kind of adapter. So the event monitoring network shown in

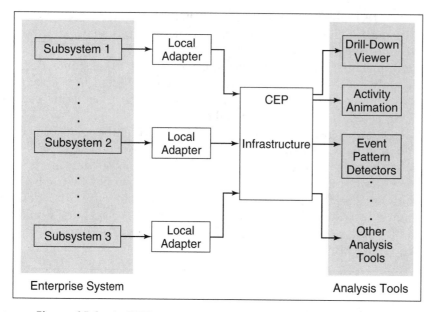

Figure 15.1: A CEP system interfaced with a target system

Figure 15.1 usually contains several different classes of local adapters, one for each local subsystem, or event source. Many applications of CEP use a homogeneous source of events and need only one adapter, or one class of adapter. But to support the general case, CEP needs a library of adapter classes with multiple implementations to cope with all the different kinds of event sources.

Normally, the infrastructure shown in Figure 15.1 executes on separate computer resources to avoid any impact on the performance of the target system. But "lightweight" complex event processing often does not even need additional resources.

15.3   CEP Adapters

In the schematic views of EPNs, such as Figures 10.1, 10.2, and 10.3 in Chapter 10, adapters are shown as agents linking an EPN with a target system's IT layer. These figures hide the role of the CEP infrastucture.

Adapters for CEP can be quite sophisticated. An adapter's job is to take events from event sources in the target system, transform them into a data structure format expected by the CEP infrastructure, and deliver them to the appropriate components of the infrastructure. These components may be merger agents, event caches, and event execution databases.

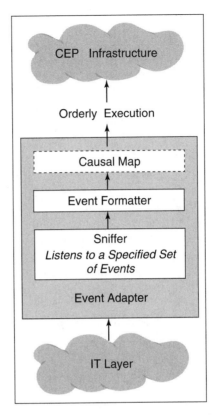

Figure 15.2: An adapter interfaces the CEP infrastructure to a target system

Typically, an adapter carries out the following steps (see Figure 15.2).

1. Listen for events in the target system's communication layer. This step is often called *sniffing* events.

    Each kind of event source requires a specialized sniffer to interact with the API for that source. For example, there are different sniffers for a CORBA ORB and for an information bus. But, apart from the sniffer interface, the other components are common to all adapters.

2. Translate events to a CEP internal format for event processing.

3. Apply a causal map to reorder events into an order consistent with orderly observation and add causal attributes.

4. Output events to the appropriate components of the CEP infrastructure.

Steps 1, 2, and 4 are mandatory—all adapters must do them.

At the most basic level, an adapter contains a *sniffer,* which allows it to interact with the event sources. For example, when publish/subscribe middleware is the source of events, the sniffer is a client that subscribes to a subset of the event traffic. The subset can be specified in advance, before the adapter begins operating, or in some cases even while it is operating. Sniffing events is a benign operation—the target will not notice it. The possibility of a small runtime resource consumption can be solved with extra hardware.

The third step requires a causal map to reorder the events into an order that conforms to *orderly observation* and add causal attributes. Because a causal map is often a complex program, encoding knowledge about the target system, the third step is optional, and most adapters may not perform it.

Events coming from the IT layer may arrive at a sniffer in a jumbled order, where events that happened later than others or were caused by other events arrive before those events. Event processing is much more efficient if the events can be processed in an order consistent with causality and timing. So we try to reorder events as soon as possible in event processing. The earliest place to do it is in the adapter. This is the motivation for adding step 3 to adapters.

The alternative to hard-coded causal maps in adapters is to use causal map agents at an early point in the EPN.

There are advantages and disadvantages to building causal maps into adapters. On the plus side, a set of reordering rules can usually be programmed in, say, Java or C++, so that event reordering is efficient and fast. If instead we write a causal map agent with rules expressed in, say, RAPIDE-EPL, the CEP application as a whole will be slower. The difference in speed may or may not be important, depending upon the CEP application.

On the minus side lie issues about correctness and flexibility in managing causal maps. How well do we understand a causal map written in, say, Java? How easily can we change the Java program to reflect changes in the system that alter the causal relationship between events, or to correct errors in the rules because of perhaps misunderstanding causality in the target system? It is much easier to correct or change reactive rules expressed in an event pattern language such as RAPIDE-EPL. In fact, a set of event pattern reactive rules would be the formal specification for the Java program.

These trade-offs are the motivation for being cautious about putting causal maps into adapters. In practice, experience tends to dictate that causal programs (encodings of causal maps) are included in adapters only when the causal relationship is simple and will not vary over time. In such cases, flexibility to change the causal map is not an issue. For example, causality between events resulting from publish/subscribe middleware would be coded as a causal program in an adapter. But causality resulting from processes with humans in the loop or high-level protocols that may change by the week is expressed in causal maps, as shown in Chapter 11.

For example, causal modeling of a process collaboration (see Chapter 12) would not be built into an adapter.

15.4 CEP Runtime Infrastructure

Figure 15.3 is a high-level view of the role of CEP infrastructure at runtime. Communicating events between adapters and EPAs, between EPAs in an EPN, and between EPAs and visual event-driven meters is made possible by a set of objects that we collectively call the *infrastructure* for complex event processing.

The event flow that we defined as connections in EPNs and architectures of EPAs in Chapter 10 (see, for example, the figures in Section 10.1) are shown as black links between the agents of various kinds in Figure 15.3. Connections are logical communication links. But what actually takes place is shown by the broad links between the agents and the infrastructure. Whenever an event is communicated between two agents, the event is placed in the infrastructure by the sending agent and is then accessed by the receiving agent. The receiving agent has registered a request for the event with a notification component in the infrastructure. The notification component sends the event on to the requesting agent when it arrives.

The infrastructure is the medium that implements the logical links between agents in an EPN. As an analogy from an everyday situation, think about sending e-mail. We like to think (logically) of sending e-mail to one another. But what actually takes place involves a lot of lower-level network

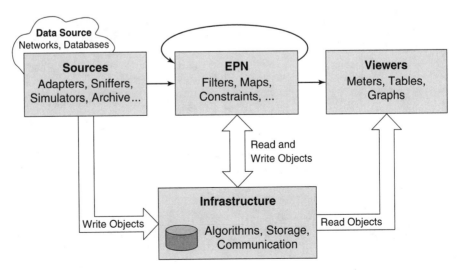

Figure 15.3: Infrastructure supporting EPNs

name servers, mailers, and network protocol activity to make the e-mail happen.

15.5   Infrastructure Interfaces and Components

What kinds of components we should expect to find in a CEP infrastructure, and how can they be used by CEP applications?

Figure 15.4 shows a more detailed view of a CEP system. The view of the CEP infrastructure as a black box in Figures 15.1 and 15.3 has been expanded to show some of its components.

The suppliers of events in Figure 15.4 can be, for example,

1. Application programs running in a target enterprise system
2. Components of an enterprise system, such as ORBs and databases
3. Adapters hosted on event sources such as information buses
4. Event-driven simulators

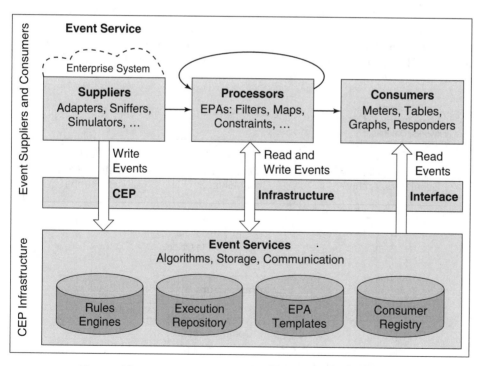

Figure 15.4: A more detailed view of a CEP system

The consumers of events in Figure 15.4 are the analysis tools in Figure 15.1. And the EPAs that constitute the actual CEP application are both consumers and suppliers (called processors in Figure 15.4).

The same CEP infrastructure can process events from a simulation of an enterprise system or from an actual enterprise system. This supports the lifecycle vision from design and simulation through deployment of a CEP application, as we discussed in Chapter 4. The *CEP infrastructure interface* shown in Figure 15.4 makes possible this flexibility to process events from many different sources.

Suppliers and consumers are shown writing and reading events into various components of the infrastructure across a CEP infrastructure interface. Suppliers and consumers need only use methods in the interface and need not use or depend upon what is behind it in the infrastructure. The infrastructure must implement the interface. The role of the interface is to separate the infrastructure from the target system and from the CEP application. This is standard object-oriented design in today's software systems technology.

There are many examples of similar interfaces in commercial applications, from the CORBA and J2EE standards to various commercial application servers now in the marketplace. These kinds of interfaces are emerging in different areas of event-driven systems. Some of them are industry standards or proposed standards, and some are simply de facto standards. At present there is no standard for a CEP infrastructure interface. The only existing example is the set of interfaces used in the CEP experiments on the Stanford Rapide research project. But it is only a small step from current standards in event processing applications today to a CEP standard.

15.5.1   Functionality of the Interface

The CEP infrastructure's facilities are represented by several functional groups that define methods or processes in the interface. We call this the *functionality* of the interface. Effectively, an interface is a composition of several interfaces. Here is a sample of functional groups for CEP.

- *Execution management:* Facilities for storing and accessing event executions. The infrastructure is a repository for executions and other system information. In addition to event executions, it may also store information about the target system—for example, static compile-time information about the components and dynamic information about changes in the target's architecture during execution.

    The functions and methods in the interface for execution management are used by CEP analysis tools for animation, viewing, and diagnostics.

An execution manager relies on relational databases. One of the main jobs of an execution manager is to store executions so that they can be searched efficiently by pattern matching engines and by analysis tools. It must enable fast retrieval of events in an execution according to their causal and timing relationships. Postmortem analysis requires that storing executions will be persistent.

- *Hierarchy management:* Facilities to store and access hierarchically related executions generated by a CEP application. This involves keeping track of aggregation relationships (for example, trigger sets; see Section 8.4) between complex events in different executions at different abstraction levels.

    Again, these capabilities are important for building diagnostic tools.

- *Event communication servers:* Facilities for communicating events between EPAs. This set of facilities may involve functionality such as registration for and notification of events. A client such as an agent can register interest in certain events and receive those events (notification) when they arrive.

    Event communication servers implement both static and dynamic connections between EPAs (see Chapter 10).

- *Compilation of EPNs and dynamic reconfiguration facilities:* These facilities handle deployment of EPNs and changes to EPNs made by users in real time.

- *Pattern matching and rule execution engines:* The fundamental runtime facilities for pattern matching and rule execution.

This is a short list of functionality to give the flavor of infrastructure facilities. It is not a complete list. A CEP infrastructure will implement these facilities.

CEP will rely on many different implementations of its infrastructure. Some, for fast, lightweight processing, will be completely in-memory. Simple implementations will rely on a single processor and use disk storage, while more sophisticated implementations will be multi-threaded or distributed on multiple processors. Libraries of component classes for infrastructure must be developed, with class implementations conforming to the interfaces.

This may seem like a lot of development work. But the foundations for much of this work are already provided by the emerging generation of event-driven application servers in the commercial marketplace.

CEP infrastructure can be expected to evolve to meet the demands of growing sophistication of CEP applications. Some of this evolution will involve issues that at this time belong to the applied research domain.

For example, the infrastructure may be required for some applications to have facilities to merge the local event executions, say, from local adapters, into a single CEP execution signifying the activity in the whole target system. To do this consistently with causality and time is a subject of ongoing experiments.

This task of merging local event executions has to solve issues arising because the local adapters are distributed around the target system, and their event collection is not necessarily coordinated. The execution merger should recognize events that signify the same instance of an activity—duplicate events, so to speak—and merge them into one causal equivalence class of events. It may have to complete the construction of local causal relationships into a global causal relationship. For example, causally related events may be received by different local adapters and therefore be unrelated when they arrive at the merger. And it may have to reconcile timestamps from different local clocks. To do its job well, an execution merger will depend on having built-in knowledge about the system.

15.6 Off-the-Shelf Infrastructure

Some application servers provide an opportunity to rapidly develop CEP infrastructures.

There has been a recent proliferation of so-called "application servers" entering the middleware marketplace.[2] Some industry reports put the application server market in 2000 at $2.2 billion.

However, the current market space for these products is chaotic. There are no standard specifications for application servers, or even reasonably comprehensive descriptions. Essentially, the *app server* evolved from early middleware products of the 1990s in an effort to gain competitive advantage in the middleware market. The app server packaged, along with the middleware, more of the processing common to customers' applications that were being hosted on the middleware and on the Internet. A typical advertising claim was "enables enterprises to easily develop, deploy, and manage business-critical Internet applications." The idea was to facilitate the development of "thin clients," thereby reducing the customer's time and expense in building business applications.

We can reasonably think of an app server as including messaging middleware, databases, and a bundle of other facilities on top of them, as depicted in Figure 15.5. These additional facilities include security, fault tolerance, object libraries, adapters, various programming and systems development and version control products, and so on. Some app servers provide workflow

---

[2]A Web search on "application server" will result in an extensive list of products.

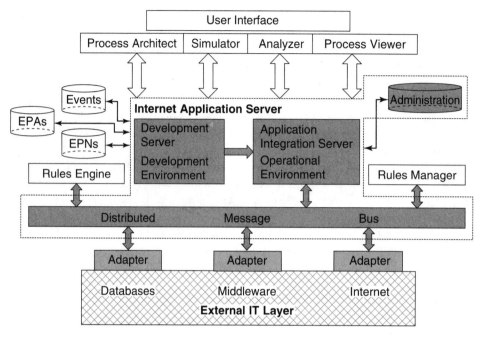

Figure 15.5: CEP infrastructure architecture using an Internet
Application Server

products and process engines. There are biases toward different software
development worlds. Some app servers fall completely in the Java world
supplying J2EE, while others support development of applications in competing programming worlds. And some are freely available in the open software world.

For us, the interesting question is how much of a CEP infrastructure
will be supplied off-the-shelf by app servers. Figure 15.5 shows an approach
to building CEP infrastructure on top of a suitable Internet app server.

The gray components in Figure 15.5 are supplied by the app server.
They include

- Object libraries and program development environments that would
  facilitate building libraries of EPAs, EPNs, and multilayer architectures of EPNs
- Configuration, deployment, and rudimentary runtime monitoring tools
- Messaging middleware and servers that would enable distributed
  communication between components of the CEP infrastructure and
  would also enable CEP applications (EPNs) to be distributed
- System administration tools

- Load balancing of client clusters, such as clusters of rules engines, each executing the rules for a group of EPAs within a large EPN
- Runtime security and fault-tolerance components

In addition, the repositories for event executions and EPA libraries may be built on top of databases supplied in the app server.

All this in one package removes a lot of the effort of implementing and deploying CEP applications. This is particularly true if the customer for CEP is using the same application server as the CEP application developer. Then the problem of integrating the CEP application with the event sources in the customer's system may be very simple, depending upon which facilities of the app server the customer is using. If the customer is using the messaging middleware layer, the deployment and integration problems should be vastly simplified.

So one strategy in developing CEP applications is to host CEP on top of various app servers. The problem of integrating CEP applications running on different app servers will have to be tackled sooner or later. But this problem will be faced by many B2B developers other than the CEP application developer. Also, we expect that future app servers will tend to add facilities trending towards CEP capabilities.

As the app server approach to building electronic enterprises and B2B collaboration matures, the CEP developer might well wonder what will remain to be done in the future. These are shown as unshaded components in Figure 15.5.

1. Event patterns language and rules languages
2. Pattern matchers, rules engines, and constraint checkers
3. Adapters to CEP event formats
4. Causal event execution repositories
5. Rules managers
6. EPA and EPN libraries
7. CEP simulators
8. Hierarchical, event execution analysis tools, supporting drill-down (Section 14.6.1)
9. Visual EPN architecture composition tools (Section 10.6)
10. Event-driven viewers (Section 14.5)

Some of these tools will also be developed with the aid of off-the-shelf components, such as relational databases and visual programming tools. The core components, central to CEP, are the ones whose development needs to be accelerated. These are powerful event pattern languages with features including those of RAPIDE-EPL, pattern matching for these languages, rule execution, constraint checkers, rules managers, capabilities for creating event hierachies, and hierarchical analysis tools. We will say a little more about these core components in the final sections that follow.

15.7   Event Pattern Languages

An event pattern language gives the user a succinct notation for expressing a pattern of events. The goal of succinct notation is to let the user express the pattern correctly and "see" instantly that it expresses what was intended.

When we build EPAs for CEP applications, we have a choice of many different event pattern languages. The event patterns that trigger the EPAs can be written in any pattern language we choose. The choice of pattern language usually boils down to speed of execution versus power of expression. For example, these are some categories of event pattern matching in increasing order of complexity and difficulty of implementation.

- *String pattern matching:*   If we want to search for very simple patterns, usually single events, and our internal representation of executions is a sequence of strings (highly inflexible, reasonable only for very low level events), we might use Perl or some similar pattern extraction language.[3] This kind of matching is often used at, say, the network packet level.

- *Single-event, content-based matching:*   We would choose this kind of pattern matching if we need to match single events, using content-based matching. The content of the event is used to decide the success or failure of a potential match. To do this, we need a pattern language with more power of expression than string matching, and a richer internal representation for events and data types.

   Message routing based upon content of the message is an example of single-event, content-based matching.

- *Multiple-event matching with context:*   Matching patterns of several events, or using context in the matching, requires yet more power of expression in the pattern language and representations of sets of events. Patterns must include the logical relational operators (**and, or,** and so on; see Section 8.7.1) and guards with expressions that

---

[3]Perl (Practical Extraction and Reporting Language) was originally designed for analyzing text represented in string format. It has since been extended with many higher-level programming features.

can reference context (for example, database queries, expression evaluation).

High-level security applications, such as correlation of alerts from intrusion detectors or context-sensitive message routing, are examples.

- *CEP matching:* Here we need pattern languages comparable to RAPIDE-EPL in power of expression, with the full set of relational operators (see Section 8.7.1), context guards, and pattern macros. Representation of event executions with causal, aggregation, and timing relationships are needed. Representations of executions must enable the event relationships to be traced easily by pattern matchers and analysis tools.

Complex event pattern matchers for a language such as RAPIDE-EPL are not yet to be found commercially and certainly not in the present generation of app servers, even though some of these products have acquired and incorporated reactive rules engines for very simple event pattern triggers.

Looking to what we can expect in the near future, it is a reasonable guess that one line of attack on developing event pattern languages and reactive rules languages will be to design them as extensions of modern, multiprocessing programming languages. The job of executing the body of a reactive rule once its trigger has matched can be handed off to the programming language or a subset of it. So this means that the design of the event pattern language is the critical part of a reactive rules language.

Pattern language design is complicated by two competing issues.

First, there is the *ease-of-use* issue. Some event pattern languages will be intended for use by non-programmers. They will employ graphics to express patterns. An example of this was our use of tabular format for patterns in STRAW-EPL in Chapter 6. Although hardly "graphical," it attempts to make the format of patterns more accessible to non-programmers. The tabular format can be supported by simple GUIs that guide the user interactively. But as we discussed, STRAW-EPL commits us to a considerable lack of power of expression. Truly graphical formats for representing event patterns cannot be expected to be more powerful.

Second, there is the tension between *power of expression* and *efficient pattern matching.* The trade-offs between these concerns will be decided by the intended applications and the need for expressive power versus efficiency. These trade-offs will be a continuing problem because as CEP applications become more complex, *both* expressive power *and* efficient matching will be needed. The pattern matcher becomes a central concern as the demand for scalability—that is, real-time event processing throughput—increases.

15.8   Complex Event Pattern Matchers

We discuss briefly some of the issues surrounding implementing matchers for complex event patterns.

As the event patterns become richer, the pattern matching becomes more difficult. The design of pattern matchers becomes an interesting topic with commercial potential. This is becoming evident in the commercial marketplace. Some simple commercial designs, capable of only content-based matching with Boolean **and,** or **or,** of events, have been the subject of recent patents.

15.8.1   Quest for Scalability

The pattern matcher is a central battleground to attain scalability of CEP applications. Some applications will demand performance on the order of testing thousands of complex patterns with context guards for matches, on event inputs at the rate of thousands of events per second, in real time.

15.8.2   The Naive View of Pattern Matchers

Conceptually, a pattern matcher may be viewed as taking as input a set of patterns to be matched and a stream of events on which the patterns must be tested for matches. As output, a pattern matcher generates a stream of matches—that is, pairs of patterns and placeholder bindings. The matches are output to rules engines that trigger and execute rules.

Under this view, these are the main functions of a complex event pattern matcher.

- Each time an event is delivered, test for a match of the pattern triggers of rules.
- Notify a rules engine when a rule's trigger has matched.
- Pass the bindings of placeholders to data objects to the rules engine. Then the rules engine can execute the rule body.
- Manage event input so that an event contributes only once to matching a pattern.

This is not an incorrect view of what a pattern matcher does. But it is not what dictates matcher design.

15.8.3   What Pattern Matchers Really Do

The fact is that most of the work of a pattern matcher is not matching patterns—that is, binding data objects to placeholder variables, as described

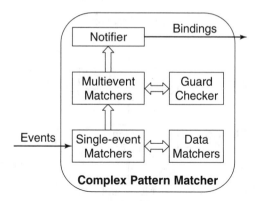

**Figure 15.6: A communicating structure of pattern
matchers and submatchers**

in Section 8.6. Rather, a complex pattern matcher spends most of its time
doing two things.

- Managing sets of patterns and partial matches of complex patterns.
  This imposes a design structure that involves multi-matchers and
  single-event matchers. The multi-matcher in Figure 15.6 has to
  manage the partial matches that accumulate.

- Avoiding attempts to match that cannot possibly succeed. The single-
  event matchers in Figure 15.6 have to do this.

15.8.4 Design Structure of Pattern Matchers

Complex event pattern matchers will likely be designed as collections of distributed communicating matchers. Figure 15.6 outlines one possible design.
A complex pattern matcher breaks down its pattern and sends the single-
event patterns to single-event pattern matchers. There may be several of
these for different formats of event patterns—say, XML, RAPIDE, and Java.
Figure 15.7 illustrates how the patterns flow downward and bindings flow
upward between the pattern matchers.

Here is a scenario of how this design works.

- The multi-event matcher splits a complex pattern into single-event
  patterns. The multi-matcher stores the logical structure of the complex
  pattern and delegates the matching of the single-event subpatterns to
  single-event matchers.

- A single-event matcher takes events as input and tries to match the
  patterns it has. Each attempt to match may require matching or

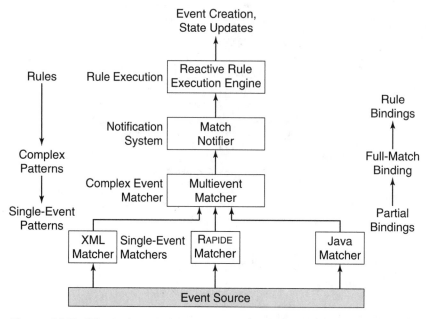

Figure 15.7: Flow of patterns down and placeholder bindings up in matcher communication

evaluating expressions of various data types: Integers, Reals, Arrays, and so on. For example:

- Does $?X + ?Y$ match $?Z$ when the bindings are $<?X \leftarrow 2, ?Y \leftarrow 1, ?Z \leftarrow 3 >$?
  Answer from integer data matcher: Yes, $2 + 1 = 3$.

- Does $A[?X]$ match $?Y$ when the bindings are $<?X \leftarrow 1, ?Y \leftarrow 3 >$?
  Answer from array data matcher depends on the value of A: No, $A[1] \neq 3$.

  Answering these examples is very simple—substitute the bindings and evaluate the expressions. Data structure matching in general can be more complicated, but expression evaluation takes care of a lot of cases.

- Bindings resulting from successful attempts as single-event matches are passed back to the multi-matcher (see Figure 15.7). The multi-matcher tries to put the bindings from single-event patterns in the same complex pattern together consistently to form a match for the complex pattern. In doing so, it may need to evaluate pattern guards that refer to context as well as to the values in the bindings (see Figure 15.6).

- Bindings for successful complex event pattern matches are passed to the rules engine.

A single-event matcher, for example, may have several thousand event patterns at any time. Each of them must be tested to see if an incoming event is a match. This search for matches is linear in the number of patterns. That means it is performed several thousand times for each input event. As a rule of thumb, far more tests for pattern matches fail on any given event than succeed. Speed-ups can be gained by organizing the patterns so that one test can be used to predict the results of lots of other tests without carrying them out. Some pattern matchers organize the patterns into a tree structure so that if a match test fails on a pattern at a node in the tree, it will also fail at patterns at nodes below it. So those tests are not performed. Organizing patterns in tree structures to guide the search for matches tends to give logarithmic or sublinear performance in the number of patterns by reducing the number of tests that result in a failure to match.

Tree organizations of patterns can be made more complicated by the data types of parameters of the events and by the use of guards in patterns to determine matches. Other kinds of speed-up strategies try to pool together similar patterns so that one test for a match is performed for the whole pool. At present, these matcher speed-up tactics are part of ongoing research into speed-up algorithms.

15.9   Rules Management

A battleground in rules-based computing is management of the rules. This becomes obvious as rule sets become more complex. To understand the role of rules management, let us look at Figure 15.5 again. How is the CEP system used?

- The *process architect* is engaged in developing or modifying an EPN. We might suppose it is a process architecture that drives and views business processes (see Chapter 4).
- As changes are made, new EPAs are added and old ones are deleted. This results in new rules being sent across the message bus to a *rules engine*. Old rules are deleted by delete messages. The triggering and execution of new rules by an engine drives the execution of new EPAs.
- The flow of new rules and deletion of old rules must take place in real time.
- Consider also that there may be several process architects sitting at different terminals and upgrading parts of the overall process architecture concurrently.

- There may also be several rules engines, each responsible for executing the rules of some group of EPAs in an EPN.

Somewhere in the communication of rules to a rules engine, and consequently to the pattern matchers, there sits a component called a *rules manager*. In Figure 15.5 a rules manager is depicted as a separate component on the message bus. There may in fact be several rules engines and rules managers sitting on the message bus.

To simplify the discussion, let us assume there is a rules manager for each rules engine. In this architecture, rules sent from the *process architect* go first to the *rules manager* before being sent on to a *rules engine*. A rules manager's job is to

- Reduce the number of rules
- Reduce *rules confusion*

Rules reduction is directly related to efficient execution of rule-based systems, as we discussed in the previous section. The speed of a pattern matcher, and the rules engine, depends upon the number of patterns it has to test for matches each time a new event arrives. In our use-case scenario— where there are a number of architects, or users who submit rules to the system—the problem of duplication arises. Duplication would be easy to deal with if it were simply a matter of exact copies of the same rule. But a rules manager has to recognize, and deal with, logical relationships between rules.

For illustration, let's take a very simple example. Suppose the CEP application is content-based message routing. Two rules, message filters, are submitted to the system in this order:

1. StockTrade(IBM, Price, LastQuote, ...) **where** Price > LastQuote+3 ⇒ **pass**;
2. StockTrade(IBM, Price, LastQuote, ...) **where** Price > LastQuote+5 ⇒ **pass**;

If these message filters are submitted by the same user, the rules manager should replace the earlier rule 1 by the later rule 2. If, on the other hand, they are submitted by different users, rule 1 should always be tested first, and rule 2 tested only if the match for rule 1 succeeds.

Rules confusion refers to the fuzzy area where new rules take over from old rules. This can lead to confusion in rule-based systems. Assuming that rules changes may be made every few minutes, we can't always halt the process system to synchronize changeover to new rules. But even when we can synchronize rule changes in the rules engine, there remains the problem of the effects of old rules. Whenever a rule is executed and, say, it creates new events, the effects of the rule progress through the EPN that controls the process, having further effects. The results of executing an old rule may still be rippling through the business processes when the changeover to the new rule takes place. Events caused by executing old rules come back to the rules engine, but the old rules that would have handled them have been deleted. This may lead to exceptional situations arising at the process level. Current ways of handling this problem, mainly by ensuring it cannot occur, are gross "stop the system" procedures. They won't work in the 24/7 electronic enterprise that is collaborating with other enterprises.

A rules manager attempts to discover relationships between a new rule and existing rules. Then it must decide on a strategy to help with the duplication and confusion problems. It controls which rules are sent to an engine, which rules are deleted, and when.

Rules are stored in search structures that enable comparisons to be made efficiently between a new rule and several thousand active rules. Even in our simple example, the rules manager has to use knowledge about the Int data structure, namely, **if** $X \leq 3$ **then** $X \leq 5$. This kind of reasoning must be included efficiently in rules managers for various data types such as Real, String, Array, etc. As with pattern matching, rule manager performance is enhanced if comparisons between unrelated rules are avoided.

To deal with rules confusion, rules managers need an ability to store and apply strategies that depend upon both the CEP application and the target system. For example, in the case of message filters in a system with multiple rules engines, one strategy is to migrate filters to rules engines closer to the publishers of the messages that are subject to the filters, thus cutting down the propagation of unneeded messages.[4]

15.10   Analysis Tools

The final core functionality of CEP infrastructure that we want to discuss here is the analysis tool set.

Four kinds of tools that get a lot of usage in applying CEP are

- Graphical event execution browsers
- Causal history–tracking tools
- Constraint checkers
- Animation tools

Analysis tools for CEP are event driven. They use the event executions, causality, aggregation, event attributes, and in some cases, additional data like architectural information. Analysis tools are consumers of information

---

[4]A. Carzaniga, D. S. Rosenblum, and A. L. Wolf. Design and evaluation of a wide-area event notification service. In *ACM Transactions on Computer Systems*, pages 332–383, August 2001.

provided by the CEP infrastructure. In fact, they are very similar to EPAs in that they require as input an event execution, and they react by searching for specific patterns. They differ in that they interact with the user and output information in a human-readable form such as a table or a graphical representation.

Simple analysis tools present events and statistics about events in a graphical form—for example, how many kinds of events in specified categories. A lot of these kinds of event viewers, which are listed in Figure 15.4, are already supplied by the CASE tool industry for specific types of event inputs—network-level events, events from simulators, and so on. Added flexibility is needed to deal with different types of event inputs, perhaps defined by the user. As one example, we can see recent developments of the Visio graphics tool toward adding a capability to build visual event-driven viewers for events specified by the user.[5]

However, we won't find the analysis tools that are specific to CEP "on-the-shelf" at the moment because they must utilize the event relationships (causality, aggregation, timing) in event executions. They must give users the capabilities illustrated in Chapter 14 to view concurrently a set of event executions that are related hierarchically by aggregation relationships between their events. They must also be able to use additional data such as architectural representations of the target system. The purpose of these tools is to use all the information CEP can deliver to help us find out what is happening in the target system.

A short list of features for a CEP analysis tool set includes the following interactive capabilities.

- *Represent posets, event aggregation, and event timing graphically.*
  CEP analysis tools must present posets and time histories in graphical formats. See, for example, the figures in Chapter 14.

- *Display the parameters and attributes of an event.* This is the simplest facility for searching an execution. We start with events and their relationships. A user needs an ability to look at the details of a chosen event or events without being overloaded with details of all events at once. Details include data parameters and predefined attributes (see Section 8.4) such as the generating component and timing. See, for example, the pop-up windows in Figures 14.9, 14.10, and 14.11.

- *Trace the causal history of an event in an event execution (poset).*
  A user can choose an event and ask to be shown the events that caused it, that caused them, and so on. This is backwards tracking of causal history. A similar feature is an ability to trace forward from a

---

[5]Web site: http://www.microsoft.com/office/visio

chosen event to the events that it causes (or participates in causing). These features help to locate the causes and effects of events.

- *Graphically present event timelines.* Similar to tracing causality is an ability to display graphically the timing relationships between events and to relate the graphical displays for causality and timing (see, for example, Figure 12.7). These features aid in understanding *how* activities happened. Used interactively, they often suggest hypotheses to the users.

- *Search an execution by pattern.* When surprises or exceptional situations happen, we often need to know if or where certain patterns of events did or did not occur in an execution. The user may be trying to answer questions such as "This rule is supposed to handle this situation—did it trigger?" So, a search for matches of the rule's trigger, perhaps within the causal history of an event, would help answer the question.

- *Interactively test constraints on executions.* Similar to search by pattern is an ability to submit constraints interactively and have the analysis tool check them on an execution. This would be done, for example, to test whether a proposed constraint would warn of an exceptional situation that has happened without warning in an execution.

- *Drill down using event abstraction hierarchies.* Show lower-level member events of a selected event. This is a basic capability to trace event aggregation in supporting hierarchical drill down, from higher-level events that are humanly understandable to the lower-level detailed events that caused them. See Section 14.6.1.

- *Relate an event to a component in an architecture diagram and to a reactive behavior rule.* This is the first in a class of features that support graphical architecting. They relate events with their origin in the target system. This class of features links a user's activities at the early lifecycle design/redesign phase with the later test and operational viewing phases, as discussed in Chapter 4 (see Figure 4.1). A user can select an event in an execution and ask, "Where did this come from in the system?" A component, or a behavior rule, in the system architecture is highlighted.

  Other features in this class include animation of system activity on architecture diagrams. This class of features use event attributes and architecture representations.

Analysis tools with these capabilities were built experimentally on the RAPIDE project.

15.11   Summary

Trends in the commercial event processing world, particularly in middleware, indicate that much of the functionality of a CEP infrastructure is, or soon will be, provided by commercial products such as application servers and CASE tools. Consequently, to build a CEP system, it may be only necessary to focus upon building the core infrastructure. We can imagine cutting down even more of the core list in Section 15.6 by omitting a CEP simulator and assuming that suitably flexible event viewers will appear among the CASE tools. This leaves the following short list:

- Complex event pattern languages and rules languages
- Pattern matchers, rules engines, and constraint checkers
- Causal event execution repositories
- Rules management
- EPA and EPN libraries
- Hierarchical, causal event execution analysis tools supporting drill down
- Visual EPN architecture composition tools

This list could be even shorter for most early CEP applications. We might expect to be "up and running" our first CEP applications with no rules management, very small EPA libraries, and only modest EPN composition tools and analysis tools.

So the bare-bones basics are (*i*) an event pattern language and a rules language of reasonable power of expression, (*ii*) a pattern matcher, a rules engine, and a constraint checker, (*iii*) a causal event execution repository, and (*iv*) a modest hierarchical execution analyzer. These capabilities could be added on top of many application servers today.

Bibliography

[1] C.Y. Chang and S.M. Sze. *ULSI Technology*. Electrical and Computer Engineering. McGraw-Hill, 1996.

[2] C.J. Fidge. Partial orders for parallel debugging. In *Workshop on Parallel and Distributed Debugging*, pages 183–194, Madison, WI, May 5–6, 1988. ACM SIGPLAN/SIGOPS.

[3] Colin J. Fidge. Timestamps in message-passing systems that preserve the partial ordering. *Australian Computer Science Communications*, 10(1):55–66, February 1988.

[4] Colin J. Fidge. Logical time in distributed systems. *Computer*, 24(8):28–33, August 1991.

[5] Benoit A. Gennart and David C. Luckham. Validating discrete event simulations using event pattern mappings. In *Proceedings of the 29th Design Automation Conference (DAC)*, pages 414–419, Anaheim, CA, June 1992. IEEE Computer Society Press, Best paper award.

[6] D. Harel. Statemate, a working environment for the development of complex reactive systems. *IEEE Transactions on Software Engineering*, 16(4):403–414, April 1990.

[7] D.P. Helmbold and D.C. Luckham. Debugging Ada tasking programs. *IEEE Software*, 2(2):47–57, March 1985. Also Stanford University Computer Systems Laboratory Technical Report No. 84-262.

[8] IEEE, Inc., 345 East 47th Street, New York, NY, 10017. *IEEE Standard VHDL Language Reference Manual*, March 1987. IEEE Standard 1076–1987.

[9] International Organization for Standardization. *Information processing systems—Open Systems Interconnection—Specification of Basic Encoding Rules for Abstract Notation One (ASN.1)*, December 1987. International Standard 8825.

[10] L. Lamport. Time, clocks, and the ordering of events in a distributed system. *Communications of the ACM*, 21(7):558–565, 1978.

[11] David C. Luckham. *Programming with Specifications: An Introduction to ANNA, A Language for Specifying Ada Programs*. Texts and Monographs in Computer Science. Springer-Verlag, October 1990.

[12] David C. Luckham and Brian Frasca. Complex event processing in distributed systems. Computer Systems Laboratory Technical Report CSL-TR-98-754, Stanford University, March 1998.

[13] David C. Luckham, John J. Kenney, Larry M. Augustin, James Vera, Doug Bryan, and Walter Mann. Specification and analysis of system architecture using Rapide. *IEEE Transactions on Software Engineering*, 21(4):336–355, April 1995.

[14] David C. Luckham and James Vera. An event-based architecture definition language. *IEEE Transactions on Software Engineering*, 21(9):717–734, September 1995.

[15] David C. Luckham, James Vera, Doug Bryan, Larry Augustin, and Frank Belz. Partial orderings of event sets and their application to prototyping concurrent, timed systems. *Journal of Systems and Software*, 21(3):253–265, June 1993.

[16] David C. Luckham, James Vera, and Sigurd Meldal. Key concepts in architecture definition languages. In Gary T. Leavens and Murali Sitaraman, editors, *Foundations of Component-Based Systems*. Cambridge University Press, February 2000.

[17] F. Mattern. Virtual time and global states of distributed systems. In M. Cosnard, editor, *Proceedings of Parallel and Distributed Algorithms*. Elsevier Science Publishers, 1988. Also in Report No. SFB124P38/88, Department of Computer Science, University of Kaiserslautern.

[18] Sigurd Meldal, Sriram Sankar, and James Vera. Exploiting locality in maintaining potential causality. In *Proceedings of the Tenth Annual ACM Symposium on Principles of Distributed Computing*, pages 231–239, New York, NY, August 1991. ACM Press. Also Stanford University Computer Systems Laboratory Technical Report No. CSL-TR-91-466.

[19] Bertrand Meyer. *Eiffel: The Language*. Prentice-Hall, 1990.

[20] K. Nygaard and O-J. Dahl. Simula—an algol-based simulation language. *Communications of the A.C.M.*, 9(9):671–678, 1966.

[21] V.R. Pratt. Modeling concurrency with partial orders. *International Journal of Parallel Programming*, 15(1):33–71, February 1986.

[22] N. Habermann and R.H. Campbell. The specification of process synchronization by path expressions. In *Lecture Notes in Computer Science, Vol. 16*, pages 89–102. Springer Verlag, 1974.

[23] Alexandre Santoro, Walter Mann, Neel Madhav, and David Luckham. eJava—extending java with causality. In *Proceedings of the 10th International Conference on Software Engineering and Knowledge Engineering*, pages 251–260. Knowledge Systems Institute, June 1998.

[24] James Vera, Louis Perrochon, and David C. Luckham. Event-based execution architectures for dynamic software systems. In Patrick Donohue, editor, *TC2 First Working IFIP Conference on Software Architecture (WICSA1)*, pages 303–317. Kluwer Academic, February 1999.

Index

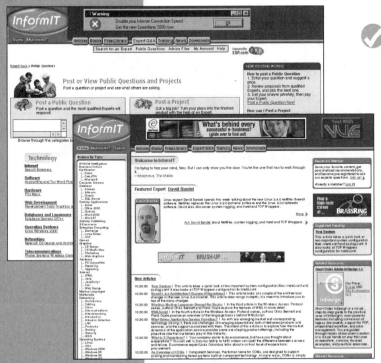